CREATE YOUR OWN
STAGE PROPS

CREATE YOUR OWN
STAGE PROPS

Jacquie Govier

Adam & Charles Black   London

First published 1984
A & C Black (Publishers) Limited
35 Bedford Row, London WCIR 4JH

Published simultaneously in the USA
by Prentice-Hall, Inc.

Govier, Jacquie
Create your own stage props.
1. Theaters-Stage-setting and scenery
I. Title
792'.025   PN2091.S8

ISBN 0-7136-2419-1

Typesetting by
Avonset, Midsomer Norton, Bath

Printed in Great Britain by
Purnell & Sons Limited, Paulton

Create Your Own Stage Props
was conceived, edited,
and designed by
Thames Head Limited,
Avening, Tetbury,
Gloucestershire
Great Britain

Editor
Alison Goldingham

Consultant editors
Barry Saltman
Head of Armoury, National Theatre, London
Elizabeth Friendship
Head of Design, Welsh College of Music and Drama, Cardiff

Art Director
David Playne

Designers and illustrators
Nicholas Rous
Tony De Saulles
Jacquie Govier
Nick Allen
Tracey Arnold
Heather Church
Nick Hand
Simon Borrough
David Chapman

Contents

Introduction

You are about to enter a world of illusion and changing identities, a world of make-believe where things are not quite what they seem.

Together with the set and costume designers, you will conspire to transport the audience across time into another world.

Prop making can be great fun and will stretch your ingenuity considerably during the process. You will find yourself in an all-embracing search into people, their habits, and their lifestyles, and your knowledge and awareness of social conditions is bound to improve!

What are props? Time and again during the writing of this book I have crossed the imaginary line from props to costume or set design in pursuit of a particular technique or idea. This has been inevitable as props, costume, and set design do not work in isolation; each is an integral part of the whole, and at times their roles are bound to overlap.

The word 'props', generally speaking, refers to most of the portable objects found on a stage set: a vase of flowers, a dish of food, weapons, armor, a wide variety of furnishings. In fact, all the paraphernalia to be found whenever and wherever the plot thickens.

It is the prop maker's skill which will enhance a production and create the bridge between actors in costume and the stage set; an influence which is felt but rarely observed by anyone other than those involved in the hard work taking place behind the scenes. It is the props which give credence to the actors' actions and movements. For this reason, the prop maker has to be prepared well in advance of any production — and certainly as soon as rehearsals begin — supplying temporary props if necessary. Where breakable props are concerned, it is best to use substitute items during rehearsals: the real thing can be used once the actors are free of scripts. The basic rule is this: something for everything. In other words, never leave an actor without a prop which is central to the action being rehearsed.

At the start of the production, make a list of all the props required. Do they have to be made? Can they be purchased or loaned? Itemize the props under the categories into which they fall. It may be easy to borrow a milk jug from a member of the cast or buy a wooden spoon, but I suggest that a Ming vase should be made! Local retailers will often loan an item, possibly furniture, in return for a free advertisement in the theatrical program.

Do not forget that many of the sources open to the prop maker are often free or can be found at give-away prices. Take another look in your garbage can — surely that plastic bottle can be utilized, and do those egg cartons really have to be thrown away, and what about that old lampshade frame? Train yourself to recognize the potential of all kinds of waste materials. Another source dear to the eclectic prop maker's heart is the junk yard. Any real hoarder surely cannot pass such a haven! I have noticed useful junk such as old bicycle parts, railings, and even old chairs which, once dealt with by a competent prop maker, can reemerge with a changed identity. What a boon we would be to the conservationists if we discovered how to recycle all our rubbish!

The philosophy of all this is not to waste anything, but to utilize all resources to the full.

Do not take shortcuts with your research. Accurate books of reference are a must for the prop maker, and it is a good idea to build up a file of pictures.

List the props in order of appearance, mapping their position on the set, drawing plans if necessary, and noting when they are to be removed.

Work with the set designer and the director to ensure that movement on stage is not obstructed by badly designed props which are incorrectly placed. Always view each segment of a scene as if it were a still photograph, checking that everything in it relates.

It is helpful to have a general discussion to discover the main objectives of the production. Will it be a stylized piece, or will everything be historically correct right down to the smallest detail? Or perhaps it will be a fun production where the absurd is the order of the day.

The choice of production, and the people working within its boundaries, will govern the mood, and a style will evolve. It is then up to the prop maker, costume and set designer to capture this style, and work, not in isolation, but hand-in-hand to make a homogenous production.

It is advisable to draw up plans for the more complicated props, no matter how elementary they may be. In fact, it will help to sort out any initial problems before you become overwhelmed with difficult materials. Do not forget to make a copy of the plans in case they get lost!

Also, remember to investigate the fire regulations in your area and make sure that your precautions are adequate. It's always wise to pay a visit to your local fire prevention officer, with the set designer and costumer, to discuss your plans and ask for advice.

Look out for
the hazard symbols
throughout the book.

The catalog of materials and techniques explored in this book will show you just how versatile they can be. There is also a separate project section containing pictorial references for hundreds of domestic, military, and ethnic objects.

Techniques

Coloring and painting

Color and characteristics of color

By the intelligent use of color, props can be brought forward in importance on the stage, or made to recede. Skillful painting makes an object appear flatter or rounder, realistic or dreamlike, cheerful or somber. Do not fall into the trap of using too many colors. The secret of a successful color scheme is the confident and clever use of a few colors, or simply many shades of the same color.

Controlling color is a logical process in which the color wheel is a valuable aid. But do not neglect the inspiration of the world around you; when in doubt careful observation is more valuable than any notebook. A logical approach only requires the understanding of three basic characteristics of color: hue, intensity and value.

Hue
The hue of a color is simply the name by which we know it — red or green or blue or yellow. Pink and maroon are both variations of the basic red hue; brown is a deep grayed orange and so on. Warm hues appear to come forward while cool hues recede.

Intensity
More often than not we use colors of less than maximum brilliance. A gray-blue is still blue in hue, but it is far lower in intensity. The color would be shown as being nearer the center of the color wheel — more gray in other words. Lowering the intensity of a hue will make it appear further away, or in shadow. It can also give the appearance of age.

Value
In addition to being blue and low in intensity, a specific color may also be light or dark: light gray-blue, medium gray-blue, dark gray-blue. This is called its value; a light value is high, a dark value is low. The value selected will create the illusion of an object being either in bright or in poor light. The highest value is a pure white, and the lowest, pure black, between which all hues and intensities can be organized within a color cone based on the color wheel.

Adjacent hues are harmonious

All hues and intensities are contained within the color cone which adds a third dimension to the color wheel

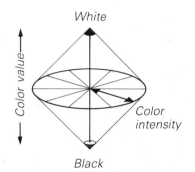

White

Color value

Color intensity

Black

Add white to increase the value

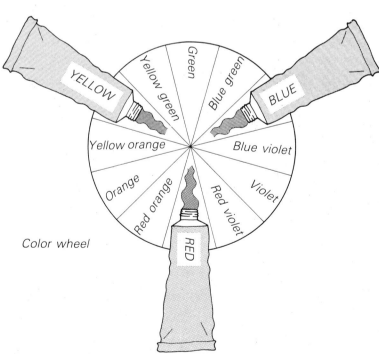

Color wheel

Opposite colors on the wheel contrast. If a small amount of contrasting color is added to a given hue, its intensity is reduced. Add more and you move to gray in the center of the wheel.

Color mixing

If you don't have the exact color you need, and if you have the three primary colors (red, yellow and blue) to work with, you can mix virtually any color you want. However, bear in mind that the resulting hue will not be as brilliant as the pure color — mixed colors always fade a little in intensity.

Colors falling opposite each other on the color wheel will produce a neutral gray when mixed. Blue and orange for example can be mixed to create gray. If only a little blue is added to the orange, the result is burnt orange. Still more blue will give varying intensities of brown. The same result can be achieved by mixing black and white with the brilliant hue, and a basic pallet of the primary colors plus black and white is often enough.

Study the color wheel and experiment with your paint until you understand how the primary colors blend together to produce intermediate hues. The addition of black or white will darken or lighten the hues respectively.

Making your own paints

If you are interested, and have the time, try making your own paints with pigment and medium.

Pigment is pure color in a powder form. It can usually be found at an art and craft or model shop, or sometimes in a liquid form from a DIY or paint stockist with mixing facilities. The range of color is enormous. When choosing a pigment, remember that the finer the ground the more superior the pigment. Metallic pigments are also available which are invaluable when making jewelry and armor (see pages 68 and 71).

The material which bonds pigment together is called medium, and is basically a glue. Size, emulsion and shellac are the most common and useful to the prop maker.

Using size

Size is the most common and cheapest medium, but it is not suitable for use on an object which is to be frequently handled, as it lacks sufficient durability and finish.

Take a gallon (4.54l) of boiling water and gently stir in 1 pound (453g) of size. While still hot pour this into a tin of color that has been previously moistened and mix to the right consistency. The lumps of pigment must be thoroughly broken up until the mixture is quite smooth. Leave it to cool before using. This solution can be made stronger, or weaker, but check with your supplier regarding the manufacturer's instructions.

Mix 1 pound (453g) size to 1 gallon (4.54l) of water.

Pour this hot mixture on to the moistened pigment

The addition of a coat of clear polyurethane varnish would solve this problem however.

Using emulsion

This is a water-plastic fluid and is mixed directly with the pigment. It can be watered down but it then loses luster and strength proportionately. It has a better finish and

binding power than size, but is also more expensive. Emulsion is used very satisfactorily in conjunction with metallic pigments.

Using shellac

This makes an excellent finishing ground on papier mâché before painting. Use also with metallic pigments and for painting furniture.

Using different paints

There are many paints, dyes and markers available these days and care should be taken to choose the most suitable and economic medium for the surface.

In some cases there is a definite fire risk. Gloss paint, for example, is exceedingly dangerous when used with polystyrene and may dissolve it.

A good way to keep within your budget is to use leftovers from home decorating or a long forgotten art class. Often this old paint will contain impurities or have developed a skin. These dregs can be removed by sieving the paint through some nylon which has been stretched and secured with elastic across a spare can.

(There is a table of paints on the following page.)

Rejuvenate old paint by sieving it through nylon

Selecting the right paint

	Oil-based gloss	Emulsion	Acrylic	P.V.A. Emulsion	Powder Color	Gloss aerosol	Felt pens and Day-Glo Pens	Other comments
Papier mâché	**LN**	**DJ** Gives uniform color and surface	**J** An excellent all round paint. Strong colors	**J**	**JHKL** Bright colors	**JLN** Gives consistent color	**KL**	Wait for papier mâché to dry thoroughly before painting
Plaster	**MJ**	**JM**	**JM**	**JM**	**JMK**	**JM**	**JKMP**	Plaster is highly absorbent, so all base coats must be thinned
Expanded polystyrene/ polyurethane	DANGEROUS Extremely dangerous in combination ◇	**J**	**JL**	**JML**	**EJ** Will run if in contact with water	**Q** Do not use, as it dissolves expanded polystyrene, unless you wish to make use of this property (see page 78)	**P**	
Fiberglass	**JR**	**DKR** Use as undercoat for less durable paints, such as powder colors	**JR**	**JR** Woodshavings, sand etc, can be added to the emulsion to change surface texture	**EKR**	**JR** Easy to blend and shade Spray metallic shades lightly over dark undercoat	**KL**	Color can be added to fiberglass props during their construction
Paper products	**Q** Not suitable: leaves stain on reverse	**AJQ** Only suitable for heavy paper and cardboard	**BJ**	**BJ**	**CHJ** Good for posters and stencil work	**J** Suitable for heavy duty paper and cardboard	**P**	
Fabrics	**AJN**	**AE** Takes on fabric, but will flake on flexible pieces if painted thickly	**N** Prime the fabric with a layer of thinned acrylic, shellac or size	**J** Looks like a plastic skin when used on a fine fabric stretched tight	**AQ** Will take on fabrics, but will flake on flexible pieces	**JN** Good for aging or implying dirt etc. Use metallic sprays for armor etc.	**CENP**	
Wood	**FJLM**	**DJ** Fine as a topcoat	**JLM** For gloss use acrylic medium	**FJL**	**JKL** Use thickly	**JL** A quick cover up	**LP** Unlikely combination	
Metal	**GJR**	**Q** Will encourage rusting	**JR** Use only acrylic medium. Prime with thinned acrylic paint	**GJR** Do not thin with water: only use P.V.A. medium	**EQ**	**GJR** Better primed, but can be used directly on metal, particularly to touch up old paintwork	**Q**	
Comments	Normally takes several hours to dry. Thin with turpentine/ paint thinner	Dries in under an hour. Thin with water. Available in matte, semi-gloss or satin finishes. Can be used as base for pure pigment	Feels like oil paint to use, but dries quickly. Will not take on a greasy surface, or one that has been primed with an oil-based paint	Similar properties to acrylic. Mix with P.V.A. to thin and give a gloss effect	Economical, though not very durable unless coated with fixative or varnish. When mixed with P.V.A. (white flexible glue) will have same qualities as P.V.A. emulsion	Fun to use. Can be expensive. Quick way to obtain a uniform covering. Use in a well ventilated area	Limited in their use: best for small detail	

A Do not use on Flexible items
B Use as watercolor or impasto
C Spray with fixative
D Useful as an undercoat

E Not very durable
F Use a wood primer
G Use a metal primer
H Not suitable for overpainting

J Good
K Protect with varnish
L Use emulsion as undercoat
M Seal with size or emulsion

N Undercoat with shellac
P Suitable for detail only
Q Not suitable
R Sand surface to give key

Choosing and caring for brushes

Good quality brushes are expensive and are made from the bristle of animals such as ox, squirrel or sable. The cheapest brushes are generally made from nylon or synthetic fibers.

Small pencil type brushes are used for fine work. They are numbered according to size: the lower the number, the smaller the brush. The sizes given for flat or round brushes indicate the width of the bristles.

All brushes should be cleaned immediately after use with the thinning medium of the paint. Do not store brushes in water overnight as this will involve having to dry them out before use. Either wrap the brushes tightly in foil or place them in a tightly sealed polythene bag. Never stand brushes on their bristle end or they will distort permanently. During a long job, brushes can be suspended into the thinning solution from a piece of wire.

N.B. A good way to maintain the shape of a fine brush is to dip it in egg white and twist it into a point.

Round headed brush for general work

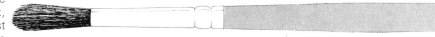

Fine brush for detail

Stencil brush for stippling

Flat headed brushes give broad, even strokes and a consistent width for painting circles

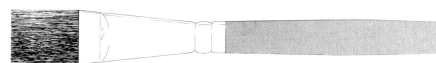

Household brushes for varnishing and painting larger areas

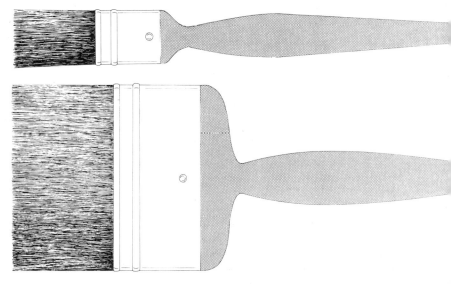

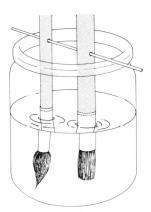

Brushes suspended from a piece of wire passed through a hole drilled in the handle

Using different adhesives

Before buying any adhesives, see what you have lurking in your garage or workshop first! There are five basic types which between them will cover most jobs.

Superglue is not included in this range. Although it is excellent for some household repair work, it has limited application for the prop maker. It can be hazardous to use and is available in very small and uneconomic quantities.

Gums and pastes
Sold in powdered and liquid form, these are very economical, but basically only suitable for sticking paper to itself and some other light materials.

P.V.A. (white flexible glue)
A good all-round adhesive which can be watered down for economy. It has the added advantage of being a 'varnish' and a 'medium'. It is sold in a liquid form in small tubes, bottles and gallon containers.

Contact cement
This adhesive has to be applied to both surfaces. After a while it becomes tacky and when the surfaces are pressed firmly together, an instant bond results. Generally it is sold in tubes.

Latex
This is basically a fabric adhesive (particularly for natural fibers), but it can also be applied to many other non-load bearing materials. It dries quickly to form strong flexible joints or seams — this makes it useful for quick hemming and also to prevent material from fraying. Latex makes an effecftive stiffener for fabrics such as lace, felt, and cheesecloth. It is available in varying quantities, from small tubes to gallon containers.

Epoxies
Almost any materials can be stuck with epoxies, but the cost make them more suitable for small jobs. Epoxies are two part adhesives; a resin and a hardener. Mixing the two together can be a messy business and hardening can take up to forty-eight hours. This process is speeded up when heat is applied. (Use a hair dryer!)

N.B. Animal glue (known as carpenters' glue) is not an essential adhesive but is invaluable in the cloth mâché process. In other cases, P.V.A. (white flexible glue) is a good substitute.

Making a spillproof bottle for P.V.A. (white flexible glue)

This homemade glue bottle is unbreakable, practically spillproof, and free! Just cut the top off a plastic bottle at the shoulder, pour in the glue and invert the top into the base.

As you use the glue, be sure to push down the top to eliminate air from the container. Most glue drips will run back into the bottle, but those that do not will peel off easily

Cut through bottle just below the neck

Invert top and push into bottom half until the air is expelled

Selecting the right adhesive

	Metal	Wood	Fabrics	Paper products	Fiberglass	Expanded Polystyrene/ Polyurethane	Plaster	Papier Mâché
Papier Mâché	Contact cements P.V.A.	Contact cements P.V.A. Resin	Contact cements P.V.A.	Gums and pastes Contact cements P.V.A.	Contact cements Epoxies	Contact cements P.V.A.	Contact cement (Prime surface first) P.V.A.	Gums and pastes P.V.A.
Plaster	Contact cements P.V.A.	Contact cements P.V.A.	Contact cements P.V.A. Latex	Contact cements P.V.A. Latex	Contact cements Epoxies	Contact cements P.V.A. Latex	P.V.A.	
Expanded Polystyrene Polyurethane	Contact cements P.V.A. Latex	Contact cements P.V.A. Latex	Contact cements P.V.A. Latex	Contact cements P.V.A. Latex	Contact cements Epoxies	Contact cements P.V.A. Latex		
Fiberglass	Contact cements Epoxies	Contact cements Epoxies	Contact cements Epoxies	Contact cements Epoxies	Contact cements Epoxies			
Paper	Contact cements P.V.A.	Gums and pastes Contact cements P.V.A.	Gums and pastes P.V.A.	Gums and pastes Contact cements P.V.A.				
Fabrics	Contact cements P.V.A. Latex	Contact cements P.V.A. Latex	Contact cements P.V.A. Latex					
Wood	Contact cements P.V.A. Epoxies	P.V.A. Epoxies Resin						
Metal	Contact cements P.V.A. Epoxies							

Working with papier mâché

Papier mâché is the theater's own special material, for it combines the cardinal qualities of strength and lightness.

The principle on which papier mâché is based is this: if many fragments of paper or cloth are soaked in glue or paste and then laid over each other, when dry they will fuse into a hard skin.

Papier mâché can be laminated — used as strips of paper and layered, or pulped — broken up until it is a homogeneous mass which can be molded into shape.

The paper does not have to be soaked in water first. Although it takes longer to dry, if it is soaked it will need less paste, and make a more satisfactory surface.

Papier mâché is stable enough to hold its own structure, or it can be supported by a frame or cast in a mold. The pulped form makes a variety of textures possible, and is best for packing, shaping and decoration.

Almost any available paint can be used on papier mâché, it only depends on how long you are prepared to wait for it to dry! Acrylic paint is very suitable as it not only dries quickly but withstands over-painting. Colors do not mix together and become muddy — a fault with powder, poster and tempera colors. Oil-based gloss paints are good but take a long time to dry.

Papier mâché is obviously not fire-proof and the appropriate fire-precautions need to be taken. Fire-proofing crystals can be made up from 15 ounces (425g) of boric acid crystals and 10 ounces (283g) of sodium phosphate in a gallon (4.5l) of water. Be careful how you spray the solution, for colors may run and delicate shapes be damaged.

The rigidity of papier mâché makes it very suitable for making large pieces of stage furniture where wood and other materials would be too heavy and clumsy. Fountains, well-heads, and so on, can easily be made in paper and will look very realistic if decorated with 'carving' in paper pulp.

Papier mâché is also useful for pieces of property that have to be maltreated during a play. A simple case, common in farces, is the hat that gets sat on. If you are doing several performances, it is almost impossible to make the hat look wearable after it has been sat on once or twice! On the other hand, a hat made up of laminated paper can be created for each performance, and will crush convincingly. Likewise, a large urn can be made to break simply, if it is first assembled jig-saw fashion to appear complete.

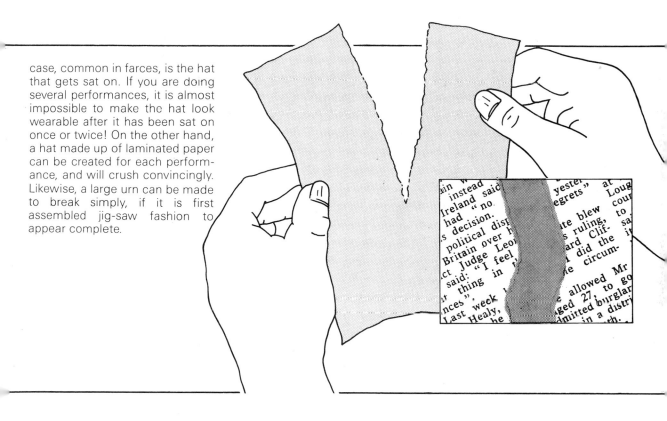

Making papier mâché from wallpaper paste and paper

Wallpaper paste is very convenient and easy to make up. It produces an ideal papier mâché mix for covering small areas or lining molds, and when pulped is excellent for imitating carved detail or texture. It lacks the strength needed for constructing large props, however.

Tear up the paper

As the machine cut edges of paper have only a little fibrous overhang, tear these off and use only the center portion of each sheet so that it mats better in the papier mâché process. Tear the central portion of the sheet into irregular shapes about 1 square inch (25mm) for small objects, 3 square inches (75mm) for medium ones and 6 square inches (150mm) for large objects — bearing in mind that the smaller the pieces, the better they bind together. Soak the paper in the bucket of water.

Make up the paste and soak the paper until saturated

Ring out the surplus water from the paper and immerse it in the paste (made according to the manufacturer's instructions). Crush and squeeze the paper until it is thoroughly impregnated with paste. Wipe off any surplus. It is now ready to use. If pulped papier mâché is required, continue the

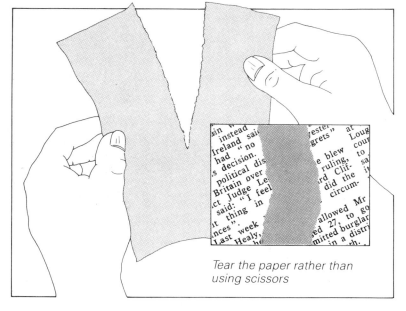

Tear the paper rather than using scissors

breaking process with the fingers, while squeezing out the surplus paste. Shape the pulp, rolling it between your hands as you would plasticine. Make it into ball or sausage shapes.

Apply the papier mâché

When applying the pasted paper, use a coarse paper first, (such as newspaper or paper towels), build up the layers, finishing with tissue paper to give a smooth finish. Leave the prop to dry in a well ventilated place and when thoroughly dry, paint it with shellac. This will give it a final bonding and provide a good surface for painting. Use white emulsion paint as an alternative to shellac — apart from sealing, this will block out any areas of newspaper print. A gloss finish is difficult to paint on with water colors. If water color paint is to be used, apply it to emulsion, and then cover the finished work with a coat of varnish or lacquer.

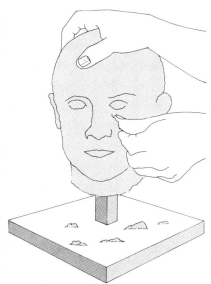

After soaking in water, the pulp should be completely saturated with paste. (Remove any surplus paste before applying the pulp to the subject.) In the case of the head illustrated above, an armature would be required. (See page 36)

MATERIALS
Any paper, ranging from toilet tissue, brown paper and newspaper, to paper towels; water; wallpaper paste; a base or a mold; shellac

TOOLS
Bucket

Making papier mâché from glue and cloth

Carpenters' glue can be used with cloth (canvas is very suitable) for a papier mâché with more 'body'. This is advantageous when making larger props, such as tree trunks or architectural shapes. The disadvantage over paste is that the glue needs to be heated and it is not always convenient to do so.

Cut the cloth

Cut the cloth diagonally across the grain, so that it will lie more easily, particularly when covering a curved surface. As with paper, sizes vary according to the job. Generally, as already suggested, cloth is best used for large objects so your pieces should range between a minimum size of 5 square inches (125mm), and a maximum size of 18 square inches (450mm).

Make up the glue and soak the cloth

Have two metal buckets or tins available, one larger than the other. Boil up a quarter of a bucket of water in the larger bucket. Put the glue block or granules and water into the smaller bucket and place this in the first bucket of boiling water. Stir the glue until it has melted into a piping hot fluid. It can be thinned with water, but its

strength will diminish proportionately. Keep the glue as hot as the hand will stand, for the hotter the glue the greater its impregnation and strength. Soak the cloth in this solution (you may find it helpful to wear rubber gloves.)

Apply the glued cloth

Having squeezed out the surplus glue, lay the cloth on to the structure — overlapping smoothly and crossing the pieces in an irregular manner. When covering a round shape, wind the pieces in a spiral, making the most of the flexibility of the cross-grain material. When

it is a good two or three layers thick, the tough, hard skin will be a good base for finishing with paper. Leave it in an airy place to dry quickly. Any glue left over can be used with torn paper. Dip unsoaked paper into hand-hot glue, squeeze it gently to rid it of the surplus glue and apply it in the same way as paste-treated paper. If you wish to build up a form, pulp the gluey paper in your hand and work it in with the flat-laid papier mâché. Glued paper will grow cold quickly, so work fast and precisely. After finishing off with tissue, leave the papier mâché to dry in a well ventilated place.

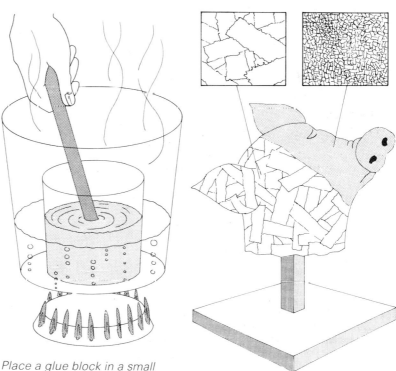

MATERIALS
Canvas or any other available cloth such as cheesecloth or factory seconds; carpenters' glue; water; strong framework on which to apply the cloth

TOOLS
Two metal buckets (one larger than the other); spoon; gas burner or other heater; tongs; rubber gloves

---

Place a glue block in a small bucket. Lower this into a larger bucket containing water which should be kept hot throughout the process

Apply larger pieces of paper first and build up with smaller pieces to achieve a fine finish

aking papier mâché from size and paper

Size is a mild glue easily made up with boiling water. It lacks the clearness of paste, but has more strength and will produce a papier mâché suitable for most prop-making. Make sure you have an adequate supporting frame for larger props.

To prepare the paper

Tear the cut edges of the paper, and use only the center of the sheet, so that the fibers will mat together during the papier mâché process. Tear this central portion into irregular shapes of about an inch square for small objects, 3 inches (75mm) for medium ones, 6 inches (150mm) for large, bearing in mind that the smaller the pieces the better the binding.

Brown paper is good for making large piece underlays. Newspaper

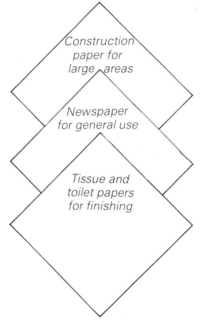

Construction paper for large areas

Newspaper for general use

Tissue and toilet papers for finishing

is useful for general purposes, and tissue and toilet papers are excellent finishers. If the papers are used in this order a smooth, strong covering should result.

To prepare the size

Place 1 pound (450g) of size in a bucket and top it up with boiling water. When size is used as a glue it should not be left to cool off.

Dip unsoaked paper into hand-hot size, squeeze it gently to expel the surplus size, and apply it to the framework. Use the larger pieces first for a base and cover them with smaller pieces. Overlay two or three times more, and finish with tissue. Leave it to dry in an airy place, and, when thoroughly dry, paint with shellac. This will give a final bonding and a good surface for painting.

Making papier mâché with flour and water

This is a fairly messy process and the result has limited use, because it lacks strength. As the surface texture is often rough, it is most suitable for small, unsophisticated objects, such as fruit or bread.

A small quantity — say 1 pound (450g) — of flour is placed in a bowl and mixed with cold water to form a creamy paste. A wooden spoon can be used to stir the paste, although using hands is probably a better way to remove the lumps.

Unsoaked paper is added to this mixture and can be applied in layers to the base or pulped for

modeling. The object has to be dried thoroughly in a well ventilated place or left in a cool oven, after which it can be finished in the same way as the method above.

Alternatively, a paste can be made by adding boiling water to a flour and water mix and bringing the whole solution to the boil for 5 minutes. When cold this will become a thick paste which can be thinned down if necessary. Use 3 ounces (85g) flour to 1 pint (562ml) water.

This will keep well in the refrigerator for 2-3 days. To add to the keeping qualities of this and the

previous 'recipe', add a small quantity of Borax to ward off any possible mold (otherwise buy a proper fungicide).

Some molded shapes need not be made entirely from mâché. Many cardboard and paper items such as cups, small boxes and cones can be used as bases and enveloped in mâché — assorted shapes make excellent rocks and boulders. Large handles are cleverly contrived by twisting wire round a length of rope to maintain the shape of the curve until the mâché is dry. These are anchored to the body, with more mâché being added at the join.

Using papier mâché on a clay form

Sometimes the prop maker may need a thin shell of papier mâché — perhaps for a mask or a plaque. Clay is an ideal substance from which to fashion a shape. The base need not be all clay. For economical reasons it could quite easily be a block of expanded polystyrene or wood over which a layer of clay is smoothly applied. Use your thumbs and forefingers to pull and push the clay into shape. Remember that the papier mâché shape will obliterate some of the detail, and therefore the clay form needs to be bold with simple sculpturing. Do not get involved in modeling any unnecessary detail. To make sure the papier mâché does not stick to the base, smear petroleum jelly all over the clay to act as a separator.

Lay the papier mâché over the surface and build it up to an even thickness of about half an inch (12mm). Although not essential, it may be useful to add a final layer of gauze dipped in paste, woodworkers' glue or P.V.A. (white flexible glue) to strengthen the shape and give a uniform surface. Leave the papier mâché to dry. (When it is hardening, but not completely dry, it can be lifted carefully from the clay, which will speed the drying process.) If more haste is necessary, heat the papier mâché in a cool oven and when it is completely dry, shellac or emulsion the entire surface. One of the advantages of emulsion is that it provides a plain background which will take felt tip markers. This technique is particularly effective for producing masks with colorful decorations.

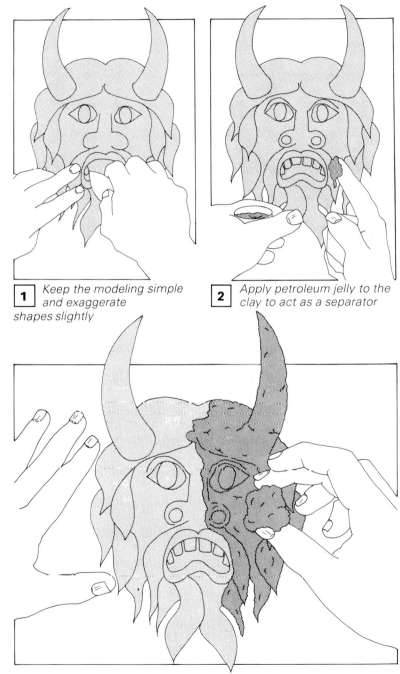

1 *Keep the modeling simple and exaggerate shapes slightly*

2 *Apply petroleum jelly to the clay to act as a separator*

3 *Papier mâché should be built up to a thickness of about half an inch (12mm)*

4 *A final layer of gauze dipped in glue will provide strength and smoothness*

Using cloth mâché on a wood and wire frame

The cloth/glue method of making papier mâché is most suitable for covering a large wood/wire base. Thus a large substantial prop like a tree trunk can be made without the disadvantage of weight.

Do not forget that textures can be added to the paint to increase surface detail. P.V.A. (white flexible glue) can be mixed with powder color to create a plastic skin-like surface, and quantities of sand, gravel, dried beans, or pasta suspended in this medium produce interesting effects.

Lath and very thin ply, which has been moistened to make it more pliable, is useful when a curved wooden framework is required. Staples should be used to secure the joints and fix the chicken wire to the wooden framework. Clothbacked adhesive tape across the joints will stabilize them until the cloth mâché is applied.

MATERIALS
Wood; nails; carpenters' glue; chicken wire; wire tape (insulation tape); paint; shellac

TOOLS
Tenon saw; hammer; buckets; wooden spoon; gas burner or source of heat; tin snips; pliers; scissors; brushes

1 *Make a wooden frame using conventional joining methods; hammer and nails, or drill and screws, or chisel and carpenters' glue*

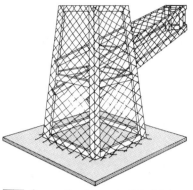

2 *Cover the frame with chicken wire. Staple the wire to the wooden frame, weaving and twisting the ragged ends of the wires together*

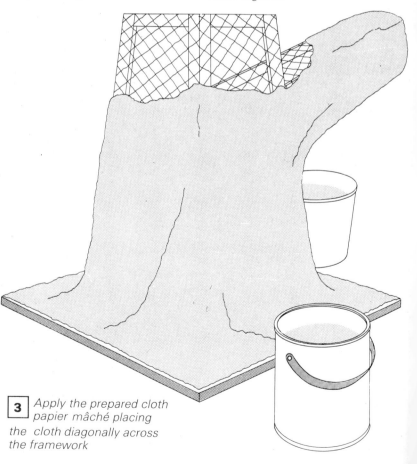

3 *Apply the prepared cloth papier mâché placing the cloth diagonally across the framework*

Using papier mâché on a balloon frame

Balloons are ideal as a shortcut to creating spherical shapes. The papier mâché covering can form the basis for such things as jugs, bowls, pots, masks, and helmets.

Prepare the paper and balloons

Tear the sheets of newspaper lengthwise (with the 'grain') into strips about 1 inch (25mm) wide. You can tell the grain direction simply because it is the direction in which the paper tears more easily. Make some strips narrower than 1 inch (25mm) if you are planning to add more detail after the basic shape is dry.

Using a large, shallow pan (a baking dish or roasting pan is practical — the paste rinses out with soap and water), pour about half an inch (12mm) of paste into the bottom. Soak the newspaper strips in the paste until they are completely saturated.

Assemble the balloons (if more than one is required), taping them with adhesive tape. Prop the balloon(s) on a stapled cardboard ring for support.

Apply the papier mâché

Lift one strip at a time from the pan and place it carefully on to the base. Smooth the pasted strip with your fingers from the middle to the ends, to eliminate any air bubbles or lumps of paste. Cover the base with one layer of strips horizontally, and follow this with a second layer at right angles to the first. Place the third and fourth layers diagonally on top of the others. Altering the direction of the newspaper strips guarantees complete, even, coverage of the base, and smoothing each strip as you apply it helps to build up a hard surface.

When the papier mâché is almost dry, pop the balloon and trim the papier mâché to shape.

Set aside the papier mâché object for a day or two, preferably in sunlight, to let all the moisture evaporate. To speed up drying you can bake it at low heat in an oven. When the object is hard and dry, decorate it with paints, paper sculptures or whatever is appropriate. Use facial tissue dipped in paste to build up small areas. A final layer of shellac or polyurethane lacquer will produce a hard, strong surface. Shellac mixed with metallic pigments is particularly effective as a finishing coat for equipment such as army helmets.

Cover the balloon with strips in the above sequence

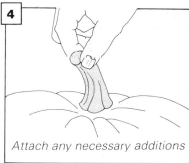

When the papier mâché is dry enough, burst the balloon

Attach any necessary additions

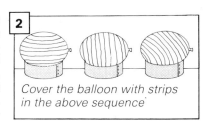

When the object is hard and dry, decorate it with paint

Support the balloon on a ring of cardboard

MATERIALS
Balloons; adhesive tape; cardboard to support balloons; papier mâché; paint; shellac

TOOLS
Scissors; large shallow pan; brushes

Using a balloon frame with other material

This Egyptian drinking cup can be made basically from papier mâché. The top quarter of a plastic bottle would be a suitable support for a hemispherical container (made from laminated papier mâché over a balloon). The handles at the sides are easily improvised depending on the materials available to you. Wires can be implanted in the bottle base and the hemispherical container molded with pulped papier mâché. Such things as lollipop sticks and cut-out cardboard may also be incorporated into the design. For any 'fretwork' carving, cardboard can be cut and shaped and a design built up with pasta or string glued on and then dipped in a mixture of P.V.A. (white flexible glue) and plaster of Paris (see page 32). The plaster will give body to the glue, and the glue will stop the plaster from being brittle. Once dried, this unit can be glued to the rest of the cup. Paint it all liberally with a slightly green-white emulsion paint.

When the paint is almost dry and has a skin over it, impress a design onto the body of the cup, with a blunt instrument to give an embossed look. When this coat has dried fully, rub some white paint here and there to give it the translucence of the original.

Exploit the wide range of balloon shapes to save unnecessary expense. A long, thin balloon, covered entirely with laminated paper, makes an excellent marrow, quiver, or stick of french bread. Round balloons are ideal for bombs, bread rolls, melons and other fruit. Do not forget about the fate of the balloon — an explosion on stage might not do much for the plot! — insert a long pin through the papier mâché.

Hemisphere of papier mâché formed on a balloon base

Decorate the surface using string dipped in glue

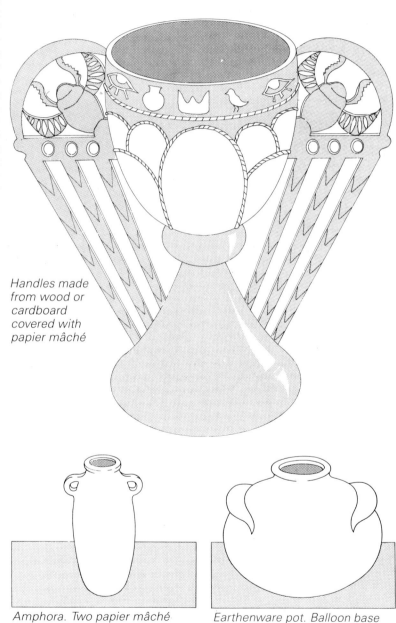

Handles made from wood or cardboard covered with papier mâché

Amphora. Two papier mâché hemispheres connected by a cardboard tube. The collar is cardboard, and the handles are wire covered with papier mâché

Earthenware pot. Balloon base papier mâché with cardboard collar and rope handles glued to the body and molded to shape with pulped papier mâché

Using papier mâché on an empty container

Instead of molding or building a base from wood or wire for your papier mâché, take advantage of the many and varied domestic containers which are always available. Some cartons or bottles are just the right size for building up a shape, while others are perfect for a particular feature: a toilet roll tube for a nose, egg carton sections for eyes. Using a disposable container for a base not only saves you time, it also cuts down on pollution, and makes practical use of what would otherwise be a piece of garbage.

Other suggestions for old containers: old tennis balls — cut in half, flower or plant pots.

When making hollow objects to contain liquid, leave the container inside the papier mâché structure.

A separator is then unnecessary. A toby jug could be assembled from the base of a plastic bottle, with a strip of plastic for a handle glued or wired into place. Cover the jug firstly with laminated papier mâché, adding pulp for the detail.

To make shallow bowls, line an existing plastic bowl with papier mâché. Do not forget to use a separator such as petroleum jelly.

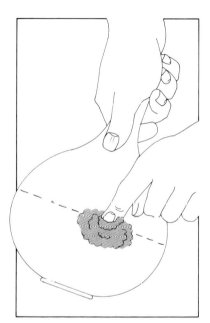

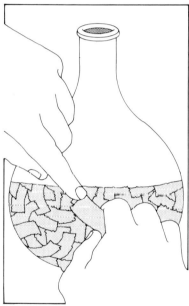

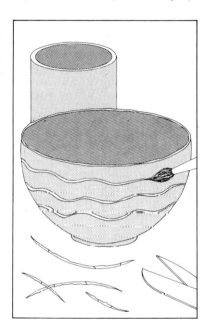

1 *Select and mark out contours on the container using a felt pen. Smear a thin layer of oil or petroleum jelly on to the shape to aid separation when the papier mâché is removed*

2 *Apply several layers of papier mâché to the container following the lines already drawn. Apply a final layer of well pasted cheesecloth to strengthen and bond the layers together*

3 *When the papier mâché is almost dry and has been removed from the container base, trim the edges with scissors. Dry thoroughly and paint. A final layer of shellac will harden off the surface and preserve the paintwork*

Papier mâché can be built onto small cardboard rolls or egg boxes to produce a variety of false noses!

Using papier mâché on corrugated cardboard

To make a coat of arms

There are many weights of corrugated paper and cardboard. Corrugated paper is best for smaller props: it is more pliable and may be cut using scissors without any distortion of the shape. Corrugated cardboard needs to be cut with a craft knife. It makes a sturdy base for papier mâché, particularly for such things as masks, shields and embellishments on furniture. You have to take care not to over wet the cardboard base with the papier mâché pulp. (Squeeze the pulp thoroughly to get rid of the excess glue). While the pulp papier mâché is wet other objects can be glued on for extra ornamentation, such as string (soaked in glue), rolls of newspaper, bottle caps, egg carton sections, marbles (excellent for eyes), beads, and so on.

Make sure these additions are pressed well into the papier mâché and are not left lying on the surface without any real adhesion.

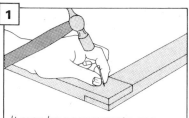

1

It may be necessary to construct a simple wooden frame for larger items

2

Cut out the coat of arms shape and glue or pin it to the frame

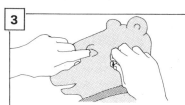

3

Press other objects well into the wet pulp to provide extra detail and to build up a three-dimensional shape

To make a palm tree

An exotic desert island location might seem a difficult set to contrive, but palm trees can be constructed simply by molding a number of cones, with slightly flared bases, in laminated papier mâché. The bottom one is glued or screwed on to a base board large and stable enough to stop the tree being top heavy. Cover the base with glue and sand, (or suitable ground foliage) and pile the rest of the cones on top of each other to make the trunk of the three. The top cone supports the leaves — cut out from green paper or thin cardboard. You can glue all of the cones together, or you can make the tree in two parts that will come apart again for storage. The use of separate cones allows you to give the trunk a graceful bend before you glue the parts together.

Use the same principle to fashion large rubber plants or swiss cheese plants

Deciduous or coniferous trees could be made using a wood and wire frame with cloth mâché (see page 24) and paper for the leaves.

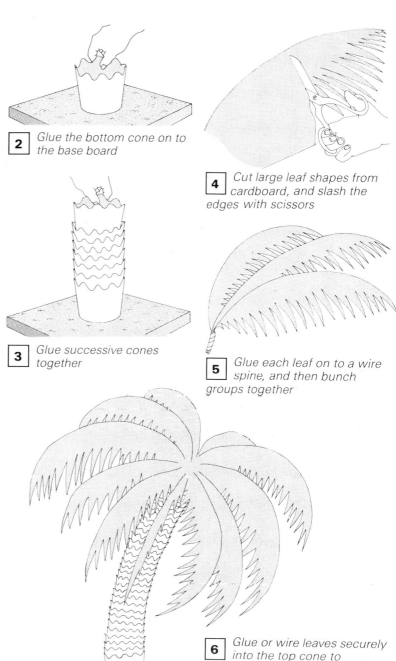

2 Glue the bottom cone on to the base board

3 Glue successive cones together

4 Cut large leaf shapes from cardboard, and slash the edges with scissors

5 Glue each leaf on to a wire spine, and then bunch groups together

6 Glue or wire leaves securely into the top cone to complete the tree

1 Pour a mixture of glue and sand on to the base board

Applying papier mâché to expanded polystyrene

Expanded polystyrene is an extremely useful material for a papier mâché base. Great bulk can be achieved and yet the object will be very lightweight. For small objects the papier mâché can be applied directly to shaped polystyrene. Larger shapes are probably better glued (with carpenters' glue or heavy wallpaper paste) to a layer of canvas or gauze first, which gives a 'key' for applying the papier mâché. For very large objects cloth mâché is a stronger, more satisfactory way of covering polystyrene.

Keep larger objects light and portable by using crushed-up paper or roughly-shaped chicken wire as a base.

Simple props like fruit and meat pies can be made very realistically with papier mâché pulp over polystyrene. They have the advantage of being non-perishable and can also be thrown about the stage without damage to themselves or the actors. If you want such things to throw at people, make them in papier mâché (in two halves) on a plasticine mold, so that they are hollow. Solid pulp is rather hard and heavy, and if you are being hit with a papier mâché pulp banana it is almost as painful as being hit with a real one!

Sometimes it is necessary to have food props that can be broken apart regularly. Here the fabric fastener, Velcro, comes into its own. If a chicken leg has to be removed from a carcass, make the body and leg(s) separately in papier mâché, then glue two pieces of compatible Velcro to the surfaces that need to be bonded together. The actor can then cheerfully rip off the chicken leg when the plot requires (and put it back for the next performance)!

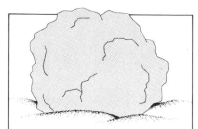

Roughly shaped and covered with glue/cloth papier mâché, this is a realistic yet light-weight boulder

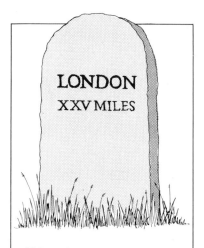

This polystyrene milestone was glued to a wooden base, then covered in cloth mâché

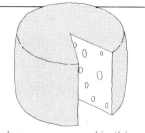

Holes were gouged in this polystyrene cheese and a single layer of gauze applied using heavy wallpaper paste or size

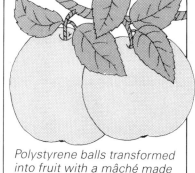

Polystyrene balls transformed into fruit with a mâché made from tissue paper. They are attached to the branches with wire

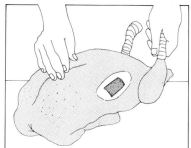

A chicken carcass made from polystyrene with wire limbs, covered with papier mâché. Velcro allows the leg to be detachable

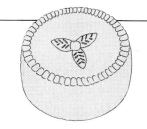

A pie made from ceiling tiles laminated together and scalloped around the edge with a hot knife. The papier mâché covering the pie is pulped on top to give an undulating surface

Using papier mâché on foil

The flexibility of foil makes it invaluable for duplicating a shape. It can be molded around part of the body, to create a mask or a piece of armor or be pressed against a plaque to reproduce an approximation of the original.

Two layers of foil need to be used, and, of course, speed is essential when molding the foil over a face. Remove frequently for ventilation. Children need to be supervised when using this process.

1

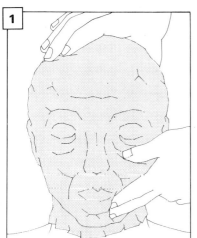

Mold foil and trim where necessary. (If modeling a face, try to work as quickly as possible so as not to cut off the person's air supply for too long.)

MATERIALS
Metal foil (not cooking foil as this is too fragile); torn paper; paste; water; gauze; shellac; paint

TOOLS
Scissors; two buckets, (one for water, one for paste); brushes

2

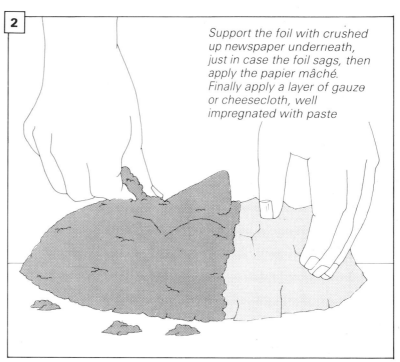

Support the foil with crushed up newspaper underneath, just in case the foil sags, then apply the papier mâché. Finally apply a layer of gauze or cheesecloth, well impregnated with paste

3

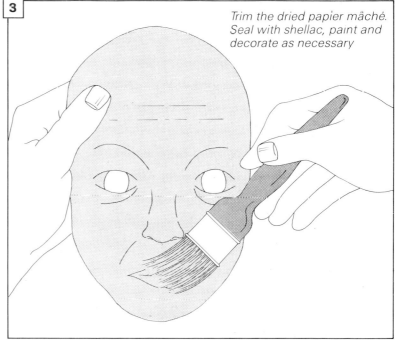

Trim the dried papier mâché. Seal with shellac, paint and decorate as necessary

Working with plaster

Plaster is, next to papier mâché, the most important material for the prop maker. Basic plaster of Paris is extremely versatile, and there is also a highly refined, purified version known as dental plaster, which sets with a harder, finer finish.

Use plaster on, or in conjunction with, wood, wire, cardboard, plastic, and many other materials. Gauze, cotton sheeting, canvas and scrim immersed in plaster and draped around a framework adds additional detail or texture. Plaster is particularly useful for making and filling molds because of its fast drying properties. It can also be carved with chisels and gouges and smoothed down with surforms and sandpaper — and its surface takes paint well.

Certain points should be noted before embarking upon plaster work.

1 The plaster/water ratio: most of the properties of plaster are dependent upon this ratio, in particular the setting time (which can vary from ten minutes upwards), expansion, surface hardness and all-over strength. The greater the water content, the slower the setting time, the weaker the plaster etc.

2 Plaster blocks up sinks and toilets efficiently — beware! Wash utensils, hands, tools, etc in a bowl, then carefully drain away the water leaving the sediment of plaster debris behind in the bowl, to be thrown out separately into the garbage can.

3 Nonrigid plastic containers are essential for mixing plaster, as well as flexible plastic spatulas to scrape the bowls clean and apply the plaster. If the plaster dries hard in a plastic bowl, it can be prized away from the sides by flexing it.

4 Plaster can irritate some people's skins and no matter how careful you are, you invariably get plastered! Disposable surgical gloves, or just rubber gloves, are ideal for plaster work as the hardened plaster will flake off.

5 Quantities: it is difficult to judge quantities needed for plaster work. It is certainly best and more economical to make and use small amounts at a time. This will prevent plaster hardening, or setting before you are ready to use

it. The best way to establish the proportion of plaster-to-water is to place the dry plaster of Paris into a bowl in such a way that it forms a peak in the middle. Slowly pour water into the bowl along the edges until it reaches the level of the peak. Mix in the plaster carefully until it has the consistency of thick cream.

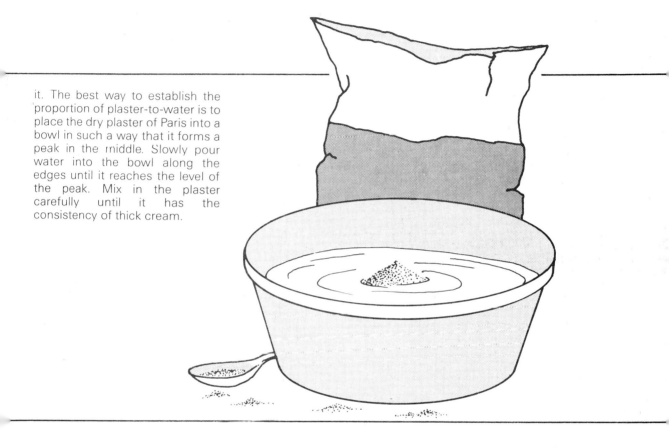

Utilizing household items for plasterwork

Every home is an ideal source of plasterwork supplies. Some items are useful for carving plasticine or clay. Others make suitable modeling shapes.

Plastic containers, as we have noted, are highly suitable for mixing plaster. Their flexible nature makes it easy to remove the plaster once it has dried.

Wire, looped and fixed in the barrel of an old ballpoint pen, makes a satisfactory tool with which to pare away surplus clay.

Containers used as molds, produce suitable casts for sculpting simple shapes and bottle caps impressed in clay add extra detail.

Rope, string, or cord dipped in plaster and applied, while wet, on an existing piece of plasterwork can create interesting architectural detail.

Egg carton sections, plaster- filled, are useful to stick on to plaster sculptures for additional dimension.

Using plaster in combination with other materials

Plaster can be used inventively for purposes other than carved shapes or molded items.

Canvas or cotton sheeting dipped in plaster and draped across a shop dummy creatively, can give just the impression of drapery found on a classical Greek statue.

Lumpy, half-set plaster can be applied quickly to give an uneven texture to an object or a wall. (Don't forget to wash the roller before the plaster sets!)

Plaster containers act as good ballast to otherwise top-heavy props. Unimpressive pictures or mirrors can be transformed with decorative ornate frames made from plaster. Plasticine is pressed on to an original ornate molding, then removed, and the impression filled with plaster. Once set, the plaster is separated from the plasticine and glued on to the plain wooden frame with P.V.A. (white flexible glue) and painted or gilded. This method is equally suitable for embellishing plain objects, such as caskets or pieces of furniture.

To make a slow drying plaster mix

Dissolve a quantity of cellulose filler in water and mix with the plaster powder, ½ pound (225g) cellulose to 14 pounds (6kgs) of plaster. Adding the filler not only makes the plaster mix easier to work with — giving it a creamy consistency that dries out very smoothly — but it also retards the setting process for half an hour or so, allowing more time to complete the job.

To make an ornate picture frame

1 Press plasticine into an existing molding. Release the plasticine and pour in the plaster

2 Separate the set plaster from the plasticine and glue it to a plain wooden frame. Finish by painting or gilding

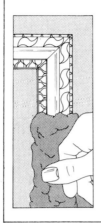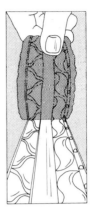

To make drapery for a classical statue

Using a shop dummy as a base, wind plastered scrim around the dummy to provide a key. Dip old cotton sheeting into liquid plaster and drape this over the dummy

To stabilize a large flower pot

To prevent a vase of artificial flowers from being top heavy, place chicken wire in the base. Push stems into the netting and fill the pot with plaster, keeping it upright until set

Making an armature

Plaster is extremely unmanageable while in a wet state (rather like cement without bricks). An armature acts as a useful skeletal frame to which the plaster can be applied. It also reinforces shape and defines size and proportion.

1 Making a wooden frame

The base is generally made up of a block of fairly heavy wood — blockboard or particle board is excellent — to prevent the structure from being top-heavy and to give proper support.

The basic structure need not be a sophisticated piece of woodwork with complicated joints. In fact nails or screws left protruding from the frame are helpful when attaching and tying the wire covering. They also provide a key when the plaster is applied.

Suitable softwood scraps including roof battening, dowelling and floorboarding will do. The only really important joint to get right, when building the frame, is the vertical support with the base, as it is very difficult to work on a nonrigid structure.

MATERIALS
Scraps of wood; oddments of bendable wire of varying thickness; wire netting or screen; clothbacked adhesive tape; staples; plaster of Paris; scrim or strips of cloth (or plaster impregnated bandage); water; emulsion paint, preferably white, for sealing; plus any paint for coloring

TOOLS
Saw; hammer; drill; screwdriver; mallet and chisel; pliers; scissors; tin snips; soldering iron; rubber gloves; plastic bowl, bucket or suitable mixing container; water container; plastic spatula; newspaper to protect working area; surform; sandpaper; paint brushes

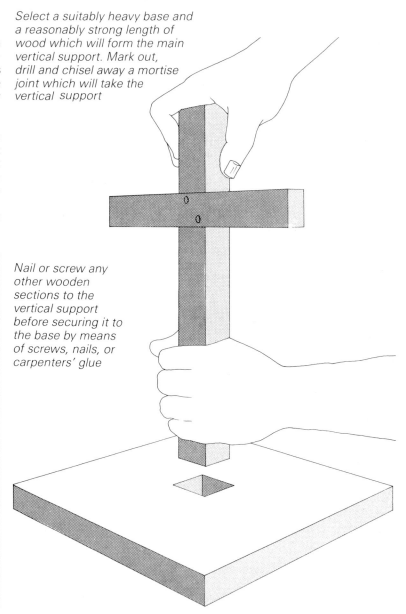

Select a suitably heavy base and a reasonably strong length of wood which will form the main vertical support. Mark out, drill and chisel away a mortise joint which will take the vertical support

Nail or screw any other wooden sections to the vertical support before securing it to the base by means of screws, nails, or carpenters' glue

2 Covering the frame with bendable wire

Once the wooden frame is completed, wire can be added. (It is not absolutely necessary but it helps to bulk-out a form and save on the amount of plaster needed.)

Wrap sturdy wire around the wooden base to form an armature, securing it with clothbacked adhesive tape, thin wire, or staples, to the base and vertical support

Cover this with chicken wire, pushing and pulling it into shape. Twist the ragged cut edges of the wire together and tape to the framework

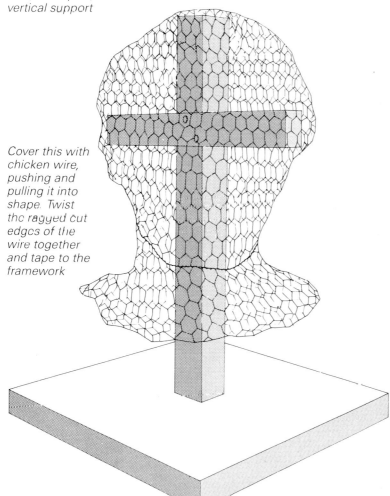

Wire of varying thicknesses (according to availability) can be wound and twisted around the wood, extending the length if necessary for slender shapes.

An armature or frame of a figure with a wooden body would need wire to create the arms and legs. The wire is attached to the wood with staples, nails or clothbacked adhesive tape. Wire in the form of chicken wire is perhaps the most expedient way to bulk-out a basic framework. Chicken wire can be pulled, pushed, and crunched into shape and is malleable enough to take on the final form desired. Thin wire can be woven to link the chicken wire together (or the ragged ends of the wire can be twisted together) and then the whole is attached to the framework with clothbacked adhesive tape.

Another method of joining wire together is by soldering. This is only really necessary when a refined frame is required or when part of the frame is exposed.

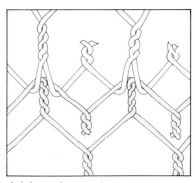

Joining wire mesh

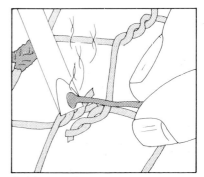

Soldering wire

Making an armature

3 Mixing and applying plaster

Have ready some scrim or strips of cloth cut to short lengths. Make up the plaster as explained on page 32. Dip the scrim or strips of cloth into the plaster and wrap it around the frame like a bandage, scraping the surplus plaster from your hands on to the frame. As the plaster begins to thicken it can be layered with the hands or a plastic spatula. (Once the plaster has started to crumble it cannot be re-constituted). If plaster-impregnated bandage is being used, cut it into small lengths, and dip each into a bowl of water before applying.. A final layer of plaster will be required on the surface if carving is necessary.

When the plaster has hardened and you have achieved an adequate thickness, chisel or gouge in the detail, and smooth off with a surform and sandpaper.

Use spare pieces mixed with P.V.A. (white flexible glue) for extra texture on other props.

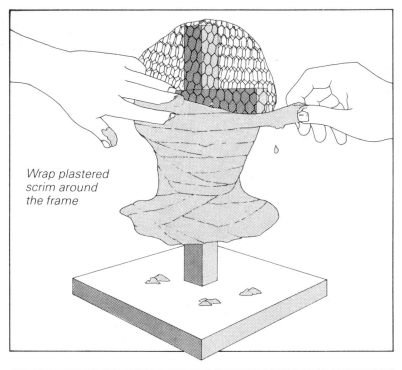

Wrap plastered scrim around the frame

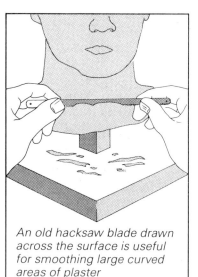

An old hacksaw blade drawn across the surface is useful for smoothing large curved areas of plaster

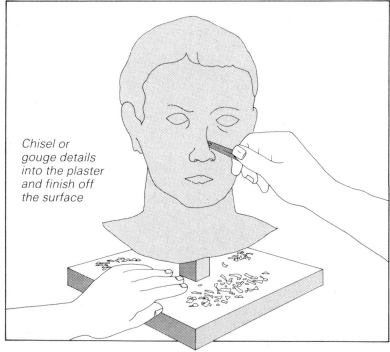

Chisel or gouge details into the plaster and finish off the surface

4 Finishing, sealing and painting the structure

Almost any paint can be used on plaster. It is best to seal with stabilizing solution and then paint with primer or emulsion — in white preferably. The wire structure underneath will rust and stain the plaster, and the emulsion will conceal this. Emulsion also helps to slow down the absorption of the final coat of paint, making it more economical and giving any color applied afterwards more resilience. Apart from this, emulsion creates a skin on the surface of the plaster which gives a greater surface strength to the finished object. If childrens' powder paint is used, color can be watered down to compensate for the rapid absorption of the paint in the plaster. If gloss is required apply a coat of glossy paint to the emulsion, or add a final coating of varnish such as shellac or polyurethane.

Add the finishing touch to a statue with hair made from string, felt laurel leaves or a chain painted with emulsion.

Making a plaster mold

Plaster molds are most economical to make. Once the technique has been mastered it is relatively straightforward to use these molds in conjunction with many other materials including papier mâché, fiberglass and latex.

Knowing how to make a mold saves considerable time and energy particularly when you have to replicate an object many times. An original clay form is hardly durable as a 'one off' on a stage set, whereas reproduced in an alternative material it will give the versatility required.

1 Making the frame and applying the clay

Make an armature or frame of wood and wire (see page 36) to resemble the basic skeletal shape of your object as closely as possible. It is best to use a small meshed wire as the final layer before the clay. Apply the clay in small flattened balls to the wire and cover the entire structure before making any attempt at detailed modeling. The most successfully cast props for stage productions are probably the simplest, made with bold modeling and form.

MATERIALS
Wood; wire; nails or screws; clothbacked adhesive tape; clay or plasticine; old tin cans or rigid metal foil; wax separator, soft soap or petroleum jelly; plaster

TOOLS
Hammer; saw; drill; scissors; mallet; chisel; tin snips; clay carving tools; tough gloves; brush; mixing bowl; water container

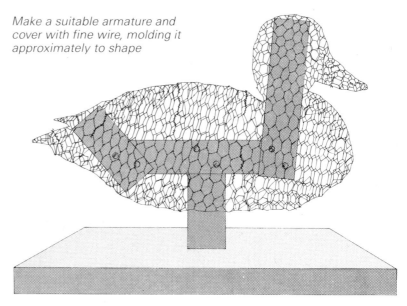

Make a suitable armature and cover with fine wire, molding it approximately to shape

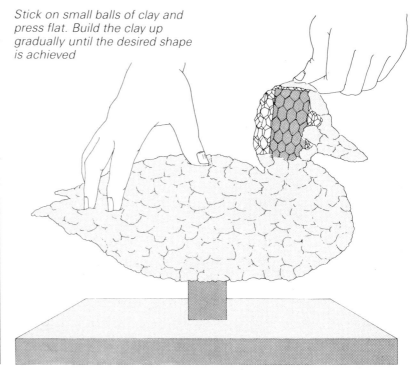

Stick on small balls of clay and press flat. Build the clay up gradually until the desired shape is achieved

To begin with, it will be difficult to see how your sculpture is developing. Position the clay model where there is a strong light source (from one side only) and look at it with half-closed eyes. This will help you see the main form clearly. When you are happy with the shape, use a ruler to tap gently all over your sculpture. Soon the surface will be free of bumps, yet with the form retained. You can now add any detail that you require.

2 Making and inserting a foil plate divider

Cut up the foil with tin snips [it would be wise to wear a pair of tough gloves when cutting the foil to avoid injury to the hands]. If foil is not available, cans are an alternative, but the cutting process is not easy! Butt and overlap the edges of the foil plates to prevent plaster seepage. The foil fence is more simple to fit together if formed in a zig-zag.

Undercutting

An undercut is the projection of part or parts of a rigid mold which prevents easy removal of the original clay form or casting material. As you will see from the illustration below much depends upon where the foil fence is situated.

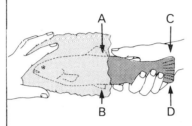

In this case it is across the form and the points A & B are deep within the mold and cannot be pulled out. If points C & D were

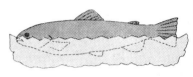

covered, they would also be obstructive. By using a longitudinal fence we solve this particular problem.

Sometimes, however a more complicated mold will have to be made, with more than just one fence. The process is identical, although the mold sections will need to be taped and wired together

If you sculpt the clay simply and avoid splaying forms many of the problems of undercutting are avoided.

The clay object is divided by a fence made up of foil plates

The fence is made in a zig-zag pattern, down the long side, to act as a key when the joint has to be matched on the mold

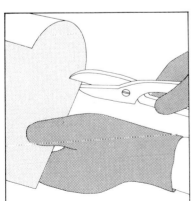

Old cans are cut up with tin snips to make the fence. Caution: wear gloves!

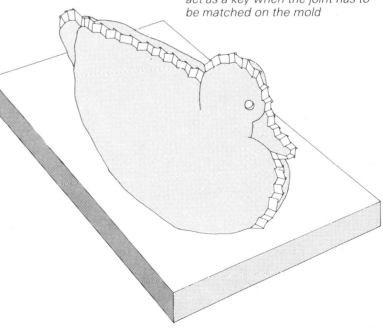

Making a plaster mold

3 Applying the plaster

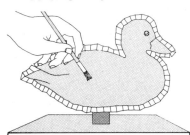

The clay is then lightly greased with petroleum jelly, oil (or another proprietary separator) which stops the clay and plaster sticking to each other

Make up the plaster (see guidelines on page 32) and flick it on to the model

As the first layer hardens, more and more plaster is applied, until the clay armature is completely buried, except for the plate fence of which just the tip should be left exposed—

4 Separating the mold

When the plaster is dry and brittle, break the mold by pulling out the plates. The two halves should come apart easily and the original is then easily removed. If necessary, use a clay tool with a wire loop to extract more confined sections (such as the beak). The clay or plasticine can then be reclaimed for further modeling. Clean the mold gently with a soft brush (like a toothbrush) under running water. Take care not to damage the zig-zag key.

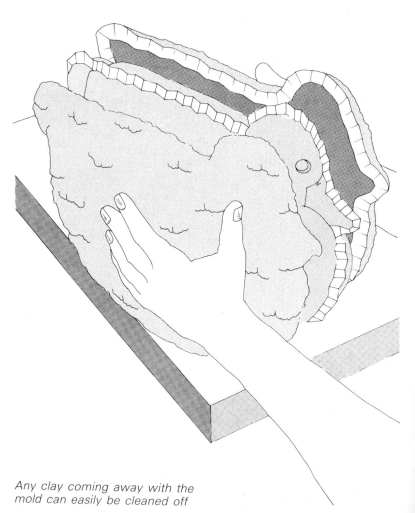

Any clay coming away with the mold can easily be cleaned off

Making replicas by filling a plaster mold

Coat the inside of both halves of the mold with a wax separator — thoroughly covering every nook and cranny. Wire the mold halves together — two people may be required for this job! Carefully fit the zig-zag edges of the long sides together whilst tying the wire around the body of the mold. Twist and tighten the two ends with a pair of pliers, until the wire is firm.

Invert and place the mold on an appropriate stand to steady it. Depending upon the shape of the mold, a suitable stand might be made from a cardboard box. Make the plaster and pour it slowly into the gap formed by the armature, occasionally banging the side of the mold to allow trapped air bubbles to surface. Continue pouring until the mold is filled.

When the plaster is dry (within 15 minutes or so), untwist the wire and carefully ease apart the two halves of the mold, revealing the plaster cast. It is then ready to finish or paint.

A hollow thin-shelled plaster object can be made by pouring plaster into the wire bound and inverted mold and by swirling it about, to cover all edges, until a desirable thickness is reached and it sets. This process is particularly useful for statues or objects that have to be broken every night.

N.B. This mold is equally suitable for lining with papier mâché.

MATERIALS
Wax separator; thin wire; plaster

TOOLS
Brush; pliers; mixing bowl; water container

1

Brush wax separator carefully into both halves of the mold

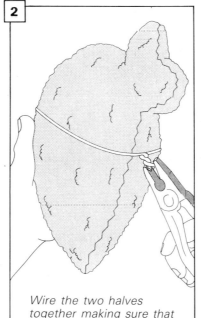

2

Wire the two halves together making sure that they fit perfectly

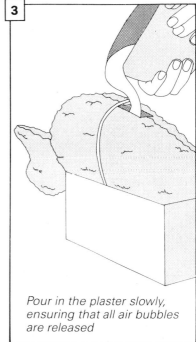

3

Pour in the plaster slowly, ensuring that all air bubbles are released

4

Once the plaster is dry and brittle, separate the two halves of the mold

Using dental moulage to make a face mask

Dental moulage is a process involving alginate, a flexible dental molding material. When mixed with water the alginate becomes thick and creamy, and, once applied, it soon sets into a rubber-like compound capable of reproducing the finest detail. Its fast setting nature means that a mold is ready to be filled within minutes of being made. This is particularly helpful when modeling parts of the human body, such as arms to add to a plaster Buddha figure, or a realistic copy of an actor's head.

There are no problems with undercutting (see page 4l) as the mold is flexible enough to release the cast. Always use dental plaster with this process, to produce the most realistic effect.

There are two types of alginate, one is reusable, the other is not. The non-reusable alginate is more readily available. The mold is only workable for a very short time and then disintegrates into a powder. Whichever kind of alginate you use, follow the manufacturer's instructions closely.

Preparing the subject

The subject is seated in a chair with a neck rest (a barber's chair would be ideal). The hair should be covered by a swimming cap, a

> **MATERIALS**
> Large plastic straw; alginate; plaster-impregnated bandage; dental plaster; water
>
> **TOOLS**
> Chair with neck rest; plastic swimming cap; rubber spatula; scissors; bowl; brush

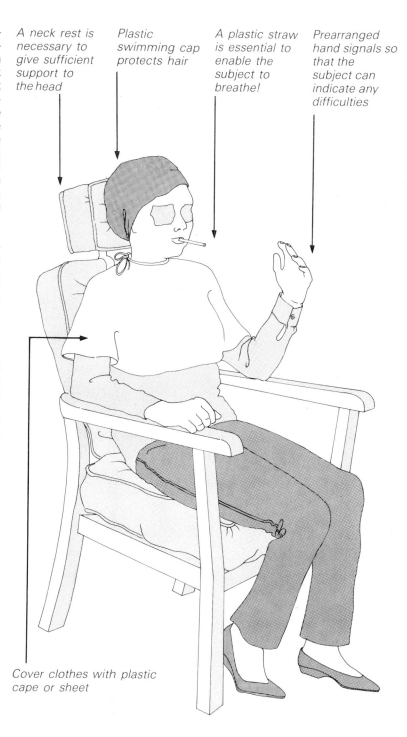

A neck rest is necessary to give sufficient support to the head

Plastic swimming cap protects hair

A plastic straw is essential to enable the subject to breathe!

Prearranged hand signals so that the subject can indicate any difficulties

Cover clothes with plastic cape or sheet

straw inserted into the mouth for breathing, and a plastic cape used for protection. Gauze, glued down with petroleum jelly must be used to cover any facial hair such as brows, eyelashes, moustache etc. Prearranged hand signals are essential as there will be no facial expressions or speech for communication. A hand held up is a good idea: when the hand drops, you're in trouble! Although not entirely necessary, it may be a good thing to plug the subject's nostrils with cotton wool balls. It will avoid panic if any alginate is inhaled.

Mixing and applying moulage efficiently

Use a rubber spatula, and only mix a small quantity of alginate at a time. It has a very fast setting time (3 minutes at 20°C) and the colder the water used the longer the setting time. It is helpful for two people to work together — one applying the moulage while the other mixes a fresh batch.

Applying plaster

Once the alginate has dried and solidified, cut strips of plaster-impregnated bandage (or make up your own plaster and use scrim), dip them in water and apply them over the alginate. The plaster acts as a strengthener, making the mold rigid and manageable without losing its shape. When a good layer of plaster has been applied and it has hardened, remove the negative mold from the subject's face. It is now ready to be cast.

Making a make plaster cast

Mix the dental plaster and fill the negative mold, tapping occasionally to remove air bubbles. Allow plaster to set hard and separate negative mold from positive cast.

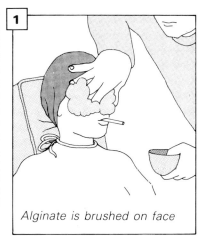

1

Alginate is brushed on face

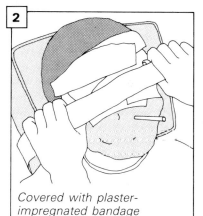

2

Covered with plaster-impregnated bandage

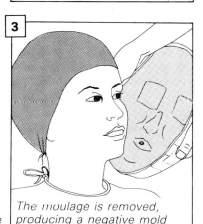

3

The moulage is removed, producing a negative mold

4

Dental plaster is brushed into the negative mold

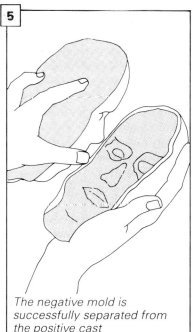

5

The negative mold is successfully separated from the positive cast

Making a sandcast

Sandcasting is a very old method of making molds. It does not have many applications for the prop maker but is a useful process to know. The rough surface texture creates an ancient weathered look suitable for plaques, gargoyles, and architectural detail on props.

Fill a bowl or tub with sand nearly to the top and level it off, moistening with water so that it will hold its shape. Use the hands or a smooth object to compress the sand and then make bold, varied impressions. A single shape such as a jelly mold could be used or the whole surface of the sand covered with a multiple design.

Make up fairly fluid plaster and, using a small plastic jar, pour it into the sand. Do this slowly so as not to disturb the fragile undulations of the cast. Continue pouring until the plaster of Paris reaches the top of the bowl, or lower if a thinner cast is required. If the cast is to be hung, insert a wire loop before the plaster sets.

When the plaster is solid — although it will not be completely dry — loosen it by drawing a knife around the edge and remove it from the mold.

Brush away the excess sand very carefully and rinse to remove the last particles. The plaster coating retains the rough texture of the sand and gives the impression of age. Pare away any unwanted plaster around the edges, using a mallet and chisel.

MATERIALS
Sand; plaster; water

TOOLS
Bowl; various objects to provide decoration

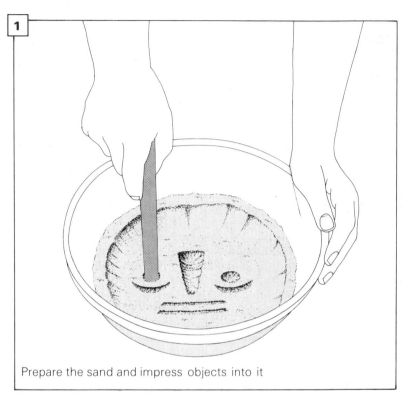

1

Prepare the sand and impress objects into it

2

Gently pour in the plaster

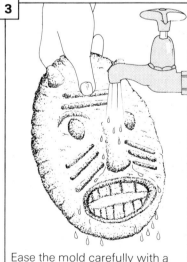

3

Ease the mold carefully with a knife and rinse under water. Remove the surplus plaster

Painting and finishing plasterwork

Type of paint	Suitability	Finish
Oil type paints (thinned with paint thinner)	Producing a glossy strong surface, needs to have the surface primed first	Glossy, semigloss
Emulsion paints, water thinned, easy to clean brushes and remove splashes	Can be used thinned as an undercoat [ratio 2 pints (1.14l) water to I gallon (4.5l) paint]	Matte or slight sheen
Acrylic or semigloss emulsion can be thinned with water	May be applied directly without an undercoat	Semigloss and matte
Powder colors tempera blocks	Cheap, very suitable for bold color, but needs to have top coat varnish to make it durable and not rub off	Any finish according to final layer of varnish
Gloss aerosol	Good, seal with emulsion	Glossy
Felt pens and day-glo pens	For detail only (see p.14)	Bold, clear colors

Use old toothbrushes to stipple almost set plaster for a change in texture. Metal bucket handles make good gauges and old hacksaw blades are useful for paring away set plaster, or for sawing off unwanted sections.

Suitable modeling shapes and bases could include: plastic bottles (cut into sections), cardboard tubes, shoe boxes, lampshade frames, or rubber gloves, filled with plaster — or wrapped around with plastered scrim.

Overalls are an absolute necessity when working with plaster. Plastic sacks make excellent substitutes, although obviously great care needs to be taken if these are to be worn by children, to avoid any risk of suffocation. Plastic carrier bags can be converted for smaller children!

Sandpaper smooth

Surform rough surfaces

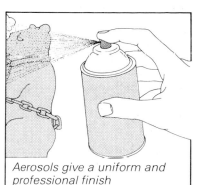
Aerosols give a uniform and professional finish

Working with synthetic materials

There are many synthetic materials available and on the whole these are lighter and stronger than many of the other methods used for making props. The prop maker has to weigh up their advantages against those of the more traditional and less expensive methods.

Expanded polystyrene fortunately does not come into the expensive category, which is probably why it is a popular material. It is very effective when used in conjunction with papier mâché or plaster. The ease with which it is cut and shaped, plus its lightness, make it a good choice for prop makers and stage hands alike. Because it is a disposable material used in packaging, large pieces may be found protecting electrical items and smaller pieces in supermarkets as meat trays and fruit trays. Most builder suppliers will sell it in a convenient sheet form.

Fiberglass is also tough and lightweight and suitable for replacing many of the cumbersome and heavier prop materials. It can be purchased at craft and model shops or at stores specializing in selling car spares and kit for car maintenance; sometimes you can buy it at garages.

Fiberglass can serve as a mold filler or can duplicate existing shapes when applied to the outside of an object. Once the fiberglass technique has been mastered, one can adapt its use in many ways. Protective clothing and good ventilation are essential when working with fiberglass as close contact with it can cause skin rashes and restricted breathing. Beware of fiberglass dust and remember that the material catches fire easily.

Both vinyl and latex are expensive to use. Vinyl molds can be justified when many objects have to be made and the convenience of having a flexible mold outweighs the expense. Latex is perhaps only suitable for a production with a reasonably good budget.

Polyurethane is becoming more fashionable for making larger props. It has similar shaping and cutting qualities to expanded polystyrene, but is obtained in liquid form. Two separate mixtures are combined to produce a solid foam.

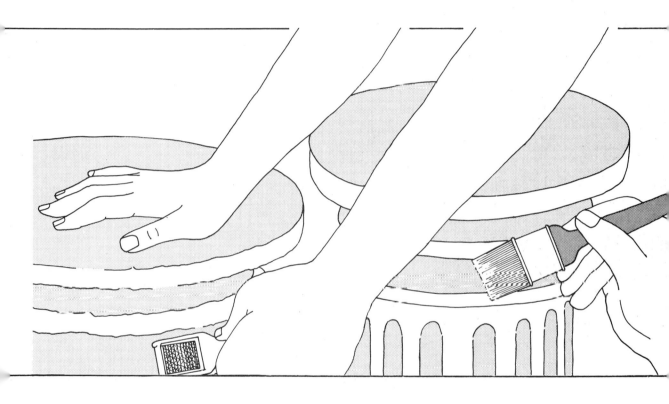

Basic techniques with expanded polystyrene

Expanded polystyrene is a light, firm, plastic solid that can be easily carved. It needs only to be covered (with papier mâché, cloth mâché, plaster or paper), to take on a new identity. Tree stumps, boulders, statues, architectural ruins are light and manageable when made this way. Food, picture frames and furniture detail can be assembled from small sections of polystyrene.

Polystyrene can be joined by gluing, by sewing, or by taping pieces together with wire to make a larger mass. Size, glue and carpenters' glue may be used as may some plastic adhesives (provided they do not melt the polystyrene).

Expanded polystyrene is also available sandwiched between two layers of fine cardboard. This foamboard is particularly useful as it has a greater rigidity than cardboard alone and therefore need not be reinforced. Sections of furniture, placards, mock books, axe heads, standards and small scenery flats are simply and quickly made by cutting out sections with a sharp craft knife.

Cutting

To cut an object from a block of expanded polystyrene, draw the front, side and top profiles on the block and cut away unwanted pieces with a saw or bread knife. Do not use these tools for delicate or close work, because they tend to rip rather than cut the material. If available an electric router would be suitable for large assemblies of polystyrene. This is an attachment to an electric drill and is usually used for shaping concrete. However, a circular wire brush fitted to an electric drill will produce the same effect as a router in sculpting the material. Use a surform to round off the edges and corners.

For precise carving, cut with a sharp knife or even better, a heated knife. For extremely delicate work, use a heated wire for each cut. Tape the wire to insulate your hand from the conducted heat. (Reheat when cold and it will cut again.) Great finesse in detail can be obtained by this method. It is now possible to buy electrically heated knives designed for this purpose.

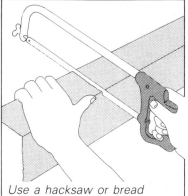

Use a hacksaw or bread knife for cutting large blocks

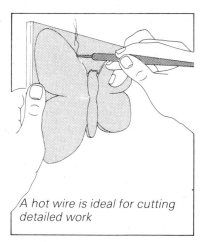

A hot wire is ideal for cutting detailed work

A Roman standard
This standard is quickly made from foamboard. A slit is cut in a thick piece of doweling and the foamboard inserted. Cover the board with foil using P.V.A. (white flexible glue)

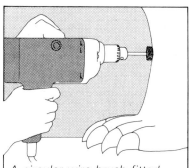

A circular wire brush fitted on to an electric drill can be used to model expanded polystyrene

Large sheets of polystyrene should be cut with a sharp knife and steel ruler

Using solvents

Solvents can be painted on to the foam, causing it to dissolve to provide varied depth. Metallic paint sprayed through a mask, such as a paper doilie, creates interesting detail. The exposed expanded polystyrene partly dissolves, leaving a raised pattern.

Fixing and assembling

Polystyrene sheets slotted and glued to make them freestanding

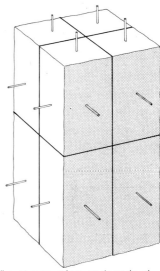

Wire straps, pins, or 'sewing' with wire will hold blocks together efficiently

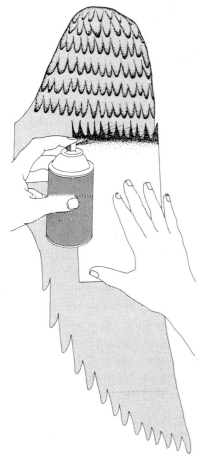

Angels' wings for a nativity play decorated with gold paint sprayed through a stencil made from stiff cardboard

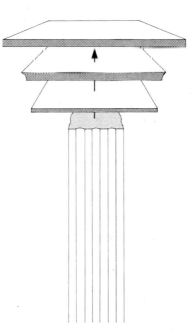

Solvents can be used on sheets of expanded polystyrene. The two surfaces dissolve, combine, then bond together

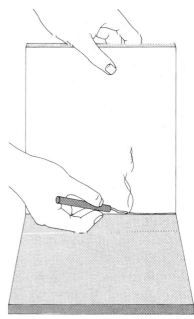

Two pieces of expanded polystyrene can be joined by running a hot wire along the two edges

Expanded polystyrene in combination with other materials

Making a sculpture of an angel

String, glued to the papier mâché surface, serves as hair

Fine papier or cloth mâché should be applied to both the wings and the body so that there is no change in the surface texture

Marbles are useful as eyes

Assemble the structure from a number of blocks of expanded polystyrene joined together with wire. Cut the rough shape with a bread knife or hacksaw, smooth with a surform and use a hot knife to add detail

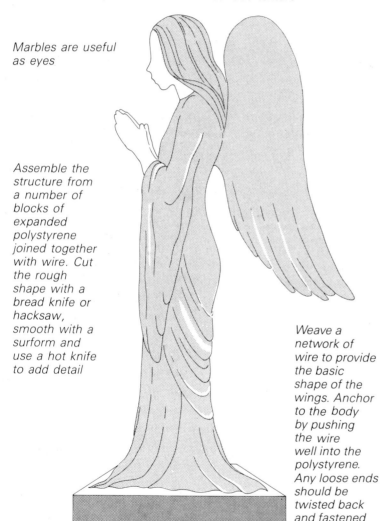

Weave a network of wire to provide the basic shape of the wings. Anchor to the body by pushing the wire well into the polystyrene. Any loose ends should be twisted back and fastened with clothbacked adhesive tape. Cover with papier mâché, using fairly large pieces of paper

Old sheets dipped in plaster and draped across the body provide added depth

Covering expanded polystyrene

Because of its plastic nature, expanded polystyrene rejects some paints, especially the oil-based variety. Therefore it is necessary to cover the surface with a layer of paintable material. Papier mâché, (cloth and glue, or gauze dipped in some binding agent like white flexible glue) is suitable for this purpose and helps to build up the desired contours. P.V.A. (white flexible glue) mixed with pigment, and textured with wood shavings or sand, can be painted directly on to polystyrene.

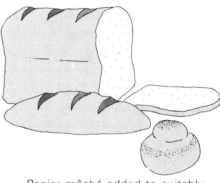

Papier mâché added to suitably shaped polystyrene

Gold bars modeled from expanded polystyrene and covered with metal foil

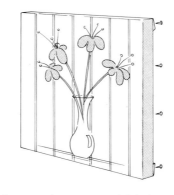

Finishing and fireproofing

As stated before, expanded polystyrene rejects some paint (particularly oil-based), so experiment for suitability with other varieties. Never use household gloss on expanded polystyrene: it becomes a lethal fire risk.

◇

Layers of papier or cloth mâché will not only strengthen the surface, but also change the texture and provide a good key.

Plaster layered on to expanded polystyrene takes most paints and will help stop surface erosion, although it may chip. P.V.A. (white flexible glue) mixed with powder color and a filler (such as sand, gravel or wood shavings) creates a different surface texture. Like its relative 'oasis' (florist's foam), which is used in flower arranging, polystyrene can act as an anchor for rods and wires. Additional shapes made from papier mâché on a wire base could have wire extensions deeply embedded into the polystyrene to make them secure.

Plaster of Paris mixed with sand applied to an expanded polystyrene base to make a realistic cake

Patterned or textured fabrics stretched over expanded polystyrene give the appearance of an artist's canvas

Felt, dipped in shellac is suitable as an alternative method of adding detail. (Especially for those who are unsure of their carving ability.) This provides a hard surface which is easy to paint.

Studs, nails and colored drawing pins are alternative decoration.

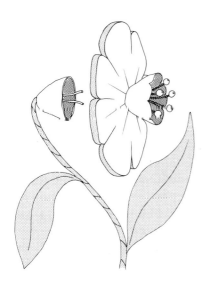

Expanded polystyrene has to be fire-proofed. If necessary you could first cover it with papier mâché. Fire-proofing crystals can be bought or a solution of 15 ounces (425g) boric acid plus 10 ounces (283g) sodium phosphate in 1 gallon (4.5l) of water made up and painted or sprayed on to the prop. Paintwork is easily damaged at this stage — take great care.

For a stylized production when realism is not important, flowers can be made of expanded polystyrene ceiling tiles with egg carton cup backs. These are fairly substantial and, suspended from the ceiling, can appear to grow if required.
Pipe cleaners threaded with beads, teazels or spirals of wood shavings are all possible centers for the flowers

Expanded polystyrene trays stuck on to the flat surfaces of cardboard furniture give an extra dimension. The trays could be assembled in the form of panelling or drawers. Do not forget to incorporate handles, hinges or escutcheons for added authenticity. These can be cut from cardboard, covered with foil, or painted, and glued on to stand in bas-relief

Working with polyurethane

Polyurethane is becoming a strong competitor to the traditional materials used by prop makers. It is carved as easily, and is as light as, expanded polystyrene, but it can also be built up in the same way as plaster. It has good stability, being based on a wooden core, and is especially suitable for tall props like columns or stairs.

There are two different component fluids from which the polyurethane foam is produced. They must be kept in separate cans, and care should be taken with their labelling.

To make a sundial

Draw a life-sized pattern by folding a piece of paper lengthwise and drawing contours on the unfolded edges. Take care not to give the shape too thin a waist.

Transfer the outline on to two pieces of ½ inch (12mm) ply. Cut out the shapes with a fretsaw, cutting a ½ inch (12mm) wide slit lengthwise half-way down the two sections, from the base on one section, and from the top on the other. Slot the two cross sections together. They should be stable enough to stand, but adjust them if necessary. Lay the wooden core with 'V' section upwards and pour in the polyurethane.

MATERIALS
Timber scraps; nails or screws; one can of each component liquid; P.V.A. (white flexible glue); muslin; emulsion or acrylic paint; lacquer

TOOLS
Saw; hammer; drill; screwdriver; mixing can; stirring stick; rasp; surform; craft knife; sandpaper; gouge; scissors; brushes

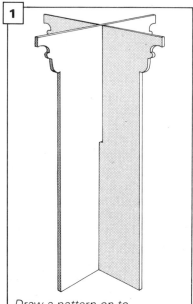

1 *Draw a pattern on to plywood, cut and slot cross-sections of core together*

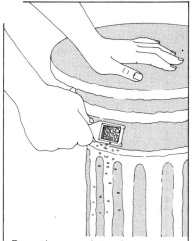

2 *Measure out an equal quantity of each liquid and mix them together thoroughly in an old can*

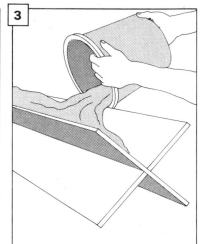

3 *When a brown foam starts to form, pour or spoon the solution into the core. Once mixed it will harden in approximately 5 minutes. (It is better to apply more foam than appears necessary.)*

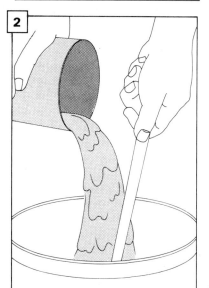

Rasp the prop into shape, being careful not to remove too much foam. A surprising amount of detail can be achieved at this stage. Sand it down evenly and remove loose crumbs

5

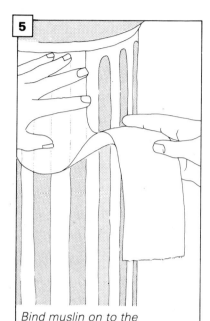

Bind muslin on to the finished object with P.V.A. for a smooth hard finish

6

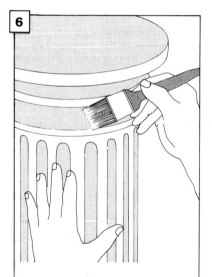

Paint and varnish with, for example, white wood glue mixed with acrylic pigment and sawdust. Two coats are needed. Sand when dry

For props requiring a wood, stone or metal finish, fill deeply carved grooves with black paint. This will give added depth to the prop and also make it look older

If you are not sure of your carving competence, cut profile templates from cardboard and work away at the polyurethane, checking your progress against the template

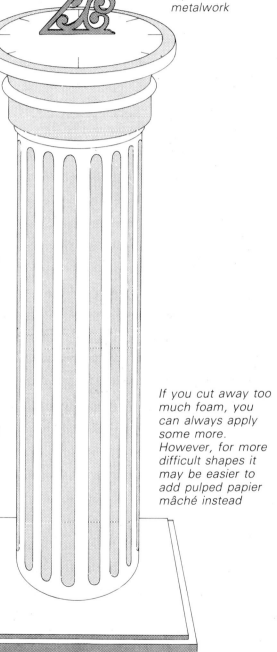

Cardboard cutout glued on to represent metalwork

If you cut away too much foam, you can always apply some more. However, for more difficult shapes it may be easier to add pulped papier mâché instead

Working with fiberglass

Fiberglass is suitable for casting in both non-flexible molds (plaster) and flexible molds (vinyl). When wrapped around shallow items it imitates their shape by creating a second skin, allowing the prop maker to replicate many times. Its facility for holding metal powder in suspension, within its gel coat, is a real boon to the armory department. Polyester resin with a metal filler converts felt shapes into hard helmets and breast plates which can then be burnished.

◇ **Warning**: Most of the materials involved with the fiberglass process are potential health hazards. Resins are a high fire risk — they have a flash point of 90°C. The hardener is an organic peroxide. Use polythene gloves and a recommended barrier cream; wear long sleeves and tight clothes. Beware also of glass dust especially when sandpapering.

Do not use for props that will touch the actor's skin.

The materials

Fiberglass is a tough lightweight plastic made up of a cold setting polyester resin reinforced with glass fiber. It is a relatively inexpensive material and requires no special skill beyond understanding the processes involved.

The polyester resin

This is a syrupy substance which is hardened by adding a liquid catalyst. This hardening or curing can take 30 minutes or more, depending on the room temperature and the amount of chemical accelerator present in the mix. The resin usually comes in cans ranging from half pint to one gallon (284ml-4.5l). The catalyst comes in smaller quantities and the manufacturer's recommended proportions of catalyst to resin should be strictly adhered to. Mix the catalyst in a separate container before adding it to the resin. Use only the minimum amount of resin, catalyst and fiberglass needed for each stage of prop-making.

The glass fiber

This is reinforcement which is required to make the resin into a tough and strong material.

There are many types of fiberglass but the following should cover most needs in prop-making.

Chopped strand mat (available by the yard or in rolls): a lightweight fiber for easy filling of awkward shapes.

Glass fiber tissue/surface mat (available by the yard or in rolls): not a reinforcement but useful for obtaining a good surface over the chopped strand mat.

Glass fiber ribbon (sold by length): used for edging and for local reinforcement.

Chopped strands (sold in l pound or half kilo packs): ideal for making resin and glass paste — very helpful for the prop maker.

The bottled liquid hardener is generally sold with a dropper fitting in a range from 50-500 grams.

The liquid accelerator is available in amounts of 15 milligrams upwards. Check the manufacturer's instructions as some accelerators can be used in conjunction with the pre-accelerated type of resin for a fast curing time. NEVER MIX CATALYST (HARDENER) DIRECTLY WITH ACCELERATOR — NOR STORE CLOSE TOGETHER.

Chemical separator or release agent

The resin is a powerful adhesive and will adhere to most non-flexible molds such as plaster. A chemical separator or release agent is necessary to act as a barrier between the mold and the cast. (If you are in doubt about a release agent, check the manufacturer's instructions, or with your retailer). There are some special release agents for plaster or porous molds. Most are sold in wax, emulsion or alcohol-based form. The sizes available vary from 210 grams to 1 gallon bottles.

Metal fillers

The surface of the fiberglass can be determined at the beginning of the process by adding fillers or pigments. Metallic fillers and inert fillers are best for making props. Brass, bronze, and copper are available in powder form and being pure metals are unsuitable for painting. These powders should be mixed with the resin in the following proportions.

Brass 5 or 6 : 1
Bronze 6 or 7 : 1
Copper 4 or 5 : 1

Your retailer will provide more detailed information or a manufacturer's list. N.B. Adding too little metal filler is as bad as having no metal filler at all.

Inert fillers have a powerful white pigmentation property. In a casting mix this will reduce the resin content and thus the cost, making a more economical mixture.

Pigment

Polyester pigments are used to color fiberglass and may be mixed directly with resin. (Greater opacity is obtained by adding an inert filler.) Again, check with the manufacturer's chart for the quantities of pigment required.

Estimating materials

Gel coat (the initial layer of resin)

1½ ounces of resin per square foot

Chopped strand mat
l ounce per square foot is normally impregnated with a resin/mat proportion of 2:1

Fillers
follow manufacturer's instructions

The method

Resin and fiberglass mat combined in layers is called laminate and the first layer of resin (either neat or with added filler) is known as a gel coat. This is brushed into place and once tacky, a further coat of resin is added followed by a layer of mat. Press and prod the mat until the glass fiber merges with the hardening resin to form a glassy mass. Repeat this once, twice, or even three more times according to the size and thickness desired.

Allow each layer to harden completely before adding another layer, making sure all bubbles are eliminated. Trim away any excess strands before applying the last layer of mat.

Fiberglass is a very satisfactory filling for a plaster mold (see page 40 for instructions on making a mold). Coat the insides of both halves very thoroughly with a wax separator before following the fiberglass process above. Remove from the mold when cured.

Sand the ragged edges and butt them together. Cover the seam with further laminated fiberglass. (Sandpapering will help to create a surface which will accept paint more readily.)

NB Polyester resin will not stick to polypropylene which makes it an ideal surface for practising laminating, or a base board for molding, or simply a precautionary cover in your working area.

Copying an original in fiberglass

Fiberglass can be used to advantage when copying an existing shape — for example, a round tray which could be converted into a large platter, a shield or a wheel hub cap. A releasing agent is then applied to the original. Resin is poured into a mixing bowl with the hardener and pigment or filler and mixed together. Cover the tray thoroughly with a thick layer of resin (the gel coat) and allow to set. Lay the mat fiber over the gel coat, pressing well into shape, then paint another thick layer of resin on, rolling or prodding well with the paintbrush to exclude all air bubbles. Repeat until the desired thickness is obtained. Trim the edges when the resin has started to set. Once dry (the time will vary according to thickness), carefully ease the original from the cast with a wooden spatula. Decorate as required.

Cylindrical molds like barrels or pipes of different thicknesses would be useful to make curved shapes like fire screens or leg guards.

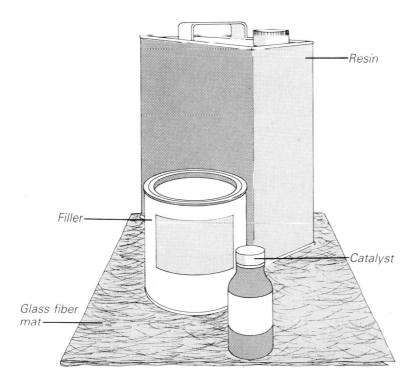

Filler

Resin

Catalyst

Glass fiber mat

Using fiberglass in a vinyl mold

Vinyl, although expensive, is a very adaptable mold material. It is as flexible as alginate (see page 44) and much more durable. Unlike a plaster mold, vinyl will reproduce deep undercuts (see page 41) and still retain fine detail and it is especially useful when many replicas of an original are required. The vinyl mold is normally filled with plaster or fiberglass.

An original object may be of wood, plaster, plasticine, clay, metal, glass or even china. Glass and china items, however, need to be heated before hot vinyl is poured over them so they will not crack.

To make the mold, place the original inside an old can and secure it to prevent it from floating up in the hot vinyl. The vinyl, prepared by slowly melting pieces in a hot-air crucible, is then poured into the container and allowed to cool. When it is hard, the mold is removed from the reservoir and slit open with a craft knife to release the original. The flexible mold is then ready for the fiberglass application of gel coat and successive layers of matted fiberglass pressed into catalyzed resin (see page 57). In the case of a goblet, this technique is first applied to the open mold halves, which are then closed and secured by tape or twisted wire, then resin and fiberglass are worked and pushed down the stem and into and around the bowl. The stem can be further reinforced by inserting a wire from base to bowl. If weight is needed in the bottom, use metallic powder, or a nut or bolt incorporated into the base. Color or metal can be introduced at the gel coat stage or the prop can be left translucent. Apply metal polish after the edges have been trimmed and sandpapered.

Making a vinyl mold

1

Place the original in an old can, weigh it down and pour in the vinyl

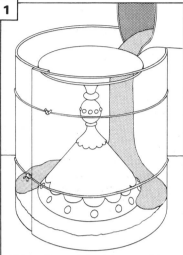

2

When the vinyl is hard, remove it from the can and slit it open to release the original goblet. Brush the inside of both halves of the mold with resin and line with fiberglass matt

Using the mold

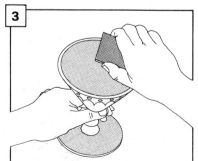

1

Wire the mold together and pour in sufficient catalyzed resin to fill the base and stem of the goblet

2

Brush catalyzed resin into the bowl of the goblet and press in a further layer of mat to line the bowl

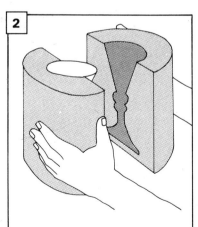

3

File away waste material and finish with fine sandpaper. Polish with metal polish if required

Using liquid latex

Liquid latex is expensive but it makes very realistic skin and likelike wrinkles! Use it also to create lightweight armor, masks, and helmets (all made from plaster molds cast from a clay positive — see page 40). Remember to shellac and grease the plaster before applying the liquid latex.

Unlike vinyl, which is used as part of the mold making process, latex is the end product itself. The hollow latex form can be filled with plaster for added weight. A full head mask would be left hollow and molded in two halves. Two slits are necessary at the bottom to accommodate the actor's ears!

Liquid latex is available from craft stores in two forms. One simply dries by contact with air and is suitable for smaller jobs. It is used like a rubberized glue to give body to fabrics. The other needs a catalyst to harden it, which can take anything from 20 minutes to several hours. (Check the manufacturer's instructions.) For larger jobs, apply a layer of fabric for reinforcement once a preliminary layer of latex has hardened.

Latex is naturally off-white, but small quantities can be colored with food coloring or dye. Larger areas should be painted.

If the prop is going to be in contact with an actor's skin, it is advisable to test a small patch first to discover if he is allergic to the latex.

> **MATERIALS**
> Clay; petroleum jelly; plaster of Paris; shellac; grease; wire; liquid latex
>
> **TOOLS**
> Bowl; brush; pliers

To make a hand by casting latex in a plaster mold

A tray should be constructed from clay with edges about 2 inches (50mm) high, and large enough to take a hand. Grease the person's hand and place it palm down in the tray with some slight support to prevent the hand flattening. Lumps of clay are distributed around the hand to serve as mold keys. Plaster is then flicked on to the top of the hand until it is covered.

When the plaster is just past the hardened stage, the hand should be removed. Shellac and grease the mold thoroughly and then replace the hand in it, this time palm upwards. The hand is then flicked with plaster again and removed when the plaster is just past the hardened stage. The shellacked and greased surface of the mold should make for easy separation and the keys will allow for the two molds to be accurately matched before being wired together.

Next the plaster mold is filled with latex. For a first attempt, an air hardening latex might be the most simply process. Follow the manufacturer's instructions and pour off any surplus at the point when the latex has begun to form an outer skin. The mold will then be lined with hardened latex which can be pulled out.

To create a gnarled or distorted hand, add clay shapes to the fingers before casting. Feet can also be made this way!

A cheaper method, but one that requires great patience, is to use a small amount of latex and gently swirl it around the mold until it hardens. You will need a chemically accelerated latex for this process.

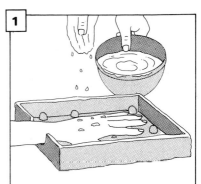

The greased hand is placed in a clay bath and plaster flicked on top

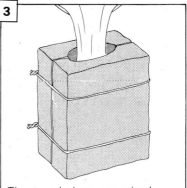

The hand is replaced in hardened plaster, but palm upwards this time. Plaster is added to create the second half of the mold

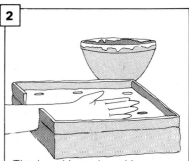

The two halves are wired together and latex poured in

Working with paper

Paper is so familiar that many of us are slow to use it in its own right and only consider it in combination with other materials. We must be ready to use our imagination and recognize paper's full potential, especially when so many varieties are at our disposal. Paper can be plasticized, surface textured, coated and metalized and what was once a material with limited uses becomes one with tremendous scope.

The packaging industry has perhaps contributed most to the variety of papers available — and the prop maker will find most choice of materials at a packaging plant. Paper's versatility means that children need only scissors, glue and paint to make a wide range of props. Paper can be cut, glued, folded, stapled, taped, linked, interlocked, woven, scored and curled. How many other materials can be thus used?

Materials to purchase:

Cartridge or drawing papers of mixed colors
Construction papers of mixed colors
Cardboard in various weights and colors
Wallpapers of any type or color
Vinyl-backed papers
Flocked wallpapers
Kitchen foil, paper cups, doilies etc.
Metalized cardboard
Acetate
Cellophane
Vilene or pelon

This is a list of suggested materials; it is by no means necessary to purchase the expensive items in quantity. It is the variety of materials that is most important, and many of these materials can be found around the house such as:

General purpose wrapping paper
Paper bags of various sizes and thicknesses
Tissue paper, i.e. fruit wrappings
Paper and vinyl egg boxes
Corrugated cardboard
Newspapers
Cardboard boxes

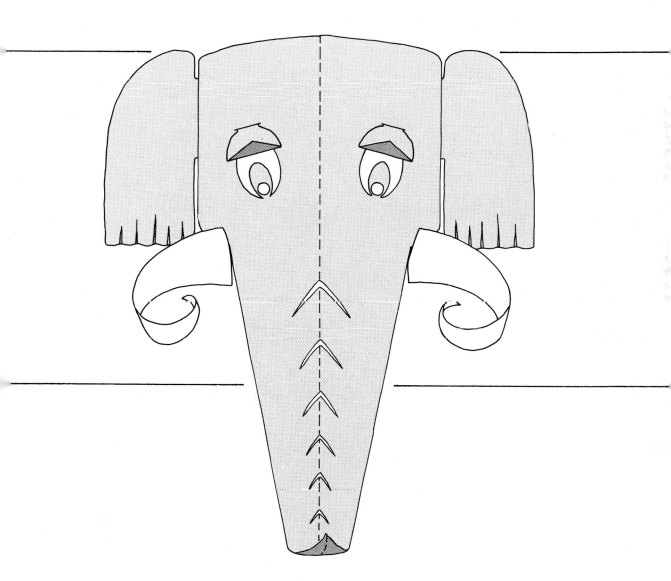

Basic techniques with paper

Cutting and scoring

Always use a sharp cutting blade for cutting, and have ready a metal ruler and a cutting board or a thick piece of cardboard to place underneath the paper. Keep fingers away from the blade area. Hold the knife firmly, and draw it along the surface of the paper slowly. Use the metal ruler for straight lines or cut freehand for curves.

For a clean, sharp fold or bend in a piece of cardboard, score the surface of the cardboard lightly using a sharp blade, or hold the scissors as indicated, to break only the surface with the blade. Then bend the cardboard into position.

When folding any paper or cardboard, and if the fold line is complicated draw the desired shape on the paper first for greater accuracy.

Press each fold line firmly by drawing the thumb or a ruler along the folded edge.

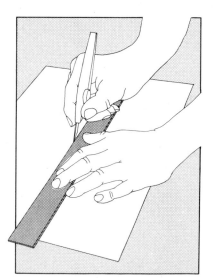

Always cut against a straight metal edge like a ruler

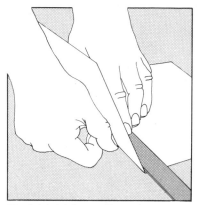

To fold thick cardboard accurately, first score it lightly with a knife against a straight edge

After scoring, fold the cardboard upwards, still keeping the straight edge firmly in place

Shaping

Shaping cardboard by means of folds and rolls is a fairly simple process which can produce useful basic sculptural forms to be used as they are, or as a base for a prop.

It is best to draw on and cut the paper while it is flat. Coloring or marbling (see pages 79 and 80) should obviously be done at this stage. Any raised areas are marked and scored lightly, then gently pressed to create not a fold, more a soft bend in the paper. This process is suitable for curves such as those found in the central stem of a leaf. Conical shapes are easily assembled by cutting a radius in a circle of paper. The two cut edges are overlapped and glued or stapled — making a satisfactory starting point for a papier mâché prop. Many geometrical shapes can be subdivided by means of scoring, and by gently bending them to create a three-dimensional object.

Curling

Strips of paper are curled by pulling the paper tightly over the back of a pair of scissors or a ruler, from one end to the other. When the tension on the strip is released, the paper should spring into a fairly tight spiral. Each different type of paper will produce a different type of curl. Generally, cheap drawing paper gives a stiffly shaped curl which has plenty of bounce.

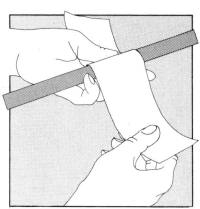

Curling paper by pulling strips tightly across a ruler

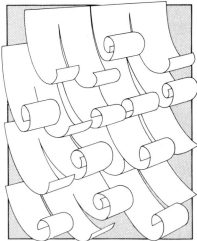

Use curled paper to create the feathers on the costume of a pantomime goose

Joining paper

There are numerous ways of attaching one piece of paper or cardboard to another. Tacks, pins, paper clips, fasteners, needle and thread and staples are just some of the means available. Tiny staplers are helpful for reaching into unusually small openings, while long staplers are advisable for larger more complicated formats.

Sometimes it is more convenient to use pieces of sticky tape, especially in inaccessible places where a stapler will not reach. Tape is handy for securing parts temporarily or for expediency when working for quick results. Paper can also be fastened by tabs and slits, and there are some very fine pastes, glues and rubber cements for special problems.

Staples

These make strong joints for medium weight paper and cardboard. Care needs to be taken to cover them as the stage lights will reflect their glint and spoil the effect of the prop. Exposed staples, of course, can be featured as part of the decoration of a prop.

Paper fasteners

The brass heads of paper fasteners may prove an attractive and useful part of the design of a prop. Paper fasteners also allow some movement between two layers of paper.

Tape

Cellophane tape is limited in its use as the glossiness repels water-based paint (apart from acrylic paint). It will also reflect stage lights when applied over a painted surface. Clothbacked adhesive tape is very strong and can be painted. Magic-tape is useful for its non-reflective properties and its

paint adhesion. Brown paper adhesive tape will cope with lightweight jobs. Vinyl, plastic, and metallic tapes are perfect when the exposed tape is an integral part of the prop. Double-sided tape, of course, is very useful for quickly securing two surfaces.

Velcro

Velcro can be glued or stapled to heavy paper or cardboard where a prop needs to be taken apart.

Gluing

This is the standard way of joining paper. Care must be taken to give good overlaps and to prevent spillage on the paper surface, as this could change the paper's ability to absorb paint. Make sure the strength of glue is matched to the strength of paper.

Sewing

Light to medium weight paper can be sewn by hand or by machine. This is a quick and efficient means of joining paper. It is also suitable for crepe papers from which whole props and costumes are made.

Lacing

Holes made in heavy paper or cardboard can be laced together with string or rope to produce a curtain effect. This could be a quick way of making a lampshade or ruffle.

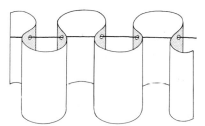

Tab and slot linking

Finally, a method of joining paper without resorting to staples, glue, or tape. This is based on a simple formula of cutting and folding. A slot is cut in one sheet of paper into which a tab from another sheet is inserted. Apart from combining paper effectively, this process will create a unique faceted surface when a large number of sheets is joined together. Three variations of tab and slot linking are illustrated but there are many other possibilities.

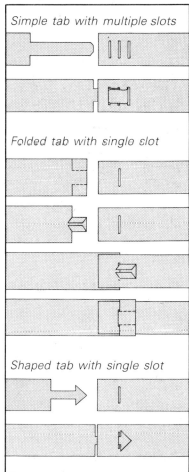

Simple tab with multiple slots

Folded tab with single slot

Shaped tab with single slot

Creating shapes from paper

To make a cone

Make a conical shape from a circle of cardboard with a line cut along the radius. If a semi-circle of cardboard is used, a taller cone will result. Include a tab, extending from the center to the circumference of the circle

To form a base, draw a larger circle around the cone on to a piece of cardboard

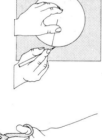

Cut tabs around the edge and fold these at right angles, before gluing and fitting the base into the cone. This will provide extra stability and permanence

To make a star

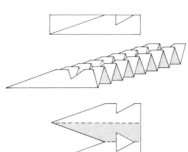

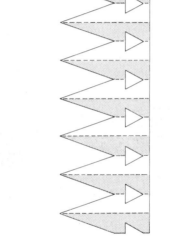

Fold a length of paper into a concertina with 12 sections. Cut as shown in the diagram. When the paper is opened out and the two ends joined together, a star shape is formed

To make a polyhedron

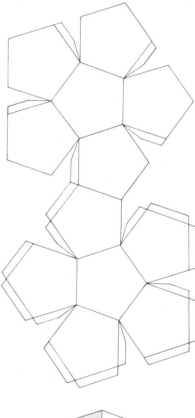

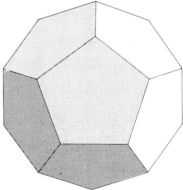

A template is first made of one of the faces, from which the others can be drawn. Score along the edges to create tabs. Paste the tabs and join the faces together

Corrugated cardboard

Light and strong corrugated cardboard can be pinned, taped, or glued to wooden frames — covering a large surface quickly and easily. This is particularly useful for a limited number of performances where effect is more important than durability. Such things as wishing wells, large ovens, cupboards, and two-dimensional (flat) carriages are suitable, subjects where lightness is important for portability and the size has to be large for authenticity. The corrugated side of the cardboard gives variety in texture, such as roof tiles. Cut up in two shapes the ridges help to make the tiles more realistic. Corrugated cardboard can also be used to give the appearance of a fluted surface on a classical column.

Tissue paper

Tissue paper is generally used for its colorful and delicate effect, although these very attributes are its weaknesses. Tissue paper tears easily and the color runs when it contacts water. For exotic productions with lots of flowers, tissue paper is ideal, fairly cheap, and easy to manage. With experience, a large variety of blooms can be fashioned (fold the paper into a flattened cone and cut the unfolded edge). These can be wired or threaded wherever necessary. Tissue paper when glued and lightly stretched across cardboard will give a stained glass effect (if there is a source of light from behind). In the case of small carrying lamps, you must keep the light source far enough away from the paper to avoid any fire risk. ◇

To make flowers from tissue paper

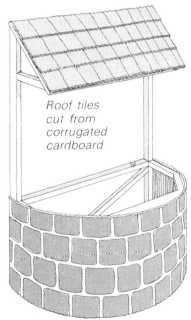

Roof tiles cut from corrugated cardboard

Wall made from corrugated cardboard, wrapped around a wooden frame. This could be painted to resemble brickwork

1

Take about 8 square pieces of tissue paper measuring no more than 12 inches (300mm) along each side. Place these on top of each other and fold twice. Cut petal shapes

2

Open up the petal shapes (still keeping the paper together), insert a wire through the center and twist it

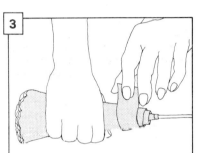

3

Gather the tissue into a cone shape and fix this to the wire with adhesive tape

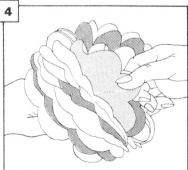

4

Fold back the petals to expose flower head. Try experimenting with different colored sheets of paper

Using paper to make animal head masks

Paper is highly suitable for making masks. The masks illustrated are simply built around a rectangle and a cylinder. Animals are used as examples, but the human face can also serve as a model for the design. In making the mask such identifying factors as the shape and position of the ears, structure of the face, snout, and other facial parts should be considered. The paper can be painted, sprayed, fringed, cut, or scored for added character and interest.

Making an ox mask from a rectangle

With careful creasing and cutting, anyone can make an imaginative mask from a folded rectangle of paper. Mark out the design on your piece of paper. Cut along the solid line and fold along the dots. Cut away the shaded area, fit the mask over the actor and overlap the back sections until a comfortable fit is achieved. Trim any untidy flaps after they have been stapled or glued together. For additional decoration, fringing made from curled cardboard can be glued across the forehead and above the eyes as eyelashes or a blaze painted on the face.

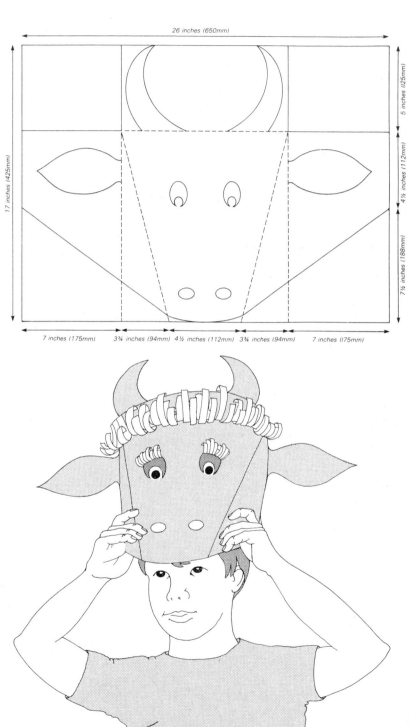

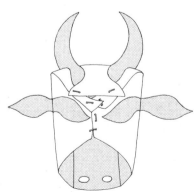

When all the flaps are gathered, they can be glued or stapled together to fit the actor's head

Making an elephant mask from a cylinder

This elephant's head is based on a cylinder. Many other masks can be made using the same principle.

Fold a rectangle of cardboard in half. Draw out the shape shown. The top measure is variable, so check the circumference of the actor's head (remembering to allow for the overlap at the back) and move the ear positions accordingly. Whilst the cardboard is still folded, cut out the eye sections, the ear and eye slits and the diagonal cuts on the trunk, using a craft knife or small pointed scissors. Cut out the ears, dividing the flange into three tabs. Cut out the eyelid, folding up the triangular section. Finally, cut out the tusks. Open up the card, insert the ear flanges into the appropriate slots, separating and gluing the tabs to the back of the mask. Slide the eyelid tabs into their slots and glue into place. Glue the tusks into place at the top of the trunk. Curl the bottom of the trunk and the two tusks. The mask is now ready to be fitted to the actor. Glue or staple the back of the mask together so it is correctly adjusted on the actor's head.

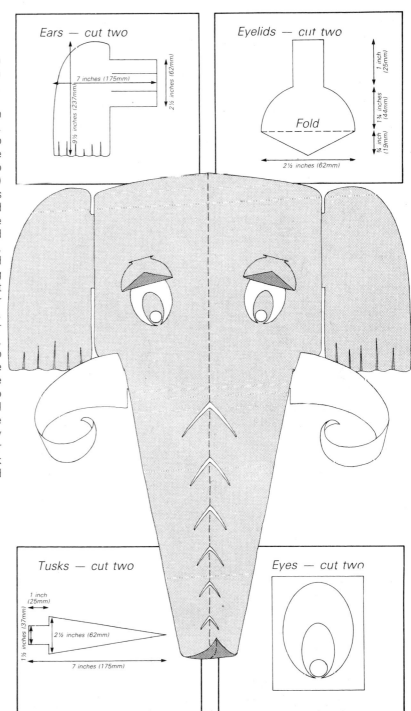

Ears — cut two
7 inches (175mm)
2½ inches (62mm)
9½ inches (237mm)

Eyelids — cut two
1 inch (25mm)
1¾ inches (44mm)
¾ inch (19mm)
Fold
2½ inches (62mm)

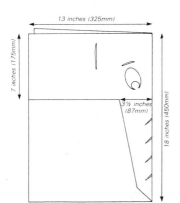

13 inches (325mm)
7 inches (175mm)
18 inches (450mm)
3½ inches (87mm)

Tusks — cut two
1 inch (25mm)
1½ inches (37mm)
2½ inches (62mm)
7 inches (175mm)

Eyes — cut two

Making use of paper products

Sweet or candy wrappers

Although small and seemingly insignificant, these wrappers, when used as embellishment, give dull and lifeless props a lift. Foil, crushed up and glued directly to a sized felt crown, will give it sparkle. Colored cellophane from the outside of small wrappers, can be folded around chunks of polystyrene, cork pieces or dried beans to resemble semiprecious stones. These are made more realistic when set in gold or silver foil, or braid to suggest a metallic mount.

Foil gives the appearance of gilt on a crown

Jewels made from small pieces of polystyrene or cork enclosed in candy wrappers

Drinking straws

Paper straws can be cut up and used as a base for beads. Thread the cut straws on a knitting needle, bandage them around with very narrow strips of papier mâché, or surround with pulped papier mâché, allow to dry in a cool oven, and dip in shellac and paint.

Added to masks, plastic straws become antennae, and straws glued to a surface suggest a different texture. An old shoe box can take on the appearance of a jewelry box made from split cane or carved wood: glue the straws side-by-side in a geometric pattern. Space-age jewelry can be given the same treatment with suitable cardboard shapes cut to fit the actor in the form of necklaces, bracelets and anklets. Straws and string, plus other available junk, can be glued on the cardboard in a distinctive pattern and sprayed with metallic paint. Careful combination of materials produces stunning results.

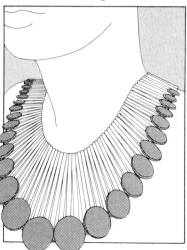

This necklace is made from cardboard with straws glued on. Painting and the addition of foil discs provide ornamentation

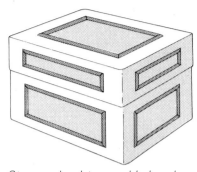

Straws glued to an old shoe box give the appearance of beading

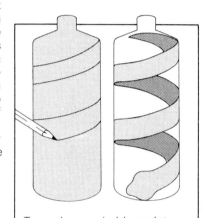

To make a spiral bracelet for an ancient Egyptian or sci-fi prop, take an old plastic bottle and mark on it the shape of the bracelet

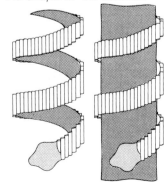

Cut out the plastic and glue on lengths of drinking straws. Spray with metallic paint

Cardboard tubes

Cardboard tubes from household goods are strong and versatile bases for many props. Glued together in a circle and placed on a round plinth, they become the base of a fluted column for a classical play. Cut in half lengthwise and mitered at the ends, they become a bold frame for a mirror or picture. Cross-sections can be used as architectural detail, or as decoration on the surface of armor.

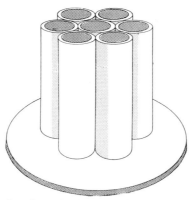

Cardboard tubes used as the base of a stone column

Paper plates

Paper plates can also be used as bas-relief for architectural detail or as additional decoration on armor. A plate provides an excellent base for a mask which is then simply colored with paint or felt pen, or built up with cardboard and papier mâché.

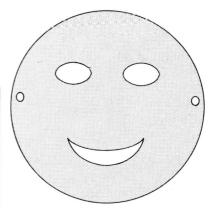

A very simple mask for a children's production made by cutting eye and mouth holes and then painting. Attach it with a loop of string

To make a picture frame

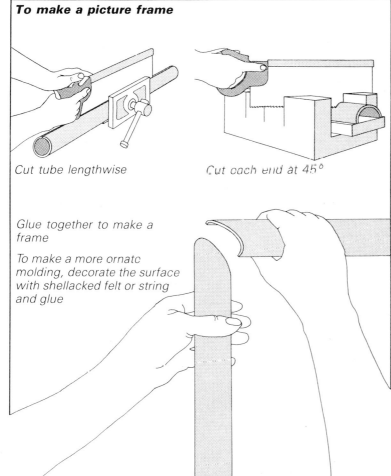

Cut tube lengthwise

Cut each end at 45°

Glue together to make a frame

To make a more ornate molding, decorate the surface with shellacked felt or string and glue

A paper plate used as the basis for a more complex mask — detail and character have been provided by modeling with papier mâché and adding a moustache made from sized string

Making use of egg cartons

Never underestimate an egg carton! The cup sections are invaluable shortcuts in the prop-making process, from cobbled streets, to the bulbous edges on a frog mask, or the wart-like surface of an old oak tree. Used on their own and covered with foil they become delicate bells or part of the architectural column detail in a classical play: the list is endless.

To make a totem pole

A totem pole can be assembled almost entirely from egg cartons:

Collect several square cardboard boxes

Use two as a base and make sure they are fixed securely with clothbacked adhesive tape

The other boxes are piled one on top of the other on this base, and glued into position

Working up from the bottom, start gluing egg cartons to the totem pole

There are many different ways to arrange the egg cartons: sometimes with the lid on the carton, sometimes with the lid off, so that the pattern inside can be seen, sometimes with the boxes on their sides

You can leave a space, and paint masks or patterns on to the pole

Put a collection of brightly colored masks or headdresses on the top. These could be made of cardboard or paper plates

Cardboard tube sections, paper sculpture and other disposable paper products make ideal decoration
(See pages 62 and 68)

Do not forget that egg cups can be cut singly, used in multiples or simply piled on top of one another for greater depth

String, beads or twisted crepe paper glued on to protruding cartons to add detail

Open the egg cartons from different angles; each will show a different profile

Large egg trays can be used to cover bigger areas

Be choosy in selecting your cartons. Many have interesting cutouts for display and handling purposes

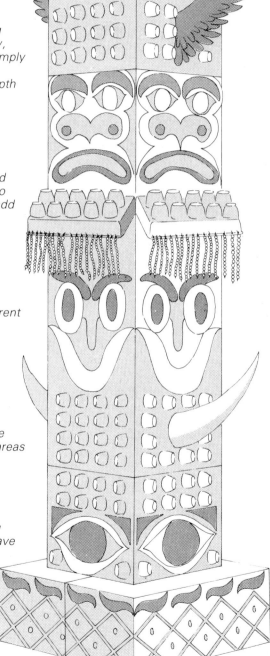

Making use of paper bags

For children's productions, large, plain grocery bags can provide many of the props and costumes desired and a simple visual theme often makes for a successful, uncluttered production. With holes for the head and arms and with careful painting or drawing, the bags can be adapted for a variety of costumes. With holes only cut out for eyes and arms, the bags become grotesque masks or just simple character faces. The advantage of this simplicity is that the actor can create his own prop or costume quickly and cheaply.

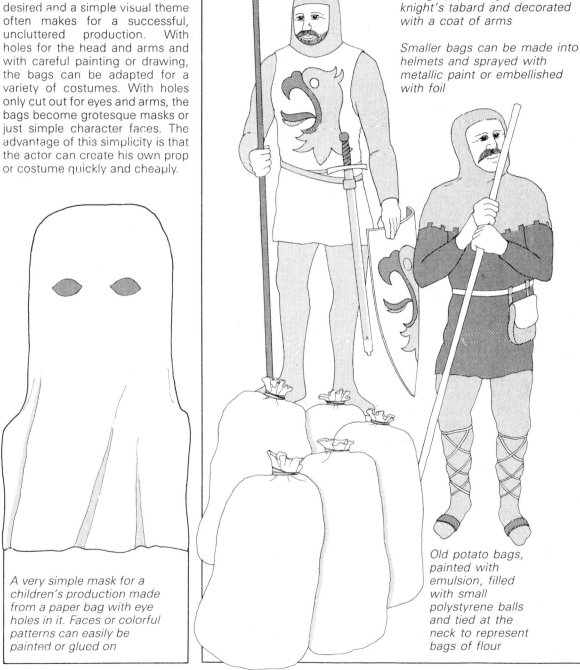

A large paper bag used as a knight's tabard and decorated with a coat of arms

Smaller bags can be made into helmets and sprayed with metallic paint or embellished with foil

A very simple mask for a children's production made from a paper bag with eye holes in it. Faces or colorful patterns can easily be painted or glued on

Old potato bags, painted with emulsion, filled with small polystyrene balls and tied at the neck to represent bags of flour

Decorating props with paper and cardboard

Using transparent plastic

The specialist theatrical and photographic suppliers stock a fire proof transparent plastic intended mainly for light filters. This material is an excellent substitute for glass, especially for small pictures, miniatures, and lanterns.

Stained glass is represented by lightly sanding the plastic to enable colored inks or french-enamel (French polish) to be applied. The lead-work can either be painted in heavy black or laid out in black, electrical insulation tape. Any fine drawing should be done with colored India inks, using tints typical of stained glass. Set the window in a wooden frame.

Sticky colored paper shapes

The use of sticky shapes is a short-cut, saving laborious hours of filling in small sections with paint. A mosaic can quickly be assembled, then matte- varnished to keep it intact. Sticky paper is particularly useful for fairly large lettering where crisp sharp lines are necessary. (Draw the letters in pencil first, then cut them with a sharp craft knife or scissors). Wall tile's can be simulated from squares — don't forget to leave gaps between the squares for the 'grouting'. Varnish with gloss afterwards. Quick change tattoos can be stuck on to forearms and foreheads — gold and silver stars and the occasional bat do wonders for a dismal witch!

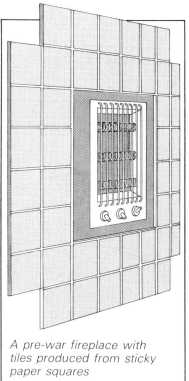

A pre-war fireplace with tiles produced from sticky paper squares

To make a stained glass window

A wooden frame painted black gives the appearance of lead-work

The design is drawn with colored inks on to lightly sanded transparent plastic

Construct the window frame from wood, and tape transparent-plastic to the back

Insulation tape can be used to imitate lead-work

Cardboard pieces for bas-relief

Using cardboard, especially the corrugated variety, is an effective way of creating additional raised detail without the hassle of intricate carving, molding or carpentry. Shapes of cardboard are built up in layers until the appropriate contours are formed. This technique is equally suitable for small objects such as the features on masks and for large areas such as a Greek key pattern along a wall.

(See also pages 62 and 65)

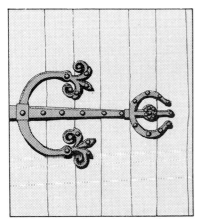

A hinge cut from layers of cardboard adds authenticity to an old door

Collage

Collage makes a good impact where there is a distinct theme in a play that needs to be emphasized time and time again. Collage is the composition and pasting together of many different pieces of paper (all with visually relevant pictures or words). Once the layers are glued, polyurethane lacquer can be painted over the collage to give it durability and strength. (Of course, you need not restrict your materials to paper.)

Flocked wallpaper

Flocked wallpaper is useful as a short cut to drawing and devising a design. The repeating patterns can be cut out and re-assembled on a group of shields when these all have to be identical. Designs on flocked wallpaper lend themselves to the flowery scroll-like shapes on a coat of arms, or oriental and extravagant costumes and headgear.

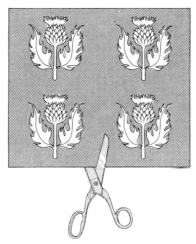

Cut up patterned wallpaper and use the design where a repeating motif is required

Silver and gold paper

Silver and gold paper in the form of chocolate and dairy product wrappings are useful folded around cardboard shapes to make bracelets, medallions or earrings. This type of paper needs to be glued down or it will unwrap itself at the most inconvenient moment! Because it is finer than foil it will mold fine detail on small objects such as coins (pieces of gold) or cardboard numerals (brass numbers on a large clock face).

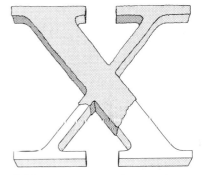

Gold paper wrapped around a cardboard number before fixing to a clock face

Crepe paper

Crepe paper has many of the same qualities of tissue paper, but it is much stronger and can stretch to an almost drum-like tautness. Care needs to be taken when gluing, as the color will run and stain other things. (It may be machine stitched instead.) Interesting shapes can be made from crepe paper by means of twisting, pulling, kinking, and folding the cut edges — possibly suitable for fronds of undergrowth or seaweed in a scenic production.

(See page 65 for making flowers)

Using foil and paper for ornamentation

Using foil to decorate a shield

Milk-bottle caps, when assembled together create a very interesting textural effect and their silver color is an added bonus. A shield is a straightforward example of this technique.

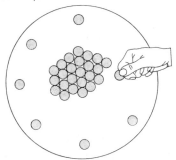

Having made your shield, work from the top downwards covering a small area at a time with P.V.A. (white flexible glue) or another strong adhesive. Gradually glue the milk-bottle caps on to the shield to create a design.

Using foil to make space age equipment

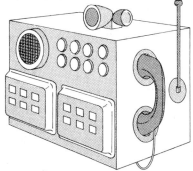

Technical appliances such as walkie-talkies, radio telephones, computers and other modern props, are easily improvised using an assortment of silver foil tops and trays. Foil push buttons, radar dishes and antennae glued on to box bases, give a realistic imitation of technical apparatus.

Using paper for ornamentation

Paper replicas of lace, such as doilies, have a variety of uses. Glued around the hilt of a sword they make fine, chiseled filigree. When cut into smaller units, paper lace may also be applied to a sword blade, wrist guard and pommel of a weapon. Some paper lace patterns actually come in gold and silver. Otherwise they can be painted black and brushed in metallic paint.

Plates and goblets decorated with lace and sprayed with gold or silver look very special

Lace used as filigree on a dress sword

A plain lampshade is transformed into a prop for a Victorian set by the addition of a doilie

Making paper and books look old

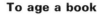

To transform paper into parchment

To make an old document take a good quality sheet of drawing paper and after writing the text with waterproof India ink, paint the paper with shellac on both sides to give it the slightly brittle quality and color desired. Color may also be achieved by painting the paper with strong tea or tearing the paper and dipping the edges in watery tea. Fold or roll the document as required. Pierce the paper with a knife, insert a red ribbon, wrap it around the paper twice and seal it with sealing wax stamped with a symbol. The stamp can be cut from lino using a lino cutter, or an impression made from a bottle cap or ring.

Instead of paper you could use fine cotton fabric. Attach this to a frame, using staples, paint it with emulsion and let it dry to produce a stiffish 'parchment'.

To age a book

To make an ancient or ornamental book, take an old and substantial volume and glue some rough paper to its spine and covers. The raised ribs of the spine can be formed from rope, and smaller ridges from string or braid. Paper lace can be glued to the book to give intricate textures. Cardboard or felt shapes or papier mâché figures may be fixed in a design. Jewels can include fruit gums, clear or boiled sweets or candy, cotton wool balls, or bits of polystyrene covered with colored transparent paper.

Spine ribs made from thick string or rope

Jewels made from cork or polystyrene enclosed in candy wrappers

A raised pattern cut from cardboard and pasted on to the cover boards

Printing with a lino block

Printing can come into its own for repeating a pattern on fabric or duplicated the same design a number of times.

Drawing the design on to the lino

A lino block is useful for reproducing small items such as banknotes. This is done by drawing the image, transferring it to a lino block and then cutting out (with lino tools) the white sections of the design, leaving only the raised printed surfaces.

MATERIALS
Paper; lino; printer's ink or acrylic paint; newspaper

TOOLS
Pencil; carbon paper; lino cutters; scissors; paper cutter; sheet of glass; roller; spatula; spoon; pegs and string line

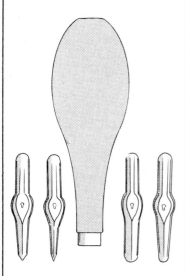

A variety of cutters are available for producing different widths of line

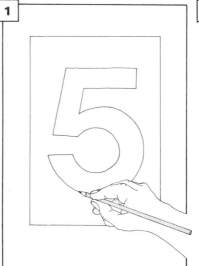

1

Draw up the design on a piece of tracing paper cut to the size of the lino block

2

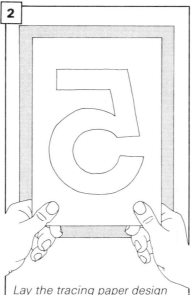

Lay the tracing paper design face down (and thus reversed) upon the carbon paper which itself is carbon side down upon the lino block. Fix with tape

3

Draw over the design, pressing heavily with a pencil or a pen, to transfer the design to the lino block

Making a lino cut

Cut the lino, remembering that the cut areas will be white or the color of the paper. Always cut in a direction away from the hands and body, with a steady hand behind the cutting hand. This is very important in order to avoid injury. If you warm the lino first with your hands, the surface will become more supple and easy to cut. For narrow lines, use an acute V cutter; for broader areas a shallow U shaped cutter is better. If too much force is used, the cutter will dig too deeply into the surface and tear the lino. Use firm pressure and gently wiggle the cutter, easing the blade along. Do not attempt to contort yourself into an awkward position when cutting curves — move the lino itself. If a lot of prints are to be made and the lino shape is difficult to hold, it may be easier to glue the lino on to a block of wood.

Inking and printing

It is most important to cut your paper in advance as it is not easy to keep cutting paper when you are covered in ink trying to maintain a printing rhythm. Squeeze the ink (a combination of colors, if necessary) on to a sheet of glass, mixing with a spatula until the correct color is reached. Work the ink backwards and forwards with a roller.

When the roller is completely and evenly covered, you are ready to transfer the ink to the lino.

Experiment with varying degrees of pressure when printing. Once the desired effect is achieved, be consistent with the amount of ink used and the pressure applied. For multi-colored printing, use a separate block for each color and, again, experiment to discover the effect of over printing with the various blocks. Study the color wheel on page 12 and try overlapping and shadow effects on large areas of lino.

Printer's ink gives a good result, the only disadvantage being that it also needs a suitable thinner. Take care — this ink stains! There are some water-based printer's inks, mainly acrylic, which adhere to most surfaces. These are easier to control and less messy to clean up. Ordinary acrylic paint is also suitable for printing (see the chart on page 14) and it dries quickly, but for a glossy finish, a gloss medium will have to be added.

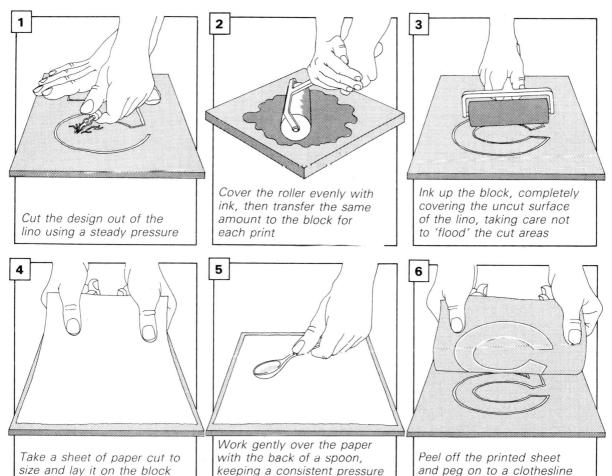

1 Cut the design out of the lino using a steady pressure

2 Cover the roller evenly with ink, then transfer the same amount to the block for each print

3 Ink up the block, completely covering the uncut surface of the lino, taking care not to 'flood' the cut areas

4 Take a sheet of paper cut to size and lay it on the block

5 Work gently over the paper with the back of a spoon, keeping a consistent pressure

6 Peel off the printed sheet and peg on to a clothesline

Stenciling

Stenciling is a speedy method of producing a constant pattern. If stencil paper cannot be obtained, sugar or construction paper, stiffened with five or six coats of shellac, will do. To make a stencil, draw the pattern in reverse (if assymetrical), cut it out with a very sharp knife and shellac the cut edges to prevent paint corrosion. To print, mix up a stiff thickness of paint (powder color, acrylics, and poster colors are fine for this purpose). Do not allow the paint to become too wet or it will leak under the stencil. Also take care not to use brushes that are too flexible, otherwise hairs might spread under the stencil and spoil the design. Stencil with a flat, thick brush. If a stencil brush is not available, spraying and splattering are other methods of applying paint to a stencil. Using a sponge is yet another. When a continuous pattern is being worked, be sure to cut marked notches at key points so that it is possible to notch and continue the flow of design.

Stencils do not have to be made from paper: interesting patterns can be produced by spraying through metal products such as perforated zinc, wire mesh, cycle wheels and colanders. Try experimenting! Children may find it fun (and messy!) to stencil around their hands or feet.

MATERIALS
Sugar or construction paper and shellac, or stencil paper; shellac; paint

TOOLS
Brush for shellac; craft knife; cutting board; brush or spray for paint; spoon

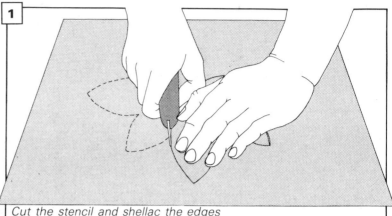

1

Cut the stencil and shellac the edges

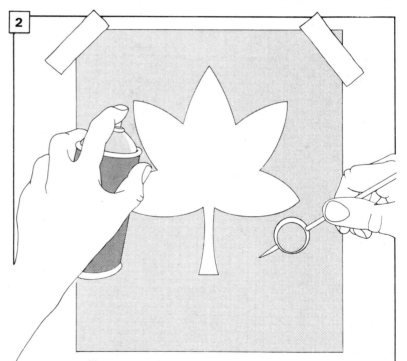

2

When stenciling a repeat pattern, you may have difficulty in positioning and holding the stencil. This can be overcome by gluing an old bottle cork to the back and attaching it to a length of coat hanger wire to form a handle

A variety of methods can be used to apply paint: stippling with a stencil brush, spraying with an aerosol, sponging, flicking, or splattering using a paint brush or old toothbrush. Wipe the stencil after each print to avoid smudging

Marbling

Marbling paper is a simple and satisfying process which produces a very attractive effect. The resulting paper can be used in the fly-leaves of made-up books, but perhaps its most effective use is when it is actually used to imitate marble! (This would be very suitable for Grecian tables, sections of pillars, and so on.) Colors need to be simple: black/gray or a mushroom/pink. It is the basic principle of marbling is that an oil-based paint, or a water repellent ink, is floated on water which has been mildly swirled about. Paper is allowed briefly to float on the stained water surface. The paper, when removed, will have lifted off a certain amount of the color creating a pleasant marble effect. The process can then be repeated. Although the marble design is haphazard, some control can be exerted if a small amount of wallpaper paste is mixed in the water and allowed to thicken slightly. Carrageen moss, instead of paste, can be used to make size on which to float the marbling colors. Use moss-size preservative adding approximately I ounce (28g) to 3 pints (1.7l) of size.

Once the color has been added and the water paste solution swirled (only very slightly) the marble design of the color will almost be 'set' on the surface. Great care has to be taken not to overdo the stirring of the water once the color has been added, as the color masses will break up into tiny globules and create a spotty design.

This activity is very enjoyable and you are bound to marble more paper than you need — not such a bad idea as you can then choose the most effective design and color flow. You may have difficulty finding adequate space to lay out and dry the paper. A simple solution to this problem is to rig up a temporary clothesline and hang the paper up by the corners.

Wallpaper-lining paper is a satisfactory paper to use for this process. It is cheap and available in long lengths — avoiding a disjointed appearance. This paper is, of course, fairly fragile and will not withstand knocks and scrapes so it is advisable to cover it with a polyurethane lacquer, sticking down the cut edges well.

A layer of clear sticky-back plastic is suitable protection for smaller props and it also gives the marble a characteristic sheen.

Remember that the size of paper is limited by that of the paint tray.

Three-dimensional objects can also be marbled. Papier mâché bowls and platters are swiftly decorated using this process. Manoeuvre the items in the marbling tray until all the surfaces are covered, then seal with varnish.

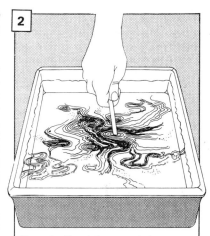

Pour in the ink or paint, stirring just enough to create a pattern

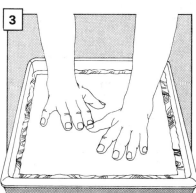

Bring a sheet of paper briefly into contact with the surface, lift it off and hang it on the line to dry

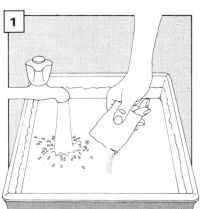

A deep tray should be half filled with water to which a little wallpaper paste is added

Painting and creating patterns

There are other methods of reproducing simple designs, perhaps more suitable for the younger prop maker. Most people are familiar with printing using root vegetables (potato being the most popular). Water-based paints are used, and designs are cut straight into the block without any attempt at transfer of a preliminary design.

Corrugated cardboard, cut into simple shapes and glued on to a wooden base, makes interesting striped prints (these printing blocks have a very limited printing life).

Thin sheets of expanded polystyrene (or tiles) are useful for printing larger areas. Polystyrene is easily cut with a craft knife, or embossed or impressed with blunt instruments. Water-based printing inks work well with polystyrene.

There are endless variations of printing blocks. String glued on to a base of cardboard, corks and bottle caps, cross-sections of wood, open weave material and match boxes all have their place in creating imaginative prints.

The quickest way to apply color to paper is with a paint sprayer or aerosol, but care needs to be taken to cover areas not required to be painted. Be careful not to over-wet the paper because it can rapidly lose its shape and strength. Obviously, the finer the paper the greater the care needed. If pigment color is added to a medium such as varnish, a fine, plastic-like skin is created over the paper, giving it greater strength. Oil-based paints are not suitable for paper (except when they are sprayed thinly), the oil stains bleed into the peripheral areas of the paper where the paint has not been applied. Water-based paints, which are not too diluted, are some of the most successful

paints for coloring or staining paper. A fine layer of varnish on strong paper, or a fixative (hairspray is good) gives greater permanence and strength. Many layers of varnish or shellac over painted paper give it some strength and rigidity and, when folded, the paper will produce a satisfyingly good crackling sound on stage like stiff parchment.

Spraying

Sprayed paint is very effective for shading and shaping flat objects to make them appear three-dimensional, and also for merging one color into another in a way that would be impossible with a brush. Use either an aerosol spray, an airbrush, or an industrial sprayer.

Aerosol cans are available in a wide range of colors from auto shops, and paints with metallic finishes are especially useful to the prop maker. When compared to emulsion, cans of spray paint are expensive for covering large areas, but they do have the advantage of being easy to apply, and quick to dry. When painting rough surfaces, or coarse fabrics, it is easier to obtain a uniform paint covering by spraying rather than brushing. Aerosol paints are cellulose and should not be used on expanded polystyrene.

The airbrush is a more sophisticated means of spraying paint and is useful for applying detail such as burn marks, rust, and shadows on stonework. The reservoir of the airbrush is filled with colored ink, water color, acrylic or enamel paint, and the instrument is connected to an air supply (either a can of propellant or a small compressor). As the air comes through under pressure, a fine jet of paint is emitted through the nozzle. The

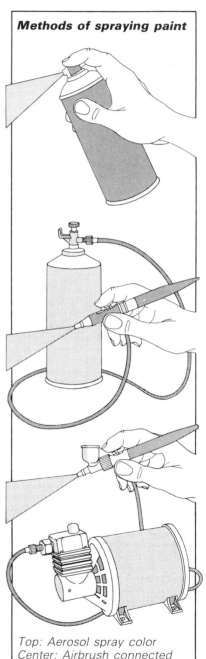

Methods of spraying paint

*Top: Aerosol spray color
Center: Airbrush connected to a can of propellant
Bottom: Airbrush supplied with air by a compressor*

airbrush is a versatile instrument, but its full potential is only realised after considerable practice.

Hand rolling

Hand rollers are a quick way of covering a flat surface. After a little practice you can also learn to draw with a roller. Make rectangular blocks or lines by just placing a paint filled roller down, and then link the lines up to create the impression of panels on a chest or wardrobe or a recess or area of shadow on a building.

Always have an imaginary light source and be consistent with the shading for greater realism.

Using rags

For irregular coloring, rub or pat cloths over paper or cardboard which has had a layer of paint applied. The rag can be dragged in lines or swirled to reveal the base color. You can also apply more color by using the same technique.

Using a pallet knife

Mix the paint with a thickening agent such as plaster, sand or flour, then use a pallet knife to produce a variety of textures from a rough surface to a planned repeating design. This process is only suitable for cardboard and rigid props, otherwise the thick paint may flake off with movement or daily handling.

Using a sponge

A sponge is very effective for delicate shading, and shapes or shadows can be implied by a greater density of the paint. It is equally useful for removing surplus paint to give the impression of fading.

Combing

The Victorian method of combing to create a woodgrain effect is particularly useful to the prop maker when trying to create the illusion of a substantial, three-dimensional wooden prop using a two-dimensional flat. A light, wood color is first applied roughly to the heavy paper, cardboard, or hardboard and is allowed to dry. A darker, heavier mix of paint is then painted over the surface, and a cardboard comb (a rectangular piece of cardboard with notches cut on one of the long sides) is then dragged along the wet surface. For a heavier mix try wallpaper paste mixed with powder color and then varnish it, or apply a light coat of colored wood varnish.

The combing must be done while this secondary layer is still wet.

Experiment by pivoting the comb to create circles, or try dragging the comb through wet plaster to give a fluted effect.

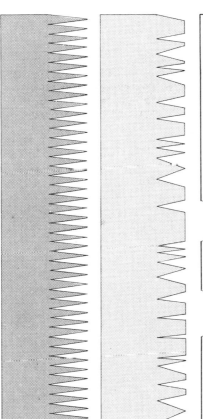

Combs cut from thick cardboard. Different effects can be made depending on the size and spacing of the teeth

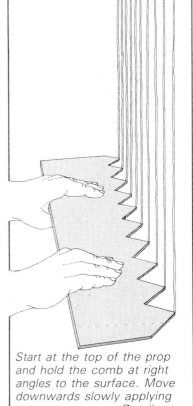

Start at the top of the prop and hold the comb at right angles to the surface. Move downwards slowly applying an even pressure. Detail such as knots for a woodgrain effect are added afterwards with a nail

Working with fabrics and cord

Fabrics and cords are not just confined to the use of the costumer. In conjunction with other materials, they can completely change their identity

Most fabrics are suitable for propmaking, especially for wrapping or molding around basic shapes. Particularly useful are felt, sackcloth, canvas, cheesecloth, gauze, lace, fur fabric, and muslin.

Generally fabrics are soaked with a hardening medium such as liquid plaster or shellac. They are then shaped, allowed to dry (and harden), and finished with paint, varnish, or shoe polish. By the time the final process is completed, the nap, pile or grain is camouflaged according to the density of the hardening medium.

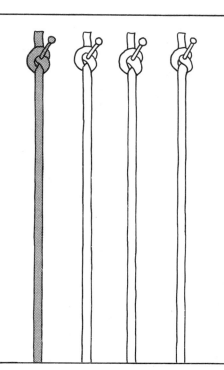

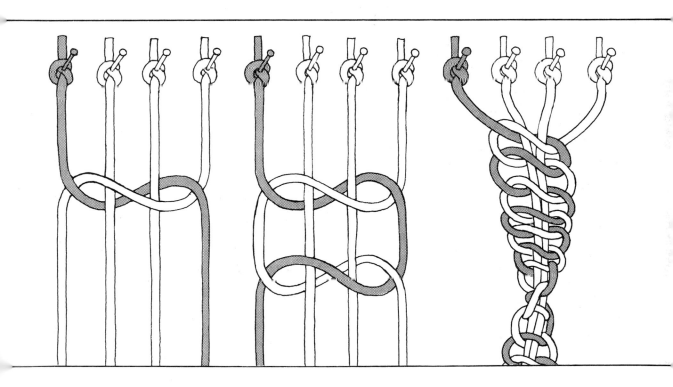

Making imitation leather from felt

Felt

Industrial felt is used for an endless number of costume accessories. It comes in many thicknesses and qualities, the best and most expensive kind being made from all-wool fibers. Cheaper felts usually contain fibers of unknown origin mixed with the wool. All-wool felt wears much better than mixtures.

Unless you live or work in a large city, industrial felt is often difficult to find. It is sold primarily for padding large, moving pieces of machinery, so if you are unable to find a felt supplier, contact a company that uses heavy machinery and they may be able to help you. It is also possible to buy end-pieces of industrial felt which may be thinner, less regular, and consequently less expensive, than the regular industrial felt. (Felt is generally sold by weight.)

A particular type of all-wool felt called orthopedic felt may be purchased from orthopedic suppliers. It is used to pad casts and is usually white Orthopedic

felt is approximately 1/8inch (3mm) thick and is excellent for constructing jewelry and crowns. (See pages 88 and 89.)

Decorator's felt may be purchased in craft shops. It can be used for covering purposes, but it needs reinforcing with some sort of strengthening.

All felt tends to shrink, although some types shrink more than others. Always steam felt before using it in order to shrink it as much as possible.

Make the article

Work out the pattern for the article using tailor's chalk. Cut and assemble either by sewing, gluing, thonging or another mechanical

method of joining. Articles suitable for making with this method would be gauntlets, jerkins, hats, aprons and spats.

Remember that methods of attaching pieces of leather have varied through the centuries, so make sure you check for historical accuracy. Joins or seams include butt joins secured with thonging, overlapped seams with the stitching showing, and seams where the stitching or gluing is concealed. Mechanical aids such as brass fasteners, rivets, and eyelets for lacing can also be employed as a means of joining two pieces of felt together.

Staples can be used as a short cut, but make sure that they are disguised effectively.

MATERIALS
Felt, preferably industrial felt; means of joining: thonging cord, latex glue, metal eyelets or brass fasteners; lava soap; brown acrylic paint; brown shoe polish

TOOLS
Scissors; bodkin or needle if sewing; bradawl or punch to make holes if thonging or using brass fasteners; rivets for putting in metal eyelets; sponge; plenty of newspaper; scrubbing brush

1 *To make a blacksmith's apron*

Cut out the pattern and assemble the pieces

2

Change the surface texture: rub the entire area with lava soap — heavily in some places and lightly in others

Scrub in brown acrylic paint with a sponge and allow it to dry

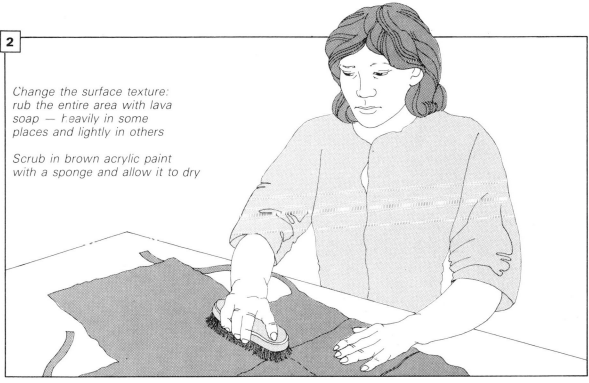

3

Rub all over with brown shoe polish and buff lightly

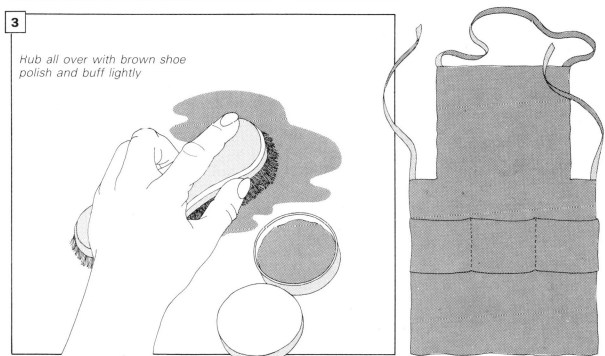

Making imitation leather and metal from felt

This process is best used when making parts for molded leather armor plates, and where the cost of real leather is prohibitive, and commercially produced plastic-based imitation leathers appear too slick and shiny.

Do not limit yourself to the more obvious leather items, however, many other props, or parts of props, can be successfully and economically created.

Try shaping felt around doweling to serve as finger shields for pistols; making leg guards for a Roman soldier by molding felt over plastic bottles and using string to provide decoration.

African hide shields can be made from felt stretched and secured across a heavy duty wire frame, and then painted in bold colors.

The flared end of a blunderbuss is simply made by shaping felt over a greased funnel and then gluing it to the barrel of the gun.

(See also page 109.)

MATERIALS
Plastic/foil sheeting; tape; string; P.V.A. (white flexible glue); size; T-pins; shellac; bottle caps; pasta or dried peas; brown acrylic paint or polish (alternatively, bronze or black pigment added to shellac for the final coat)

TOOLS
Tailor's dummy or shirt form, or a dummy assembled from cushions and foam; scissors; bowl or bucket large enough to immerse felt; awl; paint brush; scrubbing brush

---

Making a mold

Sized-felt armor is particularly good for achieving a bulky look. First you need a mold and the simplest way to make this is to pad out a male shop dummy — to correspond to the actor's measurements — with some space to spare. If a dummy is not available, try to find an old shirt-display frame at a local department store or men's shop and build it up with pieces of foam or padding material. As a final resort cushions, felt, and wadding firmly stuffed into a sack and manipulated by means of string and tape can be made to resemble the actor's shape.

Once the mold is the proper size and shape (again, do make allowance for felt shrinkage and ensure it is an ample size), cover it with a good layer of heavy weight aluminum foil, or polythene. Foil is probably better due to its superior molding qualities.

If, for example a breastplate and a back plate are required, two separate operations are necessary because you will want to extend both shoulders and sides well around the form. They can easily be trimmed back later.

Shaping the felt

Once the felt has been cut to shape, soak the pieces thoroughly with a mixture of two parts P.V.A. (white flexible glue) to one part water. When making smaller items such as gauntlets, a size solution will be sufficient.

Place the felt on the mold and work it firmly into place, pushing, pulling and stretching it until it is smooth.

Pin the felt to the mold with long T-pins or stretch it by threading string sewn from the edge of one side and pulled taut around the back of the mold to lace with the other edge.

Finishing and decorating

Allow the piece to dry: this may take several days. When it is completely dry, remove it from the mold and apply a thin layer of shellac to both sides.

Decorations on sized-felt armor are usually larger and simpler than those used on other types of prop armor. Many raised designs are possible by gluing rope, felt, string, or yarn on to the felt. Split cork balls, buttons or wooden discs also make effective decoration. A pop-riveter may be useful to secure straps to the armor for fitting and joining the sections together. After raised decorations have been applied, add a base coat of paint and then proceed with texturing. Give the entire piece of armor an under-coating of flat spray paint — brown if the surface should simulate leather, bronze or black if it must look like silver or iron. If a rough surface texture is desired, mix a little sand or sawdust in some P.V.A. (white flexible glue) and water, and lay a thin coating of this mixture over the base color. Allow the texturing to dry thoroughly.

The final layer consists of shellac colored with the appropriate pigment. Shade and touch up as desired, using shellac, lamp-black, bronzing powders, or oil paints. Alternatively P.V.A. (white flexible glue) can be mixed with brown powder color, and, when applied to the surface, it will give a hard, burnished, sealed, look. If straps and buckles are being rivetted on to armor pieces, be sure to purchase long-shanked rivets and to reinforce from behind.

1

Prepare the mold

(a) using a tailor's dummy   or   (b) by assembling cushions and
covered with foil   foam together with tape and
                                     string. Cover with plastic

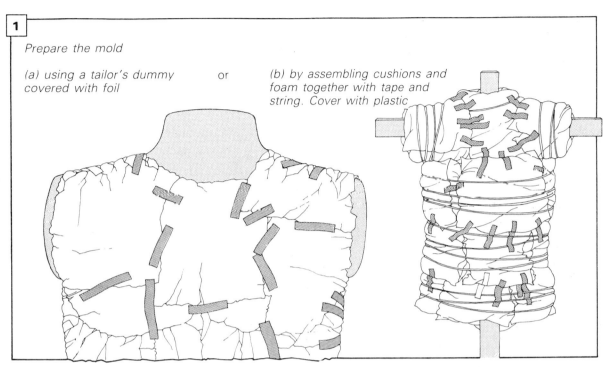

2

Cut felt to shape
and soak it in the
glue solution. Pull
felt over and
around
mold

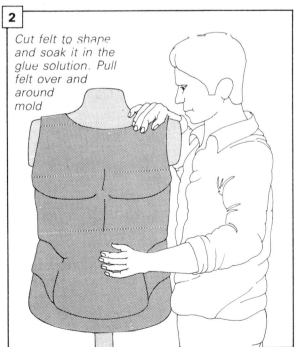

3

Remove the felt
from the mold,
then shellac, dec-
orate, and paint

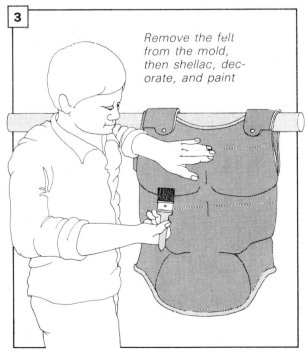

Making use of felt

For jewelry

Because it so readily takes a variety of adhesives and paints, sized felt is an extremely good foundation for making pieces of jewelry. Pendants, rings, brooches, bracelets, medals, and so on, are just a few possibilities.

First apply a flat basecoat of shellac then mix in bronzing powders with the shellac to provide color and finish. If it is necessary to attach pieces of jewelry to a garment, then use a large safety pin or kilt pin secured to the back by stitching with heavyweight thread. For more delicate jewelry involving fairly intricate gold work, stiffen bits of lace with P.V.A. (white flexible glue). These can be combined with the felt shapes and then sprayed with gold or brushed with bronzing powder suspended in varnish. A necklace can be contrived from individual stiffened lace links, which are then sprayed, or painted with shellac combined with a metal pigment, and attached to a chain.

Don't forget to make use of domestic items, such as liquid soap bottles. Sized felt can be shaped around these to produce armlets or ankle bands. Alternatively, small medicine bottles are ideal for constructing individual chain links.

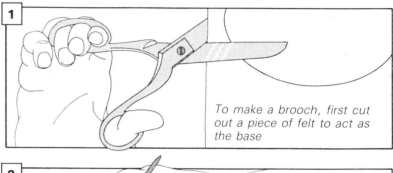

1

To make a brooch, first cut out a piece of felt to act as the base

2

Stitch on a safety pin and cover with shellac

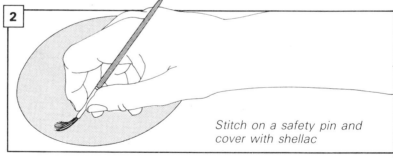

3

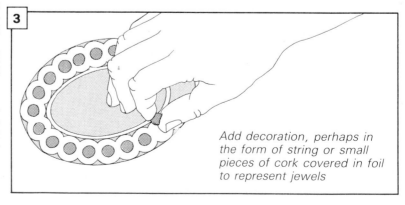

Add decoration, perhaps in the form of string or small pieces of cork covered in foil to represent jewels

For helmets and crowns

Helmets

Fiberglass resin can be combined with a metallic filler to give felt the appearance of metal for such props as helmets.

Assemble the felt helmet sections, first butting, then stitching, the separate pieces together with a wide zig-zag machine stitch or large hand sewn stitches. Adjust the shape to fit the actor's head, (making allowance for felt shrinkage) and when the shape and size are correct, place the helmet on a milliner's block. Depending on the type of headgear being made, a felt brim can be added at this stage, but it will need to be supported with cardboard. Felt shapes providing raised detail can also be glued to the headgear.

Mix resin and catalyst with the appropriate metal filler and thoroughly coat the felt. Using a file or sandpaper, smooth the edges and then burnish with wire wool. To give the feeling of antiquity, rub black paint in with a cloth, blending it into the metallic surface.

Alternatively an old felt hat (which may require altering if the helmet has to cover the ears) is a good base for a helmet. Moisten it with water and stretch it over a wooden milliner's block (or suitably shaped block of wood). Pin it down while it is allowed to dry, and then apply a thick coat of P.V.A (white flexible glue) and water: two parts glue to one part water. When the surface is firm and the helmet is completely dry, remove it from the block and paint both the inside and outside with shellac.

As already suggested, raised detail can then be glued on to the helmet, in the form of various shapes cut out of felt and stiffened, or

To reinforce a felt helmet with fiberglass resin

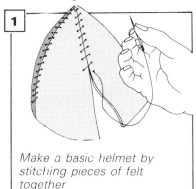

1

Make a basic helmet by stitching pieces of felt together

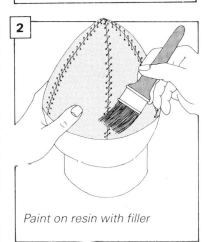

2

Paint on resin with filler

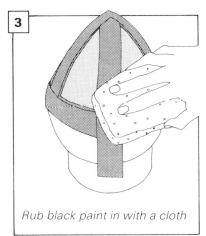

3

Rub black paint in with a cloth

string used to produce curling patterns and raised edges, or paper fasteners to represent studs. Bronze or silver sprays will give an authentic metallic finish.

Crowns

Always make a scale, cardboard mock-up of the crown which can be fitted on the actor's head and studied for size and shape.

Once the mock-up has been approved, you can go ahead and construct a felt copy. Soak it with a mixture of white glue and water (two:one as before). Allow it to dry, and decorate and color as required. To achieve a metallic effect apply a final layer of shellac mixed with metallic pigment.

Picture and mirror frames

The curved and curling shapes of ornate picture frames are easily imitated by cutting felt shapes and gluing them on to an existing plain frame. When you have built up a pattern, shellac it once and begin to mold and work the felt into its final shape. Add successive layers of shellac; the felt will become progressively harder and eventually after about five coats, it should be quite stiff when dry.

Note Too much glitter on stage must be avoided. Stage lights may pick up shiny surfaces and reflect them in a distracting way. A wash of brown, khaki, or gray paint will add age and a dull layer to jewelry.

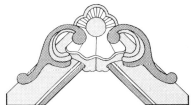

Ideas for using fabrics

Lace

Lace, when applied to a glass or metal goblet or plate, and then sprayed with metallic paint will transform plain objects into precious church plate.

To make a medieval goblet

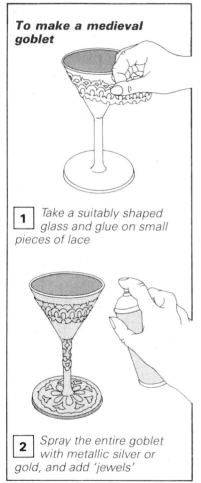

1 *Take a suitably shaped glass and glue on small pieces of lace*

2 *Spray the entire goblet with metallic silver or gold, and add 'jewels'*

Lace segments colored with metal pigments in shellac add a degree of authenticity to a reproduction sword or dagger — giving the impression of fine filigree work. A necklace can be put together from individual lace links, stiffened and sprayed and attached to a chain.

To make a necklace

1 *Cut out individual lace sections*

2 *Paint or spray the pieces gold or silver*

3 *Link together using a discarded chain*

Muslin

Soaked in P.V.A. (white flexible glue) muslin can be molded into fanciful shapes such as ears for a mask or small angel wings.

Cheesecloth

A fabric that is often used to add both strength and texture to papier mâché masks and some latex pieces (see page 23).

Canvas

Canvas forms the backing for belts and bandoliers (a shoulder belt with cartridge loops). A somewhat stylized type of armor can be made from two layers of canvas sandwiched and stiffened with P.V.A.

Fur

Some fake fur is sold quite inexpensively these days and is a boon to the prop maker; it has a wide range of uses from wall hangings and rugs to tribal equipment and exotic furniture.

Notes on sizing

Adding sizing to fabric is a way of making inexpensive, loosely woven material appear to be smoother and to have a higher thread count than it actually does. Additions of starch, gum, and resin sizings fill in the open spaces in the weave and stiffen the fabric. Most of these sizings will wash out; indeed, much will be lost through normal wear. Permanent stiffening is possible, with extra quantities of size, and in some cases desirable, (perhaps for an object which is handled frequently, or for a crown made from fabric).

Fiberglass — WARNING

Fiberglass is the trade name for a synthetic fiber used to make drapery among other things (see page 56). Under no circumstances should fiberglass be used in a costume or prop that will come in touch with an actor's skin. It is very irritating, and many people develop violent allergic reactions to it.

To make a parasol from an old umbrella

Remove the old material gently, taking care to keep the sections intact as much as possible. Use these sections as a pattern to cut the new cloth. (The panels of a parasol are often shorter than those of an umbrella, so it may be necessary to cut smaller panels, and also to cut a length off each spoke.) Sew the new pieces together and place the cover over the frame, ensuring that each seam is directly on top of a spoke in the frame. Secure the cover at the top and bottom of each spoke, stretching the fabric tightly. Add ruffles, fringe, or other decorations to the cover after it has been attached to the frame. The trim can be machine-stitched between spokes and hand-stitched over the spokes. As you work on the frame, open and close it frequently to make sure the cover doesn't interfere with the action.

Most parasols have wooden handles that can be painted to complement the cover and the costume. Use an enamel paint that will not rub off.

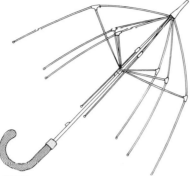

1 *Carefully strip the umbrella down to the frame*

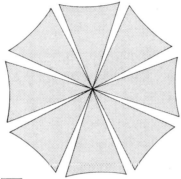

2 *Use the old sections as patterns for the new fabric: crepe polyester might be suitable*

Stitch the new panels and add frills or other decoration. The handle may need to be replaced with one that is more appropriate to the historical period

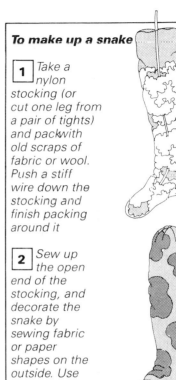

To make up a snake

1 *Take a nylon stocking (or cut one leg from a pair of tights) and pack with old scraps of fabric or wool. Push a stiff wire down the stocking and finish packing around it*

2 *Sew up the open end of the stocking, and decorate the snake by sewing fabric or paper shapes on the outside. Use buttons or sequins for the eyes, and make the fangs from wire*

3 *The stiff wire allows the snake to be coiled into any position*

To make a space age prop

An old Tiffany or billiard table lampshade covered in gauze or cheesecloth, painted with P.V.A. (white flexible glue) and sprayed silver, can resemble a radar dish, or other piece of technological apparatus for a sci-fi drama.

Using ropes, cords, and string

There are many different kinds of ropes, cords, twines, and strings available in a wide range of thicknesses. Depending on the strength and texture required you can choose from natural fibers, paper, plastic or metal threads.

Rope is versatile simply for decoration, such as winding around a column, or for forming a coil at the base and top of objects. As a flexible device it is suitable for making a snake with a felt head glued on to it, or it can be draped to liven up a decorative border. Rope can also be broken down into small curly strands or finely shredded to make hair, foliage, animal manes, or make-up. A formal hair-style, such as that used on sculpture, is achieved simply by gluing many fine lengths of string on to the object, shaping them as necessary, then hardening the result by soaking it in hot size, water paste, or plaster; shellac may also be used. It can then be painted in stone, wood or metallic colors to give the illusion of carving.

The decorative use of strings and cords, combined with felt and paper sculpture, can be quite as elaborate as you choose.

Fireproofing

Use a flame retardant, or mix 3 ounces (85g) boric acid with 7 ounces (198g) of borax and dissolve in 4 pints (2l) of warm water. Either completely soak the object in the solution or spray it on to the prop: make sure it is completely saturated. The solution has to be reapplied if the object is washed.

String or rope that has been shredded can be used as hair on masks

An ordinary hand mirror is converted into an ancient relic with string and paint

Daggers and swords gain an authentic metallic effect by binding and gluing string around the handle. Finish with bronze, gold or silver spray.

Turn glasses into goblets by gluing string around them and spraying them silver

Using string to make a mask or crown

A versatile, light structure for making helmets, crowns and masks is quickly made by wrapping string covered in glue around a balloon and allowing it to harden. The resulting framework can then be cut and painted as desired.

Rest the balloon on a cardboard collar, taping extra balloons to it if required. Paste them well with petroleum jelly and trail the string through carpenter's glue and wrap it around the balloons. The string should be applied in a random criss-cross arrangement thoroughly covering the surface. If making a mask, try to use less string where the actor will need space for vision, although this may not correspond with the eyes on the mask. In the case of a crown or head-dress, once the initial criss-crossing has been done, you can arrange a more consistent string design on top. Allow the glue to dry and harden, then pop and remove the balloons. The string shape can then be trimmed to fit the actor before finishing and decorating.

Some decorations suitable for masks and crowns can be made from sized string. String whiskers, or antennae (reinforced with thin wire and dipped in glue) will retain their shape well.

Stylized feathers are improvised by threading short lengths of string on to a piece of thin wire and then dipping them in carpenter's glue or a strong size solution. Tape both ends to a balloon-greasing underneath the string. Arrange the strands into a chevron pattern, allow to dry, and then remove from the balloon. Trim the string into a feather shape, cutting off the surplus wire. The use of aerosol paint will give subtle variations of color.

To make a mask

1 Rest the balloon on a cardboard collar and tape on any other balloons that are needed

2 Dip the string in carpenter's glue and then wrap the string around the balloon

3 Features can be painted on to the mask once the glue has hardened

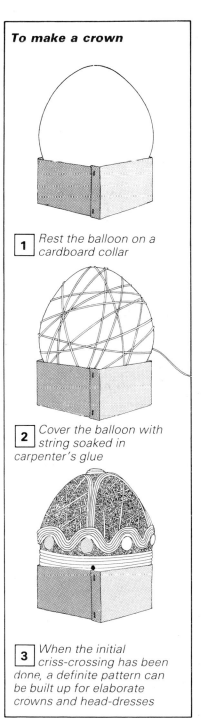

To make a crown

1 Rest the balloon on a cardboard collar

2 Cover the balloon with string soaked in carpenter's glue

3 When the initial criss-crossing has been done, a definite pattern can be built up for elaborate crowns and head-dresses

Knotting string

Knotting and pleating string — generally known as macramé — can be as complicated or as simple as you like. Twisted cords, spirals, and braids are easily made and are invaluable as a source of decoration when converting a simple prop into a more ornate one. Narrow, flat- braided macramé, sprayed with gold, silver, or bronze, is suitable as a mount for precious stones (chunks of expanded polystyrene wrapped with cellophane). Twisted spiral macramé glued in panels on a shoebox and colored appropriately, transforms the cardboard box into a carved wooden casket or treasure chest.

Making a spiral

An attractive spiral cord can be created by repeating the same knot. Choose the right thickness of string or rope to suit your practical needs. Start off with four strings knotted at the top end and secured with pins in a piece of fiberboard. The length of the string should be approximately four times the length of the desired finished result. (This, of course, will vary according to the thickness of the string.) Do not use nylon string as it slips easily and will probably untie itself. Cotlon is a good compromise and has the strength of nylon and the flexibility of cotton. To stop the cotlon from fraying, seal the end by plunging it briefly into a flame.

Heavier string can be disguised with a coating of plaster for architectural detail or, alternatively, P.V.A. (white flexible glue) mixed with sawdust and brown paint and applied to the string spiral will provide carved detail.

These methods are not restricted to string. Try using leather thonging or mock leather (see page 84) to make belts or straps.

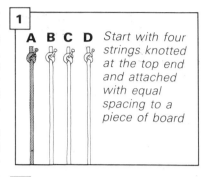

1 A B C D *Start with four strings knotted at the top end and attached with equal spacing to a piece of board*

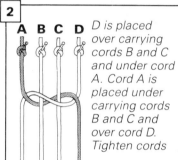

2 A B C D *D is placed over carrying cords B and C and under cord A. Cord A is placed under carrying cords B and C and over cord D. Tighten cords*

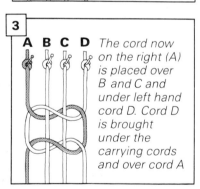

3 A B C D *The cord now on the right (A) is placed over B and C and under left hand cord D. Cord D is brought under the carrying cords and over cord A*

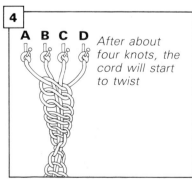

4 A B C D *After about four knots, the cord will start to twist*

Flat braiding

This braiding, based on the half hitch knot, is a flat braiding useful for making belts. It also comes into its own when decoration is needed for such things as purses, parasols and fans or for large intricate jewelry like an Egyptian necklace. Do not forget that beads, small pasta shapes, or corks can be interspersed with the knots for additional interest.

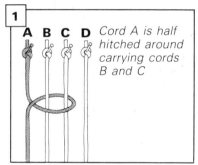

1 A B C D *Cord A is half hitched around carrying cords B and C*

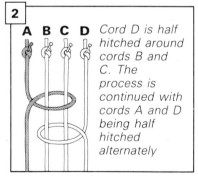

2 A B C D *Cord D is half hitched around cords B and C. The process is continued with cords A and D being half hitched alternately*

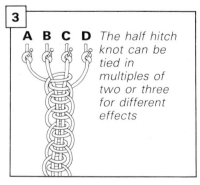

3 A B C D *The half hitch knot can be tied in multiples of two or three for different effects*

Making chain mail from string

String knitted on large size knitting needles makes very convincing chain mail. If possible, buy gray, dark green or black string. This will eliminate the need to spray the knotted chain mail with a base coat, before applying a final coat of bronzing-powder or metallic spray paint.

Helmets also look effective in 'chain mail' and are decorated in the same way as armor plates (see page 86). Make up a rough paper pattern first, to provide a good fit for the head.

You can also cut PVC into strips to be used for knitting. If using the transparent variety, fine silver lurex thread can be introduced in places to reduce transparency and to increase the sparkle of the garment — this might be suitable for part of a spacesuit prop.

To make a denser type of chain mail, nylon tights are useful. Cut across the leg in strips to make rings, and then loop these together into a length of 'string'. Knit and color as with conventional string.

For those not conversant with the process of knitting, a shortcut may be by cannibalizing an old sweater. It must be a loosely knitted sweater without any fancy stitching. Cut the garment up into sections suitable for a chain mail suit and re-assemble, oversewing the cut edges. The plain side of the garment should be the right side (generally on the inside of most sweaters) and this should be painted or sprayed as previously explained. The addition of bottle caps and studs and so on will make the garment appear more authentic. A balaclava makes an alternative chain mail helmet. Reinforce by binding the edges with silver PVC cloth.

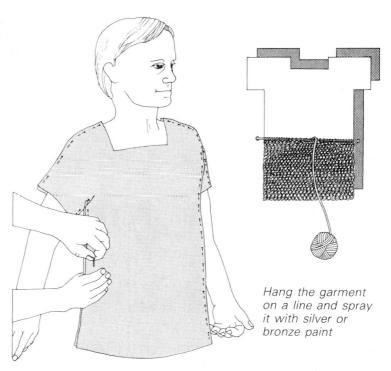

Hang the garment on a line and spray it with silver or bronze paint

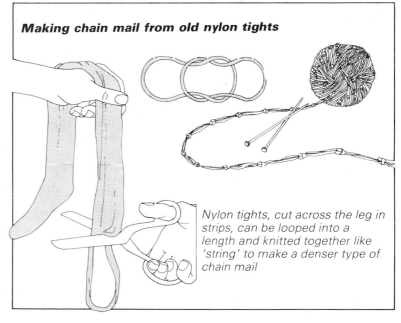

Making chain mail from old nylon tights

Nylon tights, cut across the leg in strips, can be looped into a length and knitted together like 'string' to make a denser type of chain mail

Working with wood

Wood is the basic material of many props as it is strong and easy to work with. There are many kinds. Each has a different feature that the prop maker can use to its best advantage. For instance, bamboo is rigid, cane and willow are pliable, thin-ply is bendable, and balsa is light, whereas teak and oak, being close-grained, are strong and heavy.

In this section we are not concerned with describing sophisticated joints and finishing. It must be remembered that most theatrical props have a limited life and need only be strong enough to last for the duration of the particular production. Of course, props that have to be load-bearing need to have conventional joints, otherwise shortcuts are fine, in fact preferable. The prop maker should consider his woodwork as a hammer and nail job, or make good use of glue, with corrugated fasteners and corner brackets if necessary for strengthening.

However, it is wise to become acquainted with the proprietor of the local woodwork shop, for it is there that band-saws, lathes, power drills, and other machinery for working timber will be available (at a price) to do the more laborious and excessively difficult jobs.

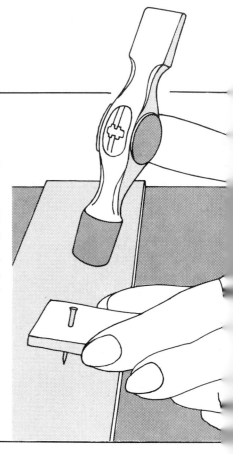

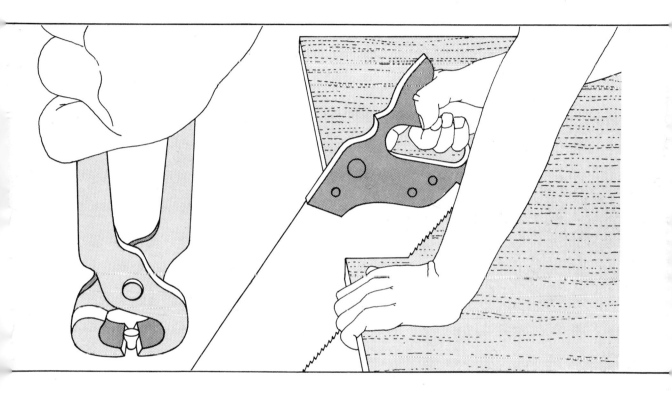

Basic techniques with wood

Marking

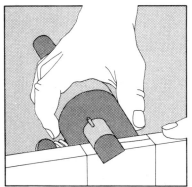

Use a marker gauge to mark out the wood

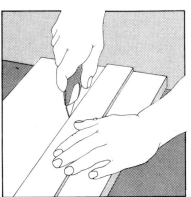

Use a knife with a metal rule to score the wood or alternatively mark with a pencil

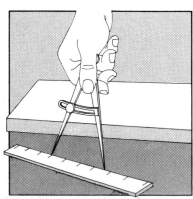

Use dividers to measure

Holding

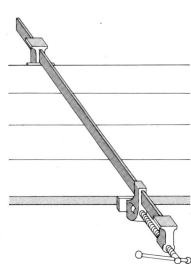

Use a sash clamp to hold work horizontally — take care not to damage the wood by overtightening

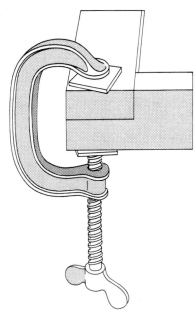

Use a G clamp to hold more than one piece of wood

Sawing

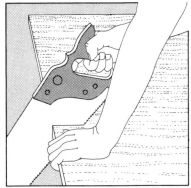

Use a rip saw to cut along the grain with short strokes first

Use a cross-cut saw across the grain applying light pressure

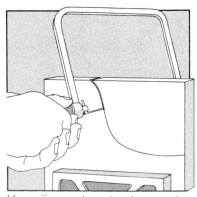

Use a jig saw to cut out accurate shapes and curves

Methods of fixing with hammer and nails

There are two basic types of woodwork hammers: the claw hammer and the ball-pein hammer. A claw hammer is a necessity, as it drives and pulls out most nails. A ball-pein hammer is a useful additional tool for hammering small pins and tacks. To start off short nails, tap them gently while holding them between the fingers until they are secure, then drive them forcefully home.

The pin hammer is the lightest version of the ball-pein hammer and is used on pins which a heavier hammer would bend. This hammer is particularly useful to the prop maker when he is economizing and using lighter, thinner varieties of wood.

The pin push is a time saver for fixing hardboard or thin ply to framing. A panel pin fits in the end tube, which is held against the hardboard or ply, and driven in by pushing on the spring-loaded handle.

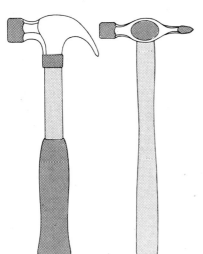

The basic claw hammer and ball-pein hammer

Use a corrugated fastener across a mitered joint

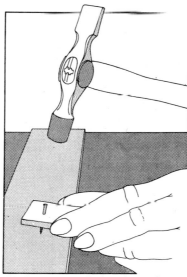

Push very small pins through a piece of expanded polystyrene. When the pin is nearly home, tear the polystyrene away

Removing nails

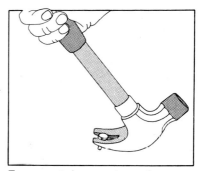

To prevent damage to surfaces, place a piece of scrap wood under the claw hammer head and use the wood as a fulcrum

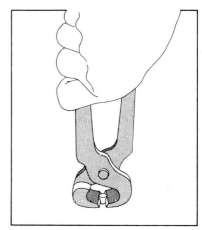

Use pincers in a series of short, sharp pulls. If you remove the nail in one pull, you will leave a large, misshapen hole

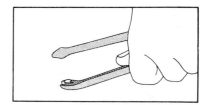

The fine claw on the end of the pincer handle slips under well-driven nails and pulls them up enough to let the jaws grip

Gluing

P.V.A. (white flexible glue). As an all-round glue this adhesive is well-suited for general woodworking and mending. It sets within 20 minutes and is completely dry in 24 hours. Surfaces must be clamped together during setting. The glue dries clear and is strong, but it will not resist high stress. Clean off excess glue with a damp cloth before it sets.

Animal and fish (Scotch) glues. These traditional adhesives, derived from hides, bones and sinews, are used by furniture makers for close-fitting wood joints not subject to moisture. Some brands come as solid bars which must be melted and applied hot; ready mixed versions harden slowly at room temperature. Joints must be clamped together. These glues dry pale brown and excess glue is cleaned off with water before hardening begins.

Acrylic cement. Obtainable from acrylic suppliers, this is a specialized adhesive for sheet acrylic. Great care must be taken when gluing acrylic as untidy joints can spoil the look of the article. When joining two flat surfaces, take care to expel all air bubbles.

Contact cement. This bonds immediately and is useful for fixing hardboard and metal to wood. The adhesive must be applied to both work surfaces and allowed to become tacky (5-40 minutes depending on instructions and room temperature). When the glued pieces are put together they are difficult to adjust. Long clamping periods are not necessary, but firm pressure must be applied initially. Most brands dry opaque, but some are transparent. Wood-to-wood bonds tend to move after long periods

Bonding wood to:	Use:
Plexiglass (perspex)	Acrylic cement
Plastic or latex foam Expanded polystyrene	Contact cement Natural latex Rubber resin
Metal	Epoxy contact cement P.V.A. (white flexible glue) Natural latex Rubber resin
Rubber	Contact cement Natural latex Rubber resin
Leather and textiles	Animal and fish glue Cellulose Contact cement Natural latex Rubber resin

of stress and are not strong enough for furniture building.

Natural latex adhesive. Used for fixing fabrics, paper and porous materials, latex adhesive sets quickly and forms strong flexible bonds. If still wet, it can be removed with a damp rag; otherwise lighter fuel or white spirit is needed. Setting time for most latex adhesives is 2-6 hours.

Rubber resin glues. These are spirit based glues used for PVC tiling, rubber, felt and asbestos-backed PVC tiles. Some brands need to be applied to both surfaces and others to only one.

Cellulose adhesive. A quick drying and useful adhesive for fixing china, glass, or any objects that are difficult to clamp together and need a strong bond.

See also: page 16, Using different adhesives.

Finishing wood and fireproofing

In prop-making, wood often has to adopt the role of another material, so advice on finishing cannot be too specific.

Most paints take well to wood. Primers must be used on some particularly absorbent woods such as hardboard and particle board. A final layer of varnish gives a painted wooden object greater surface strength — matte varnish is generally advisable to avoid glare from the stage lights.

For fireproofing paint on 15 ounces (425g) boric acid crystals and 10 ounces (283g) sodium phosphate in a solution using a gallon (4.5l) of water.

Alternatively, paint or spray on a solution of ready-made fireproofing crystals, taking care not to smudge the paintwork.

Making sticks and staffs

The biggest problem with making sticks is that they will be strong enough for their purpose. Hard woods, which are the sturdiest, are difficult to shape without a wood lathe, but softwood doweling, which is easier to carve, may not be strong enough. A bannister rod, used to construct stairway rails, often makes a handsome walking stick. It is available in a variety of different turnings and need only be cut to the correct length and stained or painted. Rubber tips to keep the stick from slipping are available in most orthopedic supply stores.

Methods of decoration

As sticks and staffs vary considerably from era to era, and depend on the character's status in life, make sure you have accurate references to work with. Rope wound around a stick in a spiral fashion, secured with P.V.A. (white flexible glue) — the knob being a papier mâché snake's head — is effective. Small, hollow rubber balls (with a small hole made to accommodate the stick) make highly satisfactory silver knobs when painted with metallic pigment suspended in shellac.

Doweling is ideal for making lightweight sticks and staffs. It is available in various thicknesses and is fairly inexpensive. By staining and polishing, you will give it the look of an older and harder wood.

Bamboo canes are particularly useful for making walking sticks and flails. Heavy duty wire can be inserted in the top to create unusual shapes and then covered with papier mâché.

Of course, an ordinary walking stick is easily transformed using scrap items about the house.

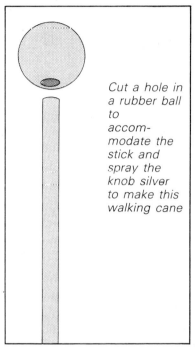

Wind rope around a length of doweling and finish with a snake's head made from papier mâché.

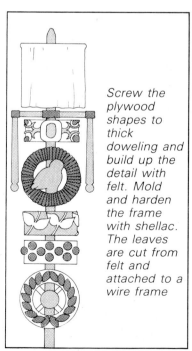

Cut a hole in a rubber ball to accommodate the stick and spray the knob silver to make this walking cane

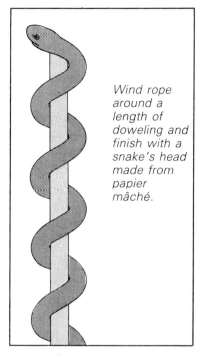

An unusual handle is made by covering a chicken wire frame with papier mâché and molding it to the shape of a bird's head. String can be entwined for added effect

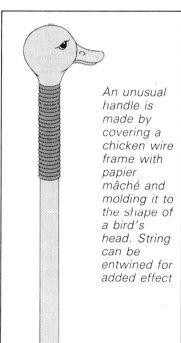

Screw the plywood shapes to thick doweling and build up the detail with felt. Mold and harden the frame with shellac. The leaves are cut from felt and attached to a wire frame

Making weapons from wood

Swords and daggers

One method of making a sword is to shape the blade in wood and add burnish to it, using a fine adhesive to glue on some aluminum foil. This way you can make a large, very light, blade. Sometimes you will not even have to make a complete sword but just the hilt and scabbard — if the sword is not drawn. The best way to make the grip is to glue an extra piece of wood each side of the blade (at the top end). Shape as required and then decorate with leather, tape, wire, or paint. One of the most effective bindings is gilt picture wire which gives a very professional finish, but must be wound very tight so as not to slip.

Quillions (cross guards). The function of this part of the hilt is to prevent your opponent's blade from sliding down your blade and reaching your hand. In most cases of theatrical swords this is purely decorative, although if there is a sword fight scene it must also look practical. A basic cross hilt can be simply made from a shortened wooden coathanger, which, when covered with aluminum foil, looks most effective. Other suitable domestic items include coat hooks and plastic ball floats (cut in half) for cup hilts.

Pommels (tops). This part of the sword is used to counterbalance the weight of the blade. As the pommel is usually ball- or wheel-shaped, the most convenient items to use would be door or cupboard handles. Other shape variations might include combinations of brass light fittings, tumblers, cardboard egg cups, and ping-pong balls. To achieve a uniformity of design, both pommels and quillions should be treated in the same way, with a brass or a silver effect.

Knives

These are made in much the same way as swords, although in many cases it is possible to utilize domestic cutlery or paper knives.

Bind handle with gilt wire

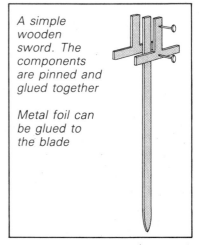

A simple wooden sword. The components are pinned and glued together

Metal foil can be glued to the blade

Two coat hooks screwed into the handle serve as a cross guard. The pommel is a brass ring from a light fitting

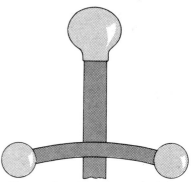

The quillion here is made from a wooden coathanger with a ping-pong ball on each end. The pommel is a round door handle

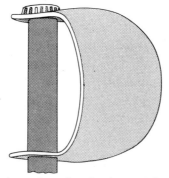

A section of a plastic container serves as the guard on this dress sword

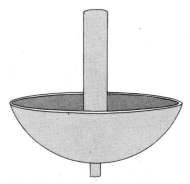

The hilt of this fencing foil is made from a section of a plastic ball float

Shields

A simple way of making a shield is to cut the basic shape out of plywood, and then give it added depth by embossing, studs, rims and raised decorative designs. A most effective round shield can be made by cutting out a disc of plywood, then covering it with, for example, red colored vinyl. Drawing pins make excellent studs with their large gold heads, and a central design and outside rim is quickly built up from gold-painted thick cardboard or felt. For a more highly polished finish, aluminum foil or various colored-foil wrappers are distinctive in detailed work. A leather strap, or wooden handle can be secured on the back — if fastening with pins, do this before covering the surface with vinyl. If a pop-riveter is being used, the projections can be included as part of the design. Take this into account when positioning the shield handle.

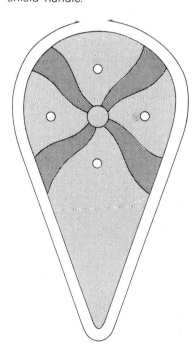

Guns

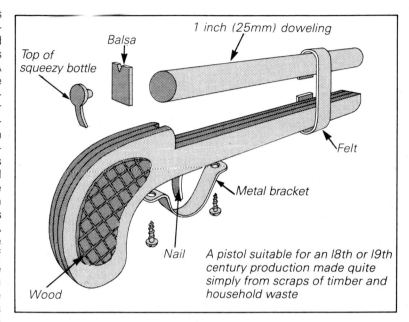

Top of squeezy bottle

Balsa

1 inch (25mm) doweling

Felt

Metal bracket

Nail

Wood

A pistol suitable for an l8th or l9th century production made quite simply from scraps of timber and household waste

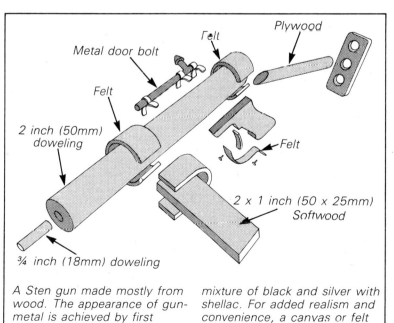

Metal door bolt

Felt

Felt

Plywood

2 inch (50mm) doweling

Felt

2 x 1 inch (50 x 25mm) Softwood

¾ inch (18mm) doweling

A Sten gun made mostly from wood. The appearance of gun-metal is achieved by first painting in black, and then working up a shine using a mixture of black and silver with shellac. For added realism and convenience, a canvas or felt strap could be added to the body of the gun

Working with metal

Some metals, generally in the form of scrap metals, are useful additions to the prop maker's store.

Chicken wire is, of course, a versatile base for papier mâché and plaster work. Some expanded metals such as zinc and aluminum, come into their own when cut and shaped into interesting sculptural shapes — suitable perhaps as antennae in a sci-fi drama. Thin drain pipes, angle iron, and railings, can be assembled together to make weird and wonderful machinery. Nuts and bolts are useful for decoration when glued on to a suit of armor. Wire is always essential for practical purposes, like threading the parts of a prop together.

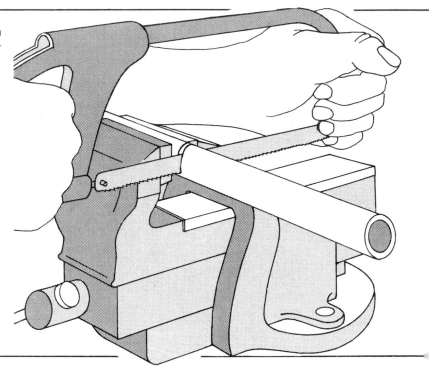

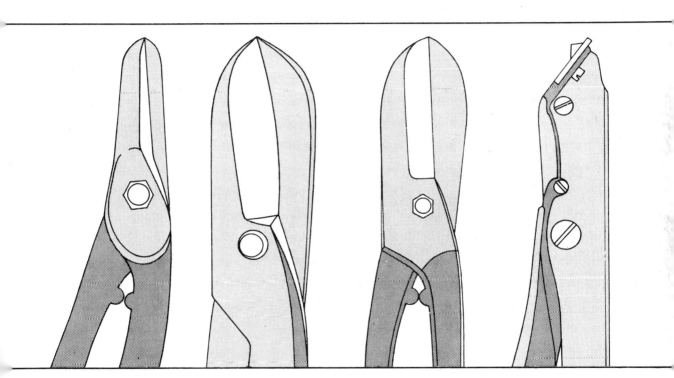

Cutting metal

Metal snips cut like scissors and are held like pliers or pruning shears. The length of the handle determines the leverage and the cutting power. This is the tool most-used for cutting sheet metal to shape. Great care needs to be taken when cutting, sawing, shaping, and grinding metal. Avoid having sharp edges, and always work tools in a direction away from the body. Always use gloves and goggles where necessary, and make sure guards on machinery are in position and are used.

Marking

Mark your cut lines using a scriber; you can easily make one from an old steel knitting needle sharpened to give a good point. Other guidelines should be made with a pencil and erased after use.

Sawing

A hacksaw is used for cutting metal. Use a standard hacksaw frame with a fine blade. Junior hacksaws and piercing saws are useful for smaller work. When sawing, always support the sheet metal to prevent vibrations which could make your cut inaccurate.

Polishing

Metal can be burnished and polished with an electric drill fitted with the appropriate attachment. Otherwise, the laborious method of rubbing down with steel wool will produce a sheen to be finished with a metal polish. To give metal an aged look, paint it black and rub areas of black paint away with steel wool to reveal parts of the metallic gleam.

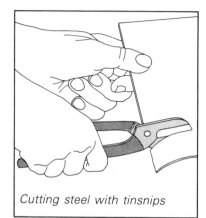

Cutting steel with tinsnips

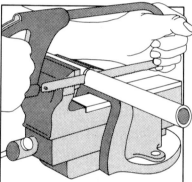

Clamp small pieces in a vice when sawing

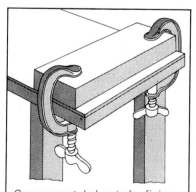

Secure metal sheets by fixing a table with wooden battens and two G clamps

Different types of tinsnips

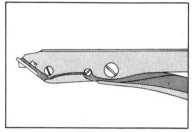

Specialized snips cut without distorting the surrounding metal

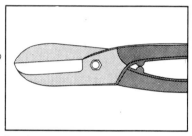

Straight snips for straight-cutting and outside curves

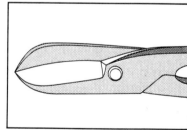

Curved snips used for cutting tight inside curves

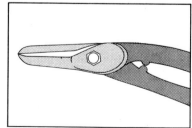

Universal snips for most shapes except small internal curves

Ideas for using metal

When selecting junk to be used it is worth remembering that generally metal is heavier and more cumbersome than many other materials available to the prop maker. Make sure that only metal can do the job before embarking on too ambitious a project.

A door knob used on top of a helmet

Part of a sieve employed as a face guard

Old litho printing plates

Litho plates are thin sheets of aluminum used for offset litho printing which, when discarded, have a variety of other applications. One example would be to glue a plate on to hardboard to give a metallic surface to a shield. The plates are also excellent as a source of metal from which to cut out the heads of axes or pike staffs. (Be careful with the ragged edges.)

Metal foil

Brass foil, glued on to cardboard with P.V.A. (white flexible glue), is a good source from which to cut hinges, ornamental sections, door plates, and finger panels.

Making foil letters in relief

Cardboard letters are cut out and glued on to a base piece of cardboard, and then a thick gauge foil is stretched over the top. Great care needs to be taken not to puncture the foil at corners — mitering will help avoid this.

Foil covered doweling

Metal foils can be shaped around almost any carvable material. For instance, cord or rope is wound around a dowel, glued, and then covered with a layer of glued foil. When dry, the spirals are emphasized with a blunt tool. This could be used as an ultra-modern lamp standard for a contemporary production, as a spring for machinery, or as part of some space gear.

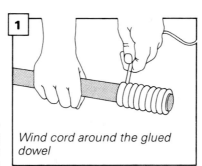

Wind cord around the glued dowel

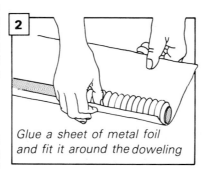

Glue a sheet of metal foil and fit it around the doweling

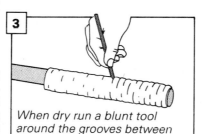

When dry run a blunt tool around the grooves between the cord

Making flowers from wire

These flowers will not go limp overnight and are economically made from florist's wire and old nylon tights! The nylon is first immersed in a proprietary dye-removing solution and then re-dyed to the desired color.

Florist's wire (available in conveniently short lengths) is then looped into rough petal shapes, and the ends twisted together.

Cut enough nylon to double over the wire petal shape. Then pull the nylon tight and gather all the cut ends to the twisted wire base and secure them by binding with a thin gauge wire. Pull the petal to the desired shape.

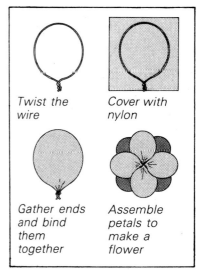

Twist the wire

Cover with nylon

Gather ends and bind them together

Assemble petals to make a flower

Finally, make a stem to wire the assembled petals together and cover the exposed wire with self adhesive green florist's tape. Arrange the petals naturally. The centers of the flowers can be contrived from any available scrap. For additional boldness flowers can be sprayed with colorful paint.

Making swords from metal

Most DIY stores stock strips of aluminum of about 1/8 inch (3mm) thick and 1-2 inch (25-50mm) wide. When shaped with a file or rasp, it can make very effective and lightweight sword blades, although they will not be strong enough for fighting! Real sword blades are generally made from tempered steel. However, this process is expensive and not generally available for small quantities. A suitable alternative would be a leaf spring from a car, shaped on a grinding wheel. Modern epee, saber and foil blades, which are comparatively inexpensive and widely available in good sports shops, make ideal blades for cup-hilt rapiers, and dress and diplomatic swords.

To make curved swords

Use sheet aluminum, such as an old litho plate, for making cutlasses and other curved swords and daggers. The sheet should be folded double and the outline of the blade scribed on to it before it is cut out with a heavy duty craft knife.

To make a scabbard

A strip of litho plate folded several times over the edge of a table, or a similar device, makes a good scabbard. If the sword has to be drawn during the production, it will make a very realistic scraping sound against the metal scabbard.

An archer's quiver could also be made from a litho plate bent into a cylinder and then glued with epoxy adhesive. Insert a thick piece of cardboard for the base, fixing it with strong adhesive tape. Cover it with dyed or painted cheesecloth or canvas and attach it with a leather thong to the archer's belt.

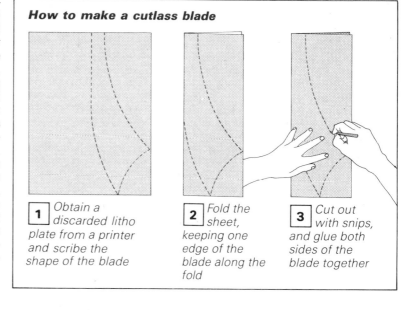

How to make a cutlass blade

1 Obtain a discarded litho plate from a printer and scribe the shape of the blade

2 Fold the sheet, keeping one edge of the blade along the fold

3 Cut out with snips, and glue both sides of the blade together

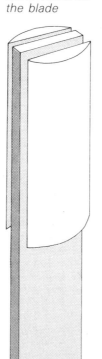

Cut and shape two pieces of wood to the same width as the blade

Fix the handle to the blade with glue or insulating tape

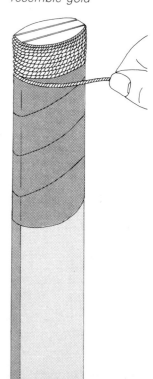

Gilt picture wire is bound around the handle to resemble gold

Making guns from metal

The majority of guns are made up of the same basic components:

Lock: the firing mechanism

Stock: the wooden support for metal parts

Barrel: the metal tube that contains the charge and projectile

Locks
The lock will be the most difficult part to make, and, unless you resort to buying a complete lock from a dealer, there is no alternative but to build it from scratch in either wood or metal. Fortunately, for stage use, you will not have to put in the fine detail.

Stocks
The stock is normally made of wood and should be carved to the shape required, according to the style of gun.

Barrels
Usually you will be able to adapt a piece of conduit or gas tubing, but any metal pipe is suitable. It should be slightly flared at the breech end (back) but this is not vital for stage use. To make the barrel for a blunderbuss, use the tube as before, but cut it shorter, fix a small decanting funnel in the end, and blend in the shape with epoxy filler.

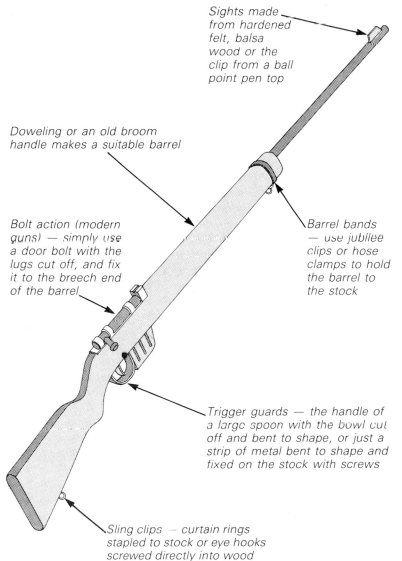

Sights made from hardened felt, balsa wood or the clip from a ball point pen top

Doweling or an old broom handle makes a suitable barrel

Bolt action (modern guns) — simply use a door bolt with the lugs cut off, and fix it to the breech end of the barrel

Barrel bands — use jubilee clips or hose clamps to hold the barrel to the stock

Trigger guards — the handle of a large spoon with the bowl cut off and bent to shape, or just a strip of metal bent to shape and fixed on the stock with screws

Sling clips — curtain rings stapled to stock or eye hooks screwed directly into wood

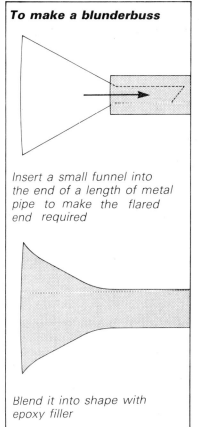

To make a blunderbuss

Insert a small funnel into the end of a length of metal pipe to make the flared end required

Blend it into shape with epoxy filler

Projects
Historical periods and specialized themes

Ancient Egypt

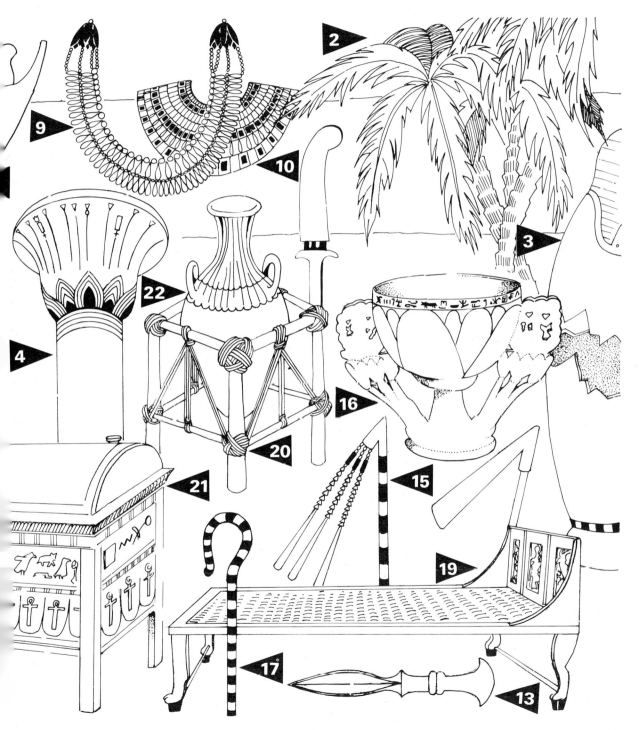

Ancient Egypt

1 Large statue

Wood wire base (see page 36). Use heavy duty wire for the arms

Fill a cardboard box with plaster for balance

Wrap plastered scrim (see page 38) around the frame

Build up with plaster, applying with hands or a spatula

Sculpt the shape using gouges and surform

Sandpaper to finish the surface

Paint using black emulsion

Use gold paint where required

Varnish well

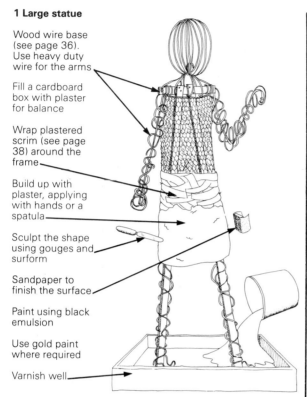

2 Palm trees

Made by using papier mâché over cardboard (see page 29). An alternative method is papier mâché over a wood/wire base (see page 24)

Watch out for instability, make sure the base is large or heavy enough

You can use paper, but sack cloth, which has been sized well, makes strong, substantial leaves

A bent wire stuck down with clothbacked adhesive tape will help to give the leaf the characteristic fall

Slash the leaves along the edges. Paint green

Position these in the top tube of the tree

3 Ushabti (A small model which accompanies a mummified body)

This small ornament is made from a plaster shell cast within a plaster mold (see page 43)

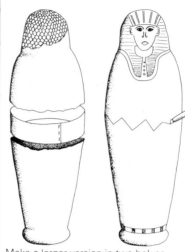

Make a larger version in two halves using chicken wire covered with papier mâché, with a central waist of cardboard cut in a zig-zag fashion to resemble a break, allowing the prop to be reassembled

4 Pillars

Hardboard or cardboard pillars curved around a semicircular framework, pinned and glued into place

The flared tops can be built up using chicken wire covered with papier mâché (see page 20). Embellish with cord and string to create a papyrus design

5 Mummy

Made from polystyrene blocks (see page 50). Cover with cloth mâché using gauze or cheesecloth

6 Papyrus design

Cut stencils (see page 78)

7 Pictogram

A sheet of 1 inch (25mm) thick expanded polystyrene cut with a hot knife (see page 50). Cut out the symbols using a hot piece of wire, shaped in a V-section — like a lino cutter (see page 76). Cut them out of paper and glue them on. Mix sand, stone colored paint and P.V.A. to create the 'stone' appearance

8 Staff and fan

A piece of cardboard or ply cut to shape, glued and wedged into a piece of heavy doweling or broom handle bound tightly with wire

Use clothbacked adhesive tape around the exposed edges

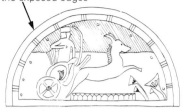

Glue a design on to the cardboard using more cardboard or odd shapes like pasta and string

Glue some brass foil over this, pressing and easing the foil around the contours of the shapes to indicate the embossed nature of the prop

(Instead of using brass foil you can paint the cardboard blue or brown and draw a design with a gold felt pen)

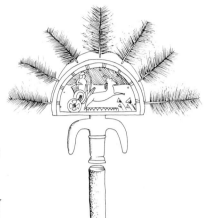

Sandwich mock feathers (see page 62) or real feathers between two pieces of cardboard for fan. Use contact glue or P.V.A. (white flexible glue) leaving under pressure for a while to ensure adhesion.

11 Owl staff

Two pieces of cardboard or felt cut to shape and glued to make a hood. Slot over a length of doweling or cane. Glue into place

---

9 Necklace

Papier mâché beads made over a knitting needle (see page 20) and threaded using strong cord. Make the lateral holes with a bodkin or large sewing needle, threaded with the cord

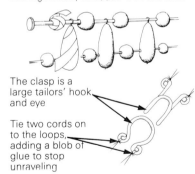

The clasp is a large tailors' hook and eye

Tie two cords on to the loops, adding a blob of glue to stop unraveling

Cut out four pieces of felt or stiff cardboard as decorative covers for the fastener

Sandwich two together, glue and shellac well

Shellac the whole necklace and paint

10 Necklace

A hook and eye sewn here

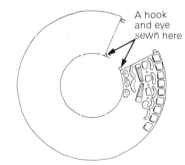

A circular collar of flesh-colored felt or gauze fashioned as a base on which to glue a variety of objects in a symmetrical design

Ideas for decoration

Pasta

Beads

Tesserae

Felt pen tops

Stones

Bolts

Crushed foil

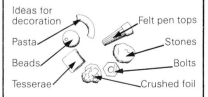

The identity of the objects is soon camouflaged with a covering mixture of P.V.A. (white flexible glue) and pigment

12 Mirror

Cut ply to shape

Use brass foil as the reflector, glued on with P.V.A. (white flexible glue)

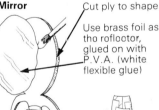

The handle is built up with papier mâché

Wrap string dipped in P.V.A. around the handle

13 Dagger

Make from ply and build up with papier mâché (see page 20)

Decorate with string. Paint the two halves in slightly different tones to give a three-dimensional quality

Ancient Egypt

14 Headgear

A Headdress made from papier mâché over a balloon (see page 25)

Cover a ping pong ball with papier mâché and add to the headgear

Build up form over an inverted balloon

Trim away surplus

Check actor's measurements with circumference of the balloon

Curl some cardboard (or stiff paper) to form the cobra. Reinforce if necessary with a spine of wire taped to the back

Staple or glue to the front of the headgear

B Headdress made from rolled cardboard

Make cone-shaped hat, trim away to the desired contours

Check dimensions of crown with actor's measurements

Curl the back 'tail' inwards (see page 62 for curling)

Add an extra curled piece of cardboard. Secure with tape or staples

C An extension of this process is to add a raised seam using strips of cardboard, or segments of expanded polystyrene, taped and covered with laminated papier mâché

D This is a combination of the rolled cardboard headdress and the papier mâché headdress

15 Flail

Insert a length of coathanger wire, bent to shape, into the top of a cane

Thread papier mâché beads (see page 115) and tie on to the wire

Wrap around with laminated papier mâché

Decorate the rod with alternate colors of tape, or colored strips of cloth mâché

16 Drinking cup

See page 26

17 Crook

Coathanger wire inserted into bamboo. Cover in laminated papier mâché and decorate as for the flail

18 Chair

There is no real shortcut, unless you have an old chair to cannibalize!

Cut the four basic shapes from blockboard or particle board, removing the rectangular sections from the back and sides. Bolt the pieces together using metal corner brackets for strength and stability

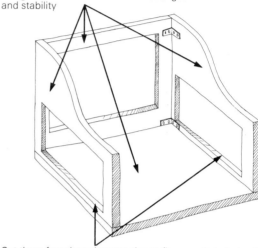

Cut three foamboard rectangles to fit the rectangles in the blockboard

Cut abstract shapes to resemble fretwork (do not cut too much away!)

Tape, then glue these sections into place in the appropriate rectangular holes in the chair

Buy cheap, screw-in legs

A good coat of emulsion or shellac mixed with pigment will unify the different materials

Leaving a gap at the bottom, build up paw shape using laminated then pulped papier mâché

Draw in detail using a felt pen over the fretwork areas. Color to fit in with the scene and varnish well

19 Bed

Using scraps of 2 inch x 2 inch (50 x 50mm) softwood assemble the legs using the simple joints illustrated

Glue then screw the joints, clamping the glued doweling into position until dry

Leave about 1 inch (25mm) clear below the ply shape, rounding off the corners if required

Backfill the ply with pulped papier mâché

Headboard and sides. Cut out the back from particle board and join to the corner piece. Use straight brackets to attach the headboard to the bed

An old door can be fastened to the frame (remove the door furniture first!)

Invert bed and screw through the cross section to door frame

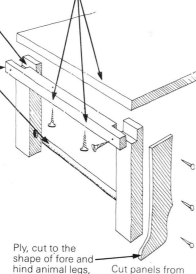

Ply, cut to the shape of fore and hind animal legs, is pinned to the four bed legs

Cut panels from foamboard and glue to the headboard to form bas-relief (see page 73 for further ideas)

21 Chest

This is a wooden framework with corrugated cardboard (smooth side out) pinned on, with curved sections of blockboard for the ends of the lid

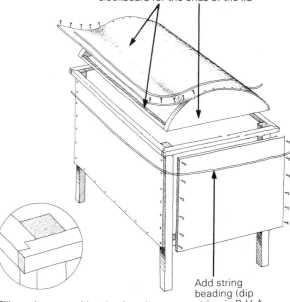

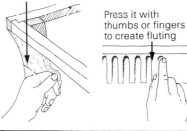

Fill cornice area with pulped papier mâché, extending it down to the level of the panel

Press it with thumbs or fingers to create fluting

Add string beading (dip string in P.V.A. [white flexible glue] then apply)

Paint thoroughly with undercoat

Use a printing block to reproduce repeat patterns (see page 76)

Finalize painting

20 Large jar stand

Narrow packaging tubes slot-jointed using sections of cardboard. Reinforce joints with adhesive tape

Make rungs from narrow doweling or cane, pegged into small holes in the legs. Reinforce with tape

Paint the legs. P.V.A. (white flexible glue) and a water soluble brown paint mixed with sand or sawdust will give a rustic effect

Dip string in P.V.A. (white flexible glue), size or shellac and tie around the joints (see page 92). This will harden when dry and give the structure stability

An old seatless stool makes a good frame for this prop

22 Jar

Basically papier mâché over a balloon (see page 25)

Add a flared collar, based upon a cone (page 64)

Handles can be rope or wire covered in laminated papier mâché. Glue well to bond the separate pieces together

Classical Greece and Rome

119

Classical Greece and Rome

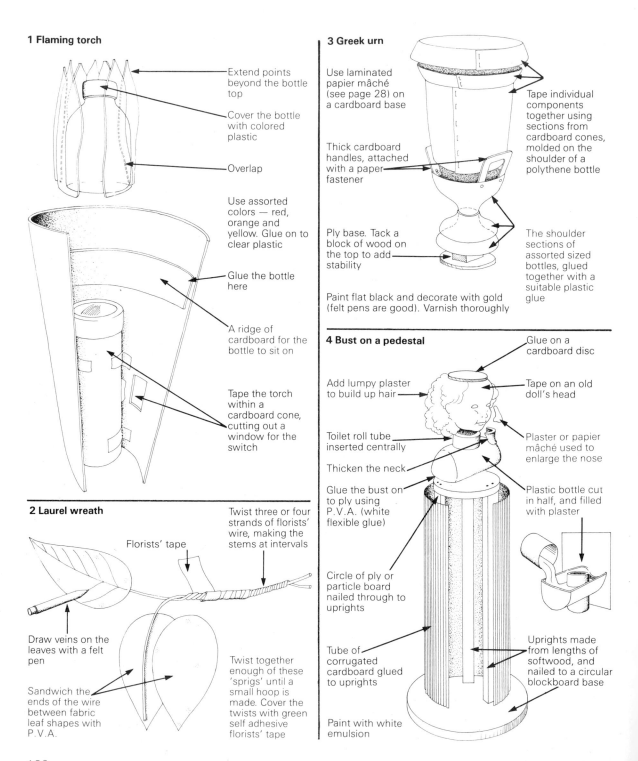

1 Flaming torch

Extend points beyond the bottle top

Cover the bottle with colored plastic

Overlap

Use assorted colors — red, orange and yellow. Glue on to clear plastic

Glue the bottle here

A ridge of cardboard for the bottle to sit on

Tape the torch within a cardboard cone, cutting out a window for the switch

2 Laurel wreath

Florists' tape

Twist three or four strands of florists' wire, making the stems at intervals

Draw veins on the leaves with a felt pen

Sandwich the ends of the wire between fabric leaf shapes with P.V.A.

Twist together enough of these 'sprigs' until a small hoop is made. Cover the twists with green self adhesive florists' tape

3 Greek urn

Use laminated papier mâché (see page 28) on a cardboard base

Thick cardboard handles, attached with a paper fastener

Ply base. Tack a block of wood on the top to add stability

Paint flat black and decorate with gold (felt pens are good). Varnish thoroughly

Tape individual components together using sections from cardboard cones, molded on the shoulder of a polythene bottle

The shoulder sections of assorted sized bottles, glued together with a suitable plastic glue

4 Bust on a pedestal

Add lumpy plaster to build up hair

Toilet roll tube inserted centrally

Thicken the neck

Glue the bust on to ply using P.V.A. (white flexible glue)

Circle of ply or particle board nailed through to uprights

Tube of corrugated cardboard glued to uprights

Paint with white emulsion

Glue on a cardboard disc

Tape on an old doll's head

Plaster or papier mâché used to enlarge the nose

Plastic bottle cut in half, and filled with plaster

Uprights made from lengths of softwood, and nailed to a circular blockboard base

120

5 Greek shield

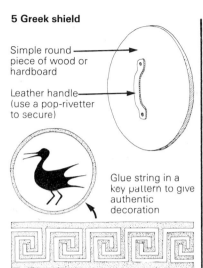

Simple round piece of wood or hardboard

Leather handle (use a pop-rivetter to secure)

Glue string in a key pattern to give authentic decoration

6 Small statues

Follow the instructions on page 36 to make a wood/wire frame, then cover with plaster (see page 38)

7 Small decorative column

Make the column using the same method for a pedestal base. Use corrugated cardboard with the corrugations facing inwards

Cut out leaf shapes from thick industrial felt. Glue on to the column using P.V.A. (white flexible glue) or latex. The felt shapes could be covered with a thin layer of plaster. The plaster itself should be fairly liquid and should be applied before it starts to thicken

Paint white

8 Two Greek helmets

Both helmets are based on balloons covered in papier mâché (see page 25) with extensions made from cardboard

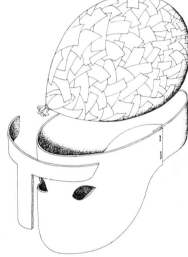

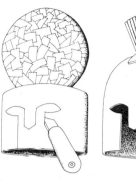

Make the plume from drinking straws glued between two pieces of cardboard. Score the cardboard and splay out the base of the fin and then glue to the helmet

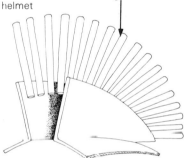

Line the crown with a ring of foam rubber for comfort and to give a good fit

Use a commercial metallic paint or make your own (see page 13)

9 Roman helmet

Use the same method as for Greek helmets

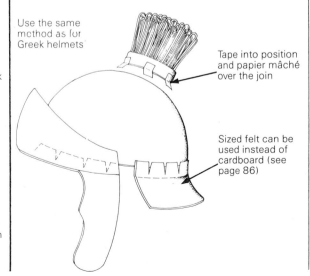

Tape into position and papier mâché over the join

Sized felt can be used instead of cardboard (see page 86)

Unravel some twine (hemp). Dip in shellac size to stiffen the strands. Wrap thick paper tightly around the twine and staple the ends. Trim off surplus and glue into position

This top fin can be extended to resemble the Greek helmet

Classical Greece and Rome

10 Two decorative Roman wine jars

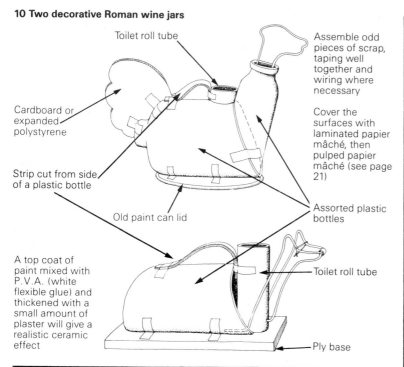

Toilet roll tube

Cardboard or expanded polystyrene

Strip cut from side of a plastic bottle

Old paint can lid

A top coat of paint mixed with P.V.A. (white flexible glue) and thickened with a small amount of plaster will give a realistic ceramic effect

Assemble odd pieces of scrap, taping well together and wiring where necessary

Cover the surfaces with laminated papier mâché, then pulped papier mâché (see page 21)

Assorted plastic bottles

Toilet roll tube

Ply base

11 Marble table

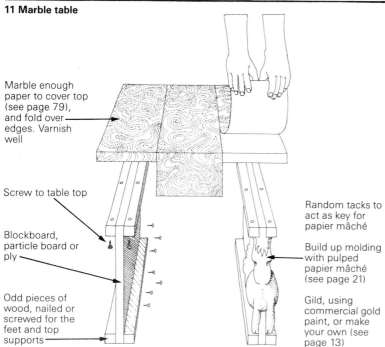

Marble enough paper to cover top (see page 79), and fold over edges. Varnish well

Screw to table top

Blockboard, particle board or ply

Odd pieces of wood, nailed or screwed for the feet and top supports

Random tacks to act as key for papier mâché

Build up molding with pulped papier mâché (see page 21)

Gild, using commercial gold paint, or make your own (see page 13)

12 Roman mosaic

Cut shallow dishes from plastic bottles as containers for paint. Mix your paints in advance and keep each color in a separate container

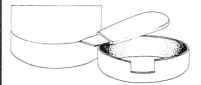

Cut suitable odd pieces of timber into wooden blocks and use to transfer color to the mosaic surface. Keep a separate block for each color. Vegetable root prints could be used as an alternative to wooden blocks

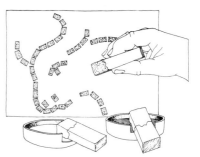

Print the blocks leaving only narrow spaces between

Make bold strong outlines. Research designs for inspiration

13 Roman shield

Cardboard cone   Hollow out handle

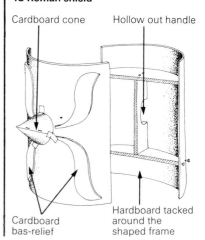

Cardboard bas-relief

Hardboard tacked around the shaped frame

14 Roman bronze mirror

Two cardboard discs covered in bronze colored foil on one side. Fold the foil around the back of each disc

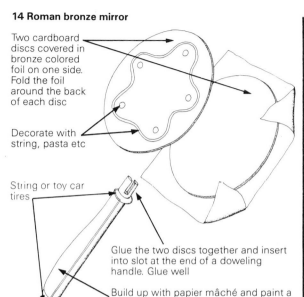

Decorate with string, pasta etc

String or toy car tires

Glue the two discs together and insert into slot at the end of a doweling handle. Glue well

Build up with papier mâché and paint a bronze color (see page 13)

15 Musical instruments

Horn

Extend the hose pipe with a small plastic funnel

Apply papier mâché to make a gradual curve

Thread wire with beads

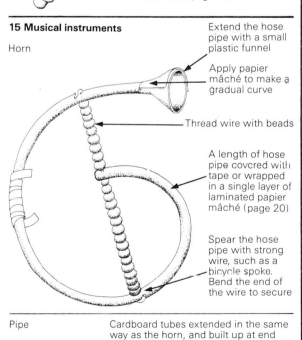

A length of hose pipe covered with tape or wrapped in a single layer of laminated papier mâché (page 20)

Spear the hose pipe with strong wire, such as a bicycle spoke. Bend the end of the wire to secure

Pipe

Cardboard tubes extended in the same way as the horn, and built up at end with papier mâché

16 Bracelet

Draw, then cut a spiral from a plastic bottle

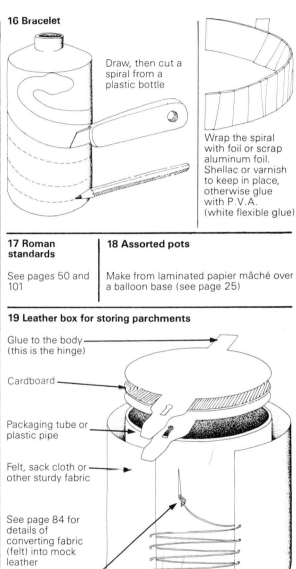

Wrap the spiral with foil or scrap aluminum foil. Shellac or varnish to keep in place, otherwise glue with P.V.A. (white flexible glue)

17 Roman standards

See pages 50 and 101

18 Assorted pots

Make from laminated papier mâché over a balloon base (see page 25)

19 Leather box for storing parchments

Glue to the body (this is the hinge)

Cardboard

Packaging tube or plastic pipe

Felt, sack cloth or other sturdy fabric

See page 84 for details of converting fabric (felt) into mock leather

Sew tightly, butting the edges

See page 75 for converting paper into parchment

To make a scroll, roll the parchment on to dowel with wooden door knobs screwed in at the ends

Medieval England

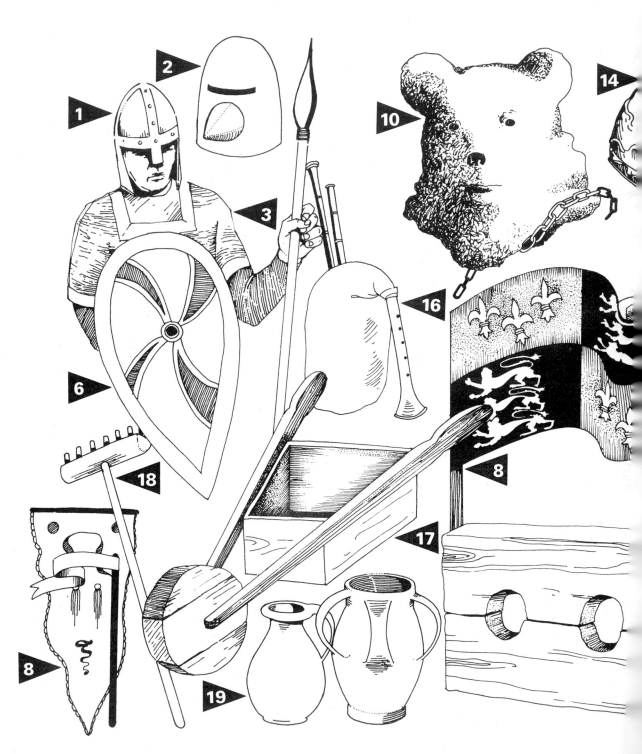

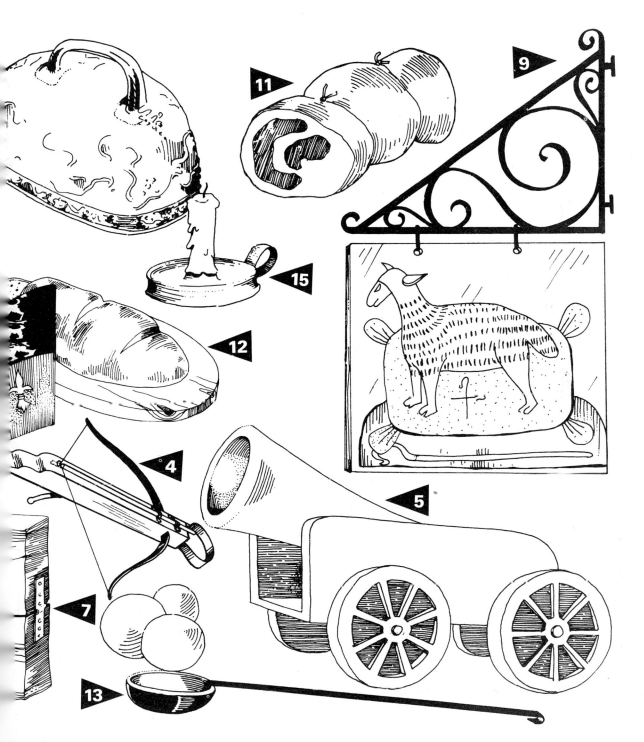

Medieval England

1 Helmet

Cover three-quarters of a balloon with papier mâché (see page 25)

Trim the edges of the papier mâché, not forgetting to cut out the nose guard

Cover the collar with papier mâché, masking the tape join thoroughly

Make sure the circumference of the helmet corresponds with the actor's head measurement

Spray silver or apply a mixture of shellac and silver pigment

Tape a collar of cardboard to dry papier mâché. Fit to the actor, cutting off the cheek guards in the correct position

Use a silver pen or silver paint to color the cut edges

Butt join the rim

Glue on split peas and paint silver

Snip the two opposite edges of the band, trim at the top and pleat as illustrated to fit the dome

Glue a decorative strip using P.V.A. (white flexible glue) or contact adhesive

Use silver PVC, metalized or plasticized silver cardboard, or even aluminum foil wrapped around cardboard

Line the crown and nose guard with felt or a narrow strip of foam rubber using latex or P.V.A. (white flexible glue)

2 Helmet

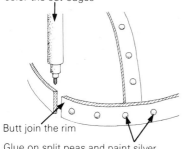

Check circumference with actor's head measurements

Finish as previous helmet

Cut away the eye slot

The crown can be packed with foam rubber to raise or lower the helmet to align the eye slot with the actor's eyes

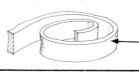

Silver bicycle or car trimming tape might be useful to bind the bottom and eye slot edges

Papier mâché over a balloon, extended over a cardboard collar (see page 25), with additional paper sculpture taped on

3 Hauberk (Norman coat of mail

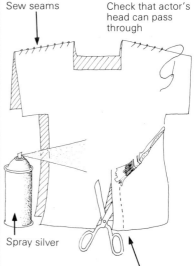

Sew seams

Check that actor's head can pass through

Spray silver

Knit front and back, following a pattern (see page 95)

Cut the crotch section. Paint cut edges liberally with latex glue

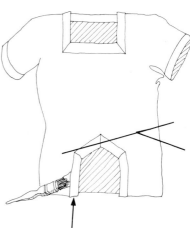

Bind the edges with a wide band of silver PVC cloth, mitering corners where necessary. Sew or glue (latex)

Most yarns can be knitted to make this garment, including yarn made from old tights (see page 95) which will make a stiff, dense, bulky material

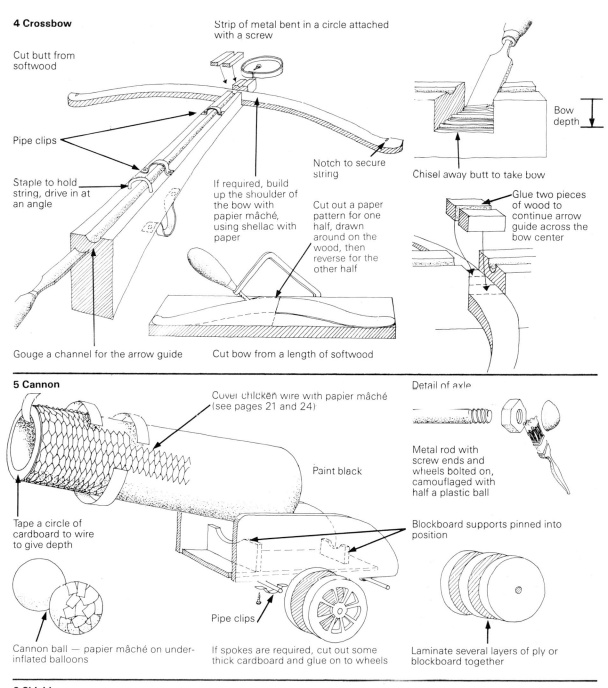

4 Crossbow

Cut butt from softwood

Strip of metal bent in a circle attached with a screw

Pipe clips

Staple to hold string, drive in at an angle

Notch to secure string

If required, build up the shoulder of the bow with papier mâché, using shellac with paper

Cut out a paper pattern for one half, drawn around on the wood, then reverse for the other half

Bow depth

Chisel away butt to take bow

Glue two pieces of wood to continue arrow guide across the bow center

Gouge a channel for the arrow guide

Cut bow from a length of softwood

5 Cannon

Detail of axle

Cover chicken wire with papier mâché (see pages 21 and 24)

Paint black

Metal rod with screw ends and wheels bolted on, camouflaged with half a plastic ball

Tape a circle of cardboard to wire to give depth

Blockboard supports pinned into position

Cannon ball — papier mâché on under-inflated balloons

Pipe clips

If spokes are required, cut out some thick cardboard and glue on to wheels

Laminate several layers of ply or blockboard together

6 Shield

Make out of hardboard with leather strap at the back (see page 84)

Medieval England

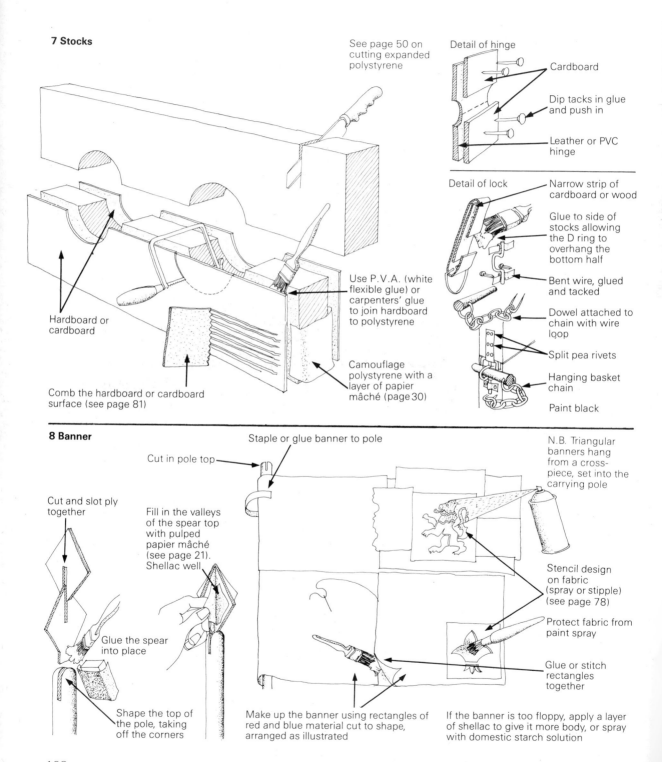

7 Stocks

See page 50 on cutting expanded polystyrene

Detail of hinge

Cardboard

Dip tacks in glue and push in

Leather or PVC hinge

Use P.V.A. (white flexible glue) or carpenters' glue to join hardboard to polystyrene

Hardboard or cardboard

Comb the hardboard or cardboard surface (see page 81)

Camouflage polystyrene with a layer of papier mâché (page 30)

Detail of lock

Narrow strip of cardboard or wood

Glue to side of stocks allowing the D ring to overhang the bottom half

Bent wire, glued and tacked

Dowel attached to chain with wire loop

Split pea rivets

Hanging basket chain

Paint black

8 Banner

Staple or glue banner to pole

Cut in pole top

N.B. Triangular banners hang from a cross-piece, set into the carrying pole

Cut and slot ply together

Fill in the valleys of the spear top with pulped papier mâché (see page 21). Shellac well

Glue the spear into place

Shape the top of the pole, taking off the corners

Stencil design on fabric (spray or stipple) (see page 78)

Protect fabric from paint spray

Glue or stitch rectangles together

Make up the banner using rectangles of red and blue material cut to shape, arranged as illustrated

If the banner is too floppy, apply a layer of shellac to give it more body, or spray with domestic starch solution

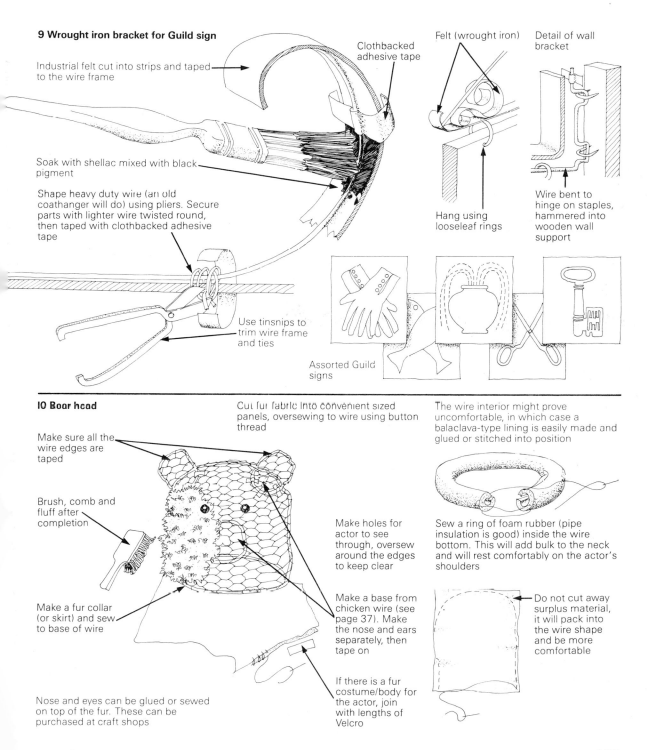

9 Wrought iron bracket for Guild sign

Industrial felt cut into strips and taped to the wire frame

Clothbacked adhesive tape

Felt (wrought iron)

Detail of wall bracket

Soak with shellac mixed with black pigment

Shape heavy duty wire (an old coathanger will do) using pliers. Secure parts with lighter wire twisted round, then taped with clothbacked adhesive tape

Hang using looseleaf rings

Wire bent to hinge on staples, hammered into wooden wall support

Use tinsnips to trim wire frame and ties

Assorted Guild signs

10 Boar head

Cut fur fabric into convenient sized panels, oversewing to wire using button thread

The wire interior might prove uncomfortable, in which case a balaclava-type lining is easily made and glued or stitched into position

Make sure all the wire edges are taped

Brush, comb and fluff after completion

Make a fur collar (or skirt) and sew to base of wire

Make holes for actor to see through, oversew around the edges to keep clear

Make a base from chicken wire (see page 37). Make the nose and ears separately, then tape on

If there is a fur costume/body for the actor, join with lengths of Velcro

Nose and eyes can be glued or sewed on top of the fur. These can be purchased at craft shops

Sew a ring of foam rubber (pipe insulation is good) inside the wire bottom. This will add bulk to the neck and will rest comfortably on the actor's shoulders

Do not cut away surplus material, it will pack into the wire shape and be more comfortable

Medieval England

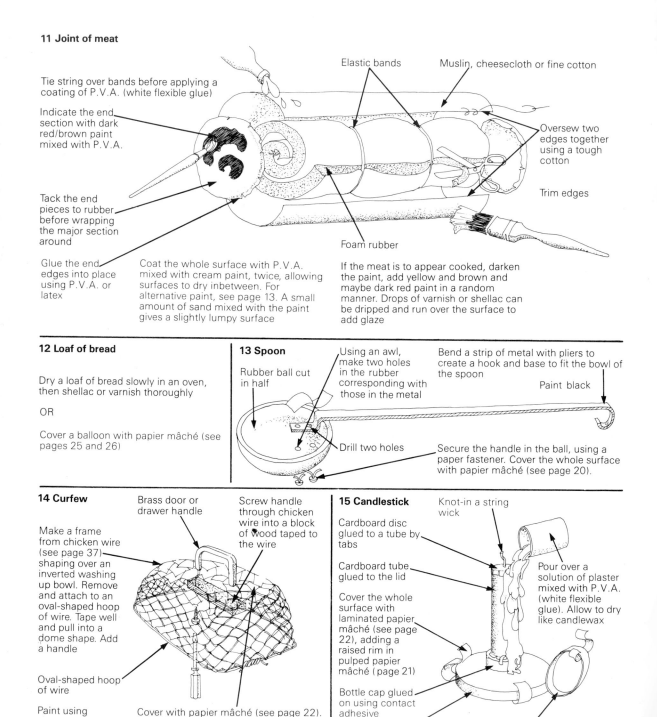

11 Joint of meat

Tie string over bands before applying a coating of P.V.A. (white flexible glue)

Indicate the end section with dark red/brown paint mixed with P.V.A.

Tack the end pieces to rubber before wrapping the major section around

Glue the end edges into place using P.V.A. or latex

Elastic bands

Muslin, cheesecloth or fine cotton

Oversew two edges together using a tough cotton

Trim edges

Foam rubber

Coat the whole surface with P.V.A. mixed with cream paint, twice, allowing surfaces to dry inbetween. For alternative paint, see page 13. A small amount of sand mixed with the paint gives a slightly lumpy surface

If the meat is to appear cooked, darken the paint, add yellow and brown and maybe dark red paint in a random manner. Drops of varnish or shellac can be dripped and run over the surface to add glaze

---

12 Loaf of bread

Dry a loaf of bread slowly in an oven, then shellac or varnish thoroughly

OR

Cover a balloon with papier mâché (see pages 25 and 26)

13 Spoon

Rubber ball cut in half

Using an awl, make two holes in the rubber corresponding with those in the metal

Bend a strip of metal with pliers to create a hook and base to fit the bowl of the spoon

Paint black

Drill two holes

Secure the handle in the ball, using a paper fastener. Cover the whole surface with papier mâché (see page 20).

---

14 Curfew

Make a frame from chicken wire (see page 37) shaping over an inverted washing up bowl. Remove and attach to an oval-shaped hoop of wire. Tape well and pull into a dome shape. Add a handle

Brass door or drawer handle

Screw handle through chicken wire into a block of wood taped to the wire

Oval-shaped hoop of wire

Paint using shellac with brass pigment

Cover with papier mâché (see page 22). Shellac well and apply string decoration (see page 92)

15 Candlestick

Knot-in a string wick

Cardboard disc glued to a tube by tabs

Cardboard tube glued to the lid

Cover the whole surface with laminated papier mâché (see page 22), adding a raised rim in pulped papier mâché (page 21)

Bottle cap glued on using contact adhesive

Cheesebox with lid

Pour over a solution of plaster mixed with P.V.A. (white flexible glue). Allow to dry like candlewax

Section from a plastic bottle, stapled to the lid and taped into position

16 Bagpipes

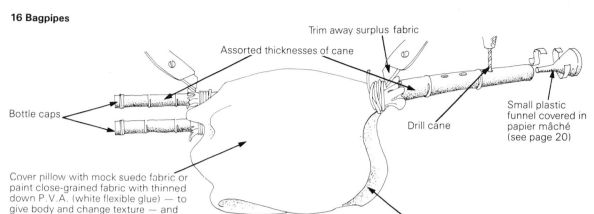

Trim away surplus fabric

Assorted thicknesses of cane

Bottle caps

Drill cane

Small plastic funnel covered in papier mâché (see page 20)

Cover pillow with mock suede fabric or paint close-grained fabric with thinned down P.V.A. (white flexible glue) — to give body and change texture — and brown paint. Experiment with a scrap of fabric first to test thinning

Use an old pillow case filled with small foam chippings

17 Wheelbarrow

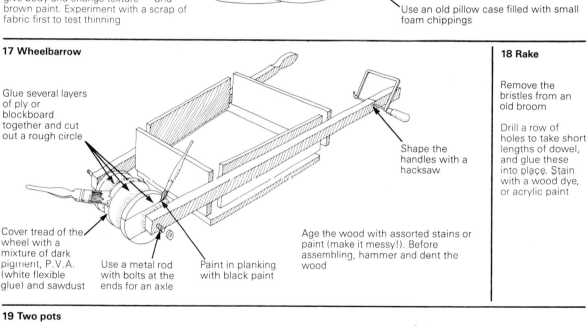

Glue several layers of ply or blockboard together and cut out a rough circle

Shape the handles with a hacksaw

Cover tread of the wheel with a mixture of dark pigment, P.V.A. (white flexible glue) and sawdust

Use a metal rod with bolts at the ends for an axle

Paint in planking with black paint

Age the wood with assorted stains or paint (make it messy!). Before assembling, hammer and dent the wood

18 Rake

Remove the bristles from an old broom

Drill a row of holes to take short lengths of dowel, and glue these into place. Stain with a wood dye, or acrylic paint

19 Two pots

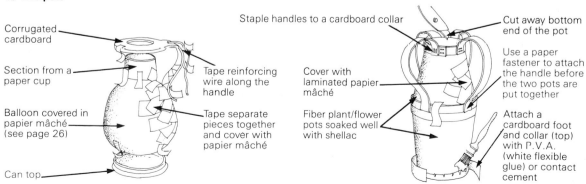

Corrugated cardboard

Section from a paper cup

Balloon covered in papier mâché (see page 26)

Can top

Staple handles to a cardboard collar

Tape reinforcing wire along the handle

Tape separate pieces together and cover with papier mâché

Cover with laminated papier mâché

Fiber plant/flower pots soaked well with shellac

Cut away bottom end of the pot

Use a paper fastener to attach the handle before the two pots are put together

Attach a cardboard foot and collar (top) with P.V.A. (white flexible glue) or contact cement

Tudor England

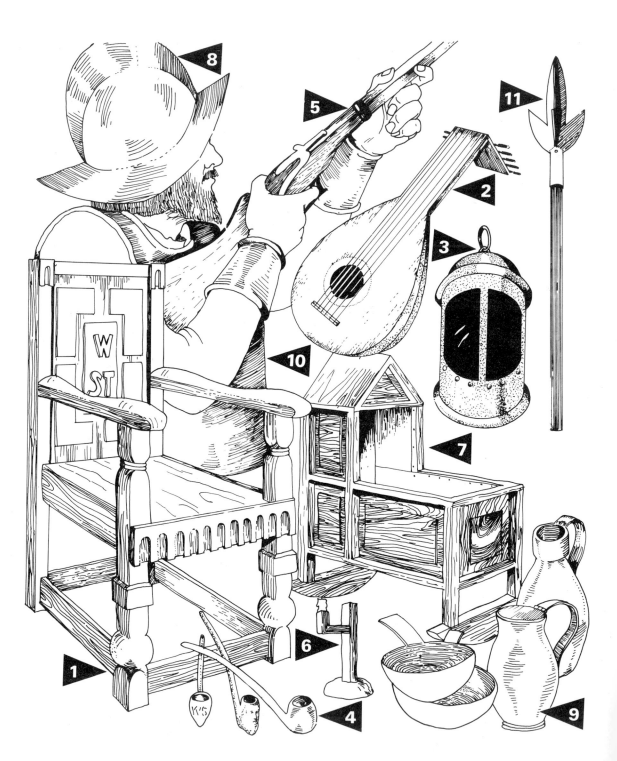

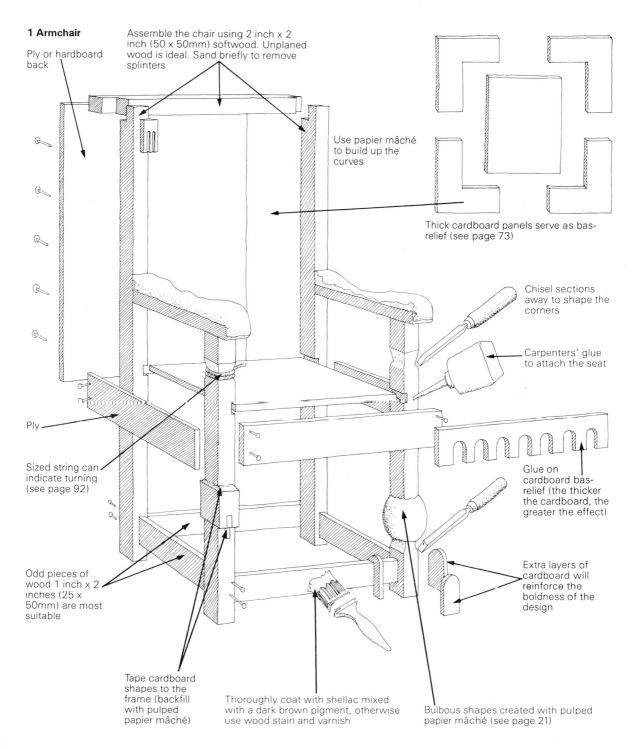

1 Armchair

Ply or hardboard back

Assemble the chair using 2 inch x 2 inch (50 x 50mm) softwood. Unplaned wood is ideal. Sand briefly to remove splinters

Use papier mâché to build up the curves

Thick cardboard panels serve as bas-relief (see page 73)

Chisel sections away to shape the corners

Carpenters' glue to attach the seat

Ply

Glue on cardboard bas-relief (the thicker the cardboard, the greater the effect)

Sized string can indicate turning (see page 92)

Extra layers of cardboard will reinforce the boldness of the design

Odd pieces of wood 1 inch x 2 inches (25 x 50mm) are most suitable

Tape cardboard shapes to the frame (backfill with pulped papier mâché)

Thoroughly coat with shellac mixed with a dark brown pigment, otherwise use wood stain and varnish

Bulbous shapes created with pulped papier mâché (see page 21)

Tudor England

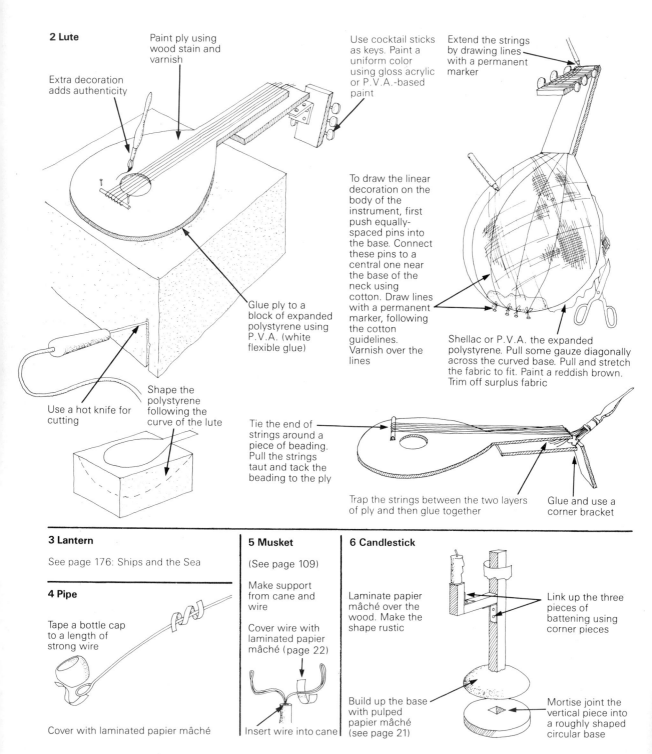

2 Lute

Extra decoration adds authenticity

Paint ply using wood stain and varnish

Use cocktail sticks as keys. Paint a uniform color using gloss acrylic or P.V.A.-based paint

Extend the strings by drawing lines with a permanent marker

Glue ply to a block of expanded polystyrene using P.V.A. (white flexible glue)

Use a hot knife for cutting

Shape the polystyrene following the curve of the lute

To draw the linear decoration on the body of the instrument, first push equally-spaced pins into the base. Connect these pins to a central one near the base of the neck using cotton. Draw lines with a permanent marker, following the cotton guidelines. Varnish over the lines

Shellac or P.V.A. the expanded polystyrene. Pull some gauze diagonally across the curved base. Pull and stretch the fabric to fit. Paint a reddish brown. Trim off surplus fabric

Tie the end of strings around a piece of beading. Pull the strings taut and tack the beading to the ply

Trap the strings between the two layers of ply and then glue together

Glue and use a corner bracket

---

3 Lantern

See page 176: Ships and the Sea

4 Pipe

Tape a bottle cap to a length of strong wire

Cover with laminated papier mâché

5 Musket

(See page 109)

Make support from cane and wire

Cover wire with laminated papier mâché (page 22)

Insert wire into cane

6 Candlestick

Laminate papier mâché over the wood. Make the shape rustic

Build up the base with pulped papier mâché (see page 21)

Link up the three pieces of battening using corner pieces

Mortise joint the vertical piece into a roughly shaped circular base

7 Crib

Cardboard stapled, pinned, or glued to the frame

Raised panels can be made from cardboard (see Armchair, page 133) or fine fabric stretched over panels of expanded polystyrene. Use P.V.A. (white flexible glue) to glue into place

Make a frame (see details of joints)

Tack ply or hardboard to the inside of the frame

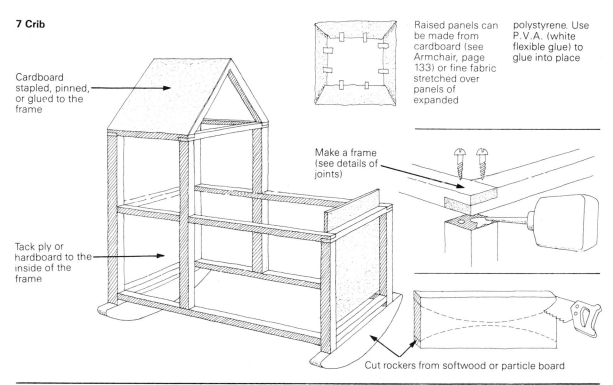

Cut rockers from softwood or particle board

8 Helmet

Balloon-based papier mâché crown (see page 25)

Cardboard covered in papier mâché (tape into position first, then papier mâché over the join)

Chicken wire covered with papier mâché (see page 20). Remember to cover the underside with papier mâché too

Paint black, or dark green, first. Allow to dry, then spray or paint using metallic paint or shellac and metallic pigment (see page 13). Rub some of the metallic paint away to reveal undercoat

Felt stiffened with shellac for an ear guard (page 88)

Line the crown with a ring of felt

9 Containers

Balloon-based papier mâché containers (see page 25) with cardboard extensions

10 Armor

Use felt as imitation metal (see page 86)

11 Spear

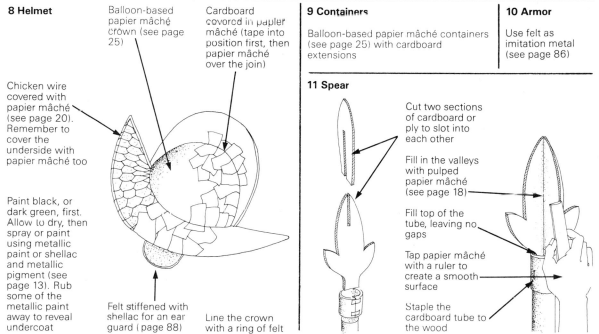

Cut two sections of cardboard or ply to slot into each other

Fill in the valleys with pulped papier mâché (see page 18)

Fill top of the tube, leaving no gaps

Tap papier mâché with a ruler to create a smooth surface

Staple the cardboard tube to the wood

135

Seventeenth and Eighteenth Century England

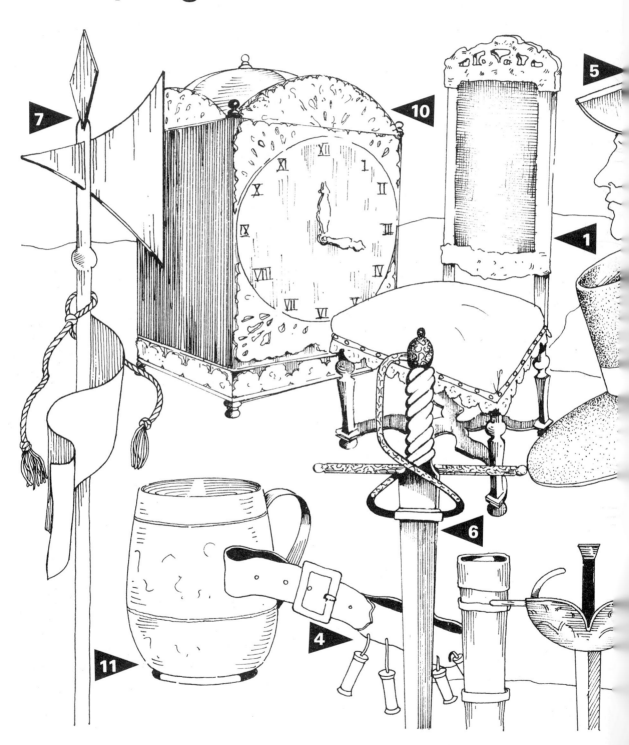

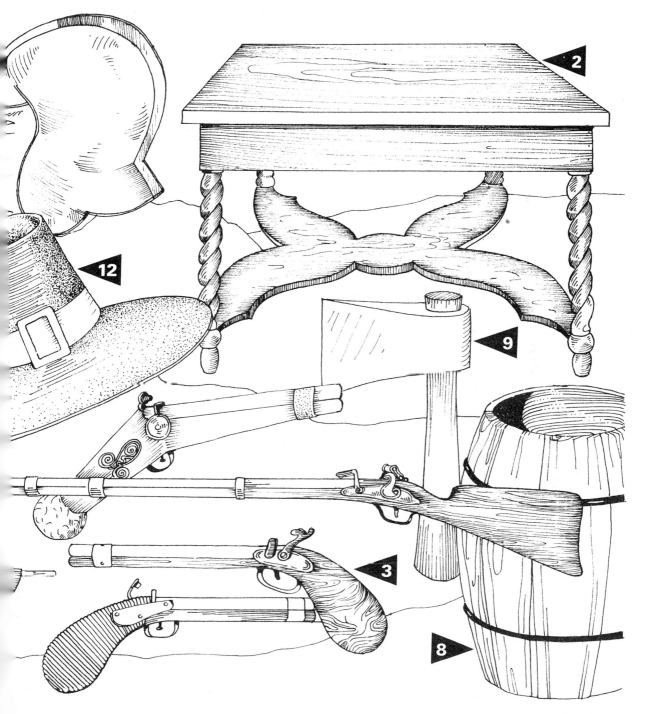

Seventeenth and Eighteenth Century England

1 William and Mary chair

Adapt an old chair. Remove stretchers, top rail and cross pieces

Shaped, pulped papier mâché

Staple open weave material to the back

Tape a plastic coathanger to the frame

Use corrugated fasteners

Add cardboard shapes to reproduce carving. Tape into place. Cover with papier mâché

Extend the vertical supports

Glue a strip of cardboard (same width as the frame) over stapled fabric

Tape plastic coathanger

Fill the seat with upholsterers' waste foam rubber

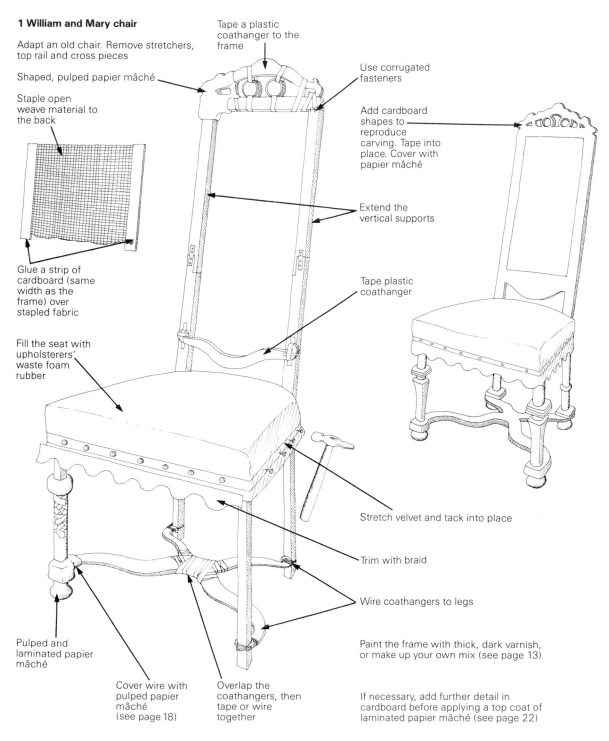

Stretch velvet and tack into place

Trim with braid

Wire coathangers to legs

Pulped and laminated papier mâché

Cover wire with pulped papier mâché (see page 18)

Overlap the coathangers, then tape or wire together

Paint the frame with thick, dark varnish, or make up your own mix (see page 13)

If necessary, add further detail in cardboard before applying a top coat of laminated papier mâché (see page 22)

2 Side table

Side table with serpentine stretchers and barley sugar legs

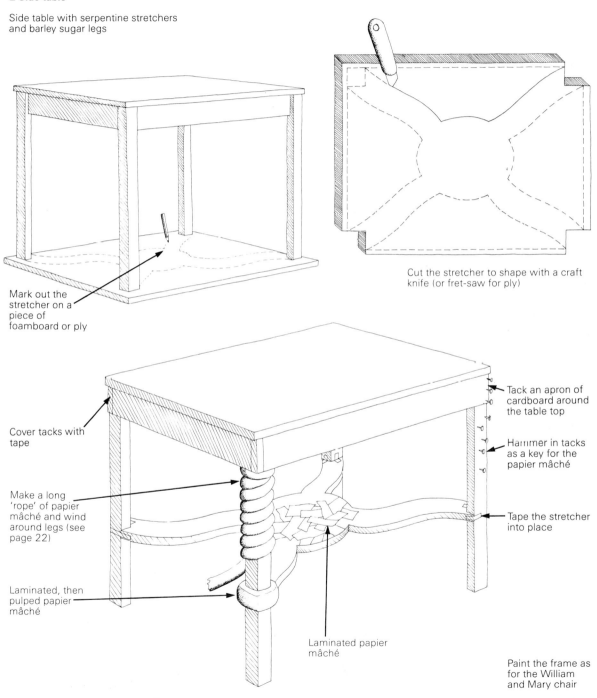

Mark out the stretcher on a piece of foamboard or ply

Cut the stretcher to shape with a craft knife (or fret-saw for ply)

Cover tacks with tape

Make a long 'rope' of papier mâché and wind around legs (see page 22)

Laminated, then pulped papier mâché

Laminated papier mâché

Tack an apron of cardboard around the table top

Hammer in tacks as a key for the papier mâché

Tape the stretcher into place

Paint the frame as for the William and Mary chair

Seventeenth and Eighteenth Century England

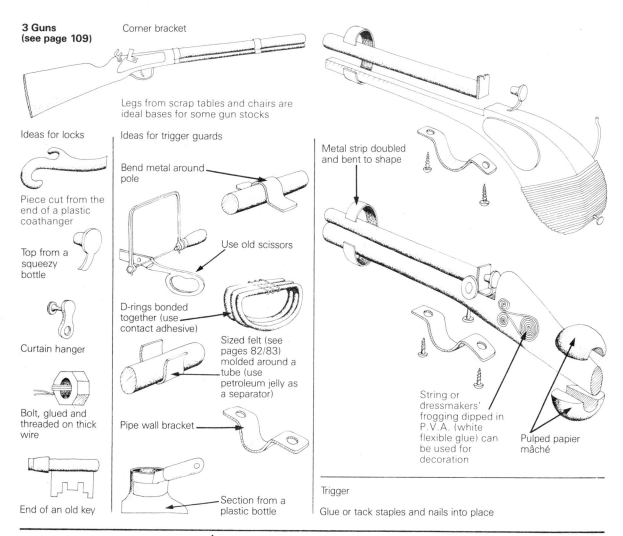

**3 Guns
(see page 109)**

Corner bracket

Legs from scrap tables and chairs are ideal bases for some gun stocks

Ideas for locks

Piece cut from the end of a plastic coathanger

Top from a squeezy bottle

Curtain hanger

Bolt, glued and threaded on thick wire

End of an old key

Ideas for trigger guards

Bend metal around pole

Use old scissors

D-rings bonded together (use contact adhesive)

Sized felt (see pages 82/83) molded around a tube (use petroleum jelly as a separator)

Pipe wall bracket

Section from a plastic bottle

Metal strip doubled and bent to shape

String or dressmakers' frogging dipped in P.V.A. (white flexible glue) can be used for decoration

Pulped papier mâché

Trigger

Glue or tack staples and nails into place

---

4 Bandolier

Old belt, or length of felt backed with sackcloth. Shellac well (see page 84 for making mock leather)

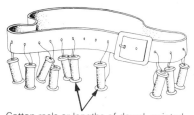

Cotton reels or lengths of dowel, painted with brass powder and shellac

5 Helmet

Papier mâché over a balloon (see page 25). Match circumference to actor's measurement

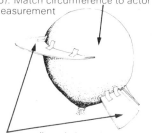

Tape a cardboard visor and neck shield before applying the papier mâché

Pulped papier mâché, raised decoration

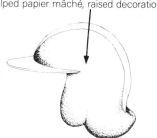

Pad out the inside with foam rubber to ensure a good fit

6 Rapier and scabbard

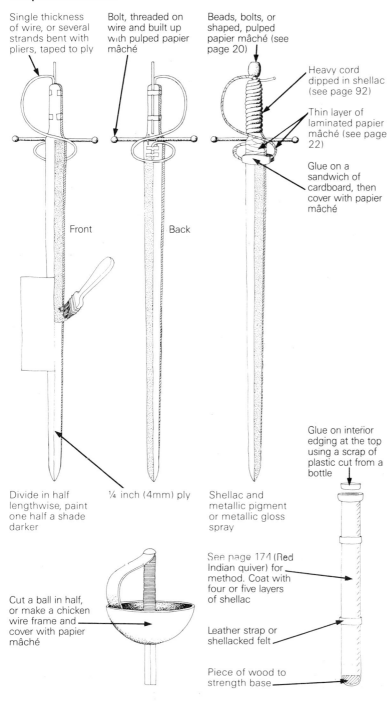

Single thickness of wire, or several strands bent with pliers, taped to ply

Bolt, threaded on wire and built up with pulped papier mâché

Beads, bolts, or shaped, pulped papier mâché (see page 20)

Heavy cord dipped in shellac (see page 92)

Thin layer of laminated papier mâché (see page 22)

Glue on a sandwich of cardboard, then cover with papier mâché

Front

Back

Divide in half lengthwise, paint one half a shade darker

¼ inch (4mm) ply

Shellac and metallic pigment or metallic gloss spray

Cut a ball in half, or make a chicken wire frame and cover with papier mâché

Glue on interior edging at the top using a scrap of plastic cut from a bottle

See page 174 (Red Indian quiver) for method. Coat with four or five layers of shellac

Leather strap or shellacked felt

Piece of wood to strength base

7 Ceremonial pole axe

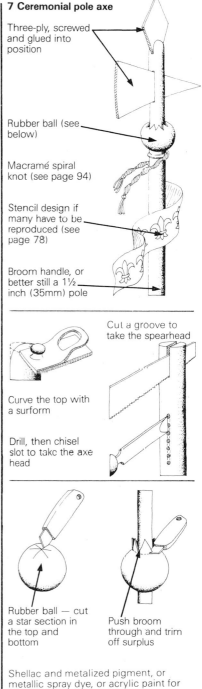

Three-ply, screwed and glued into position

Rubber ball (see below)

Macramé spiral knot (see page 94)

Stencil design if many have to be reproduced (see page 78)

Broom handle, or better still a 1½ inch (35mm) pole

Cut a groove to take the spearhead

Curve the top with a surform

Drill, then chisel slot to take the axe head

Rubber ball — cut a star section in the top and bottom

Push broom through and trim off surplus

Shellac and metalized pigment, or metallic spray dye, or acrylic paint for fabric

141

Seventeenth and Eighteenth Century England

8 Barrel

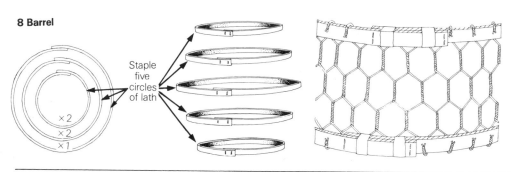

Staple five circles of lath

Shape chicken wire in and around the hoops. Tape ends and secure to lath

×2
×2
×1

Cover with laminated papier mâché (see page 24)

Use combing for wood grain (see page 81)

Paint in detail of planking. Varnish well

Make pulped papier mâché rope (see page 22)

---

9 Axe

Shape a suitable length of softwood (or use an old axe handle)

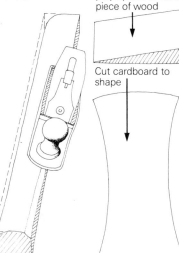

Make a wedge to hold cardboard from expanded polystyrene or odd piece of wood

Cut cardboard to shape

Glue cardboard around the handle, sandwiching wedge into position

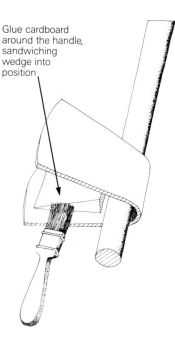

Fill and smooth edges of sandwich with P.V.A. (white flexible glue) mixed with some plaster or pulped papier mâché, pushed into the crevices

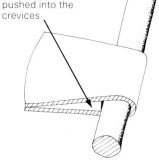

Paint with shellac and metallic pigment

10 Clock

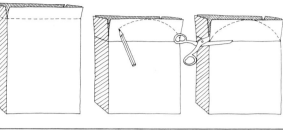

Cut a box to shape

Add four doweling legs embellished with washers, toy car tires, sized string (see page 92), or pulped papier mâché (see page 20). Paint the front black

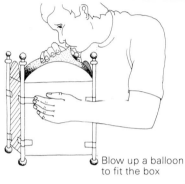

Blow up a balloon to fit the box

Cover half the balloon with laminated papier mâché (see page 25). Make crossover using curled cardboard (see page 62). Using P.V.A. (white flexible glue) at the junction, add bead or papier mâché embellishment and lodge into place within the box

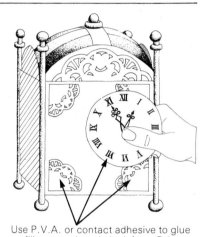

Use P.V.A. or contact adhesive to glue on filigree work and clock face. Paint body and legs of clock gold (leave black behind the doilie)

Cut sections of a gold doilie in shapes for filigree decoration and hands. Glue on to box

Circle of cardboard or paint can top painted gold

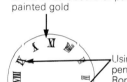

Using a black felt pen, indicate Roman numerals precisely, or give impression with zig-zag pattern

Use a brass paper fastener on a cardboard clock face if the time needs to be changed

---

11 Tankard

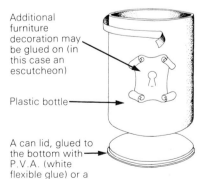

Additional furniture decoration may be glued on (in this case an escutcheon)

Plastic bottle

A can lid, glued to the bottom with P.V.A. (white flexible glue) or a contact adhesive, will give the prop an authentic metallic sound

Shellac and metallic pigment, or spray silver

Wire can be twisted around and through the holes. Cover the wire with clothbacked adhesive tape

Shape a piece of metal, or use a cabinet handle

12 Hat

Paint black

Sized felt or felt glued over cardboard

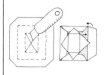

Buckram glued into place

Cardboard glued to felt

Detail of buckle

Cut a piece of cardboard to the shape of a buckle

Cover with thin foil and glue to back of cardboard. Fix to buckram to cover the join

Victorian England

Victorian England

1 Grandfather clock

Ply or cardboard glued or stapled into position

Link individual sections with laminated papier mâché (see page 22)

Beading: small packaging tubes, mitered at the corners, or tightly rolled newspaper secured with adhesive tape and mitered

Once the clockface is in position, overlay with a window mount of cellophane or clear plastic (leave this out if the hands are to move)

Paint using the combing method (see page 81). Varnish well

Assemble assorted boxes. Glue, staple or tack together and mount on a ply or blockboard base

Tape all flaps down before assembling the clock

Glue a panel of cardboard to the front

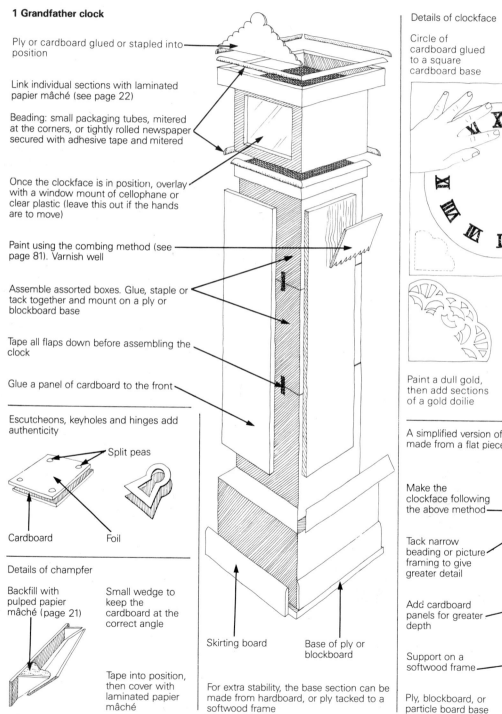

Escutcheons, keyholes and hinges add authenticity

Split peas

Cardboard   Foil

Details of champfer

Backfill with pulped papier mâché (page 21)

Small wedge to keep the cardboard at the correct angle

Tape into position, then cover with laminated papier mâché

Skirting board

Base of ply or blockboard

For extra stability, the base section can be made from hardboard, or ply tacked to a softwood frame

Details of clockface

Circle of cardboard glued to a square cardboard base

Plot the numerals from the center of the circle

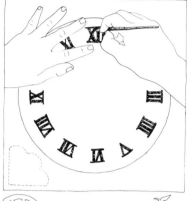

Paint a dull gold, then add sections of a gold doilie

Attach cardboard hands to clockface with a paper fastener

A simplified version of this clock can be made from a flat piece of hardboard or ply

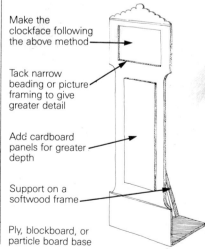

Make the clockface following the above method

Tack narrow beading or picture framing to give greater detail

Add cardboard panels for greater depth

Support on a softwood frame

Ply, blockboard, or particle board base

2 Coal scuttle

Sized felt handle (see page 86) reinforced with a narrow strip of cardboard (to maintain width of handle), and two lengths of sturdy wire (to maintain curve of handle). Pop-rivet or staple, then glue

Strong cardboard box with a tunnel of cardboard taped inside

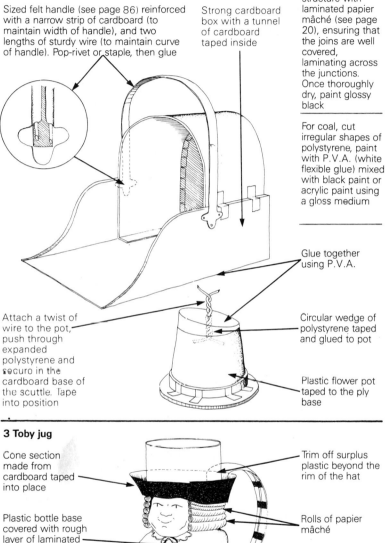

Attach a twist of wire to the pot, push through expanded polystyrene and secure in the cardboard base of the scuttle. Tape into position

Glue together using P.V.A.

Circular wedge of polystyrene taped and glued to pot

Plastic flower pot taped to the ply base

3 Toby jug

Cone section made from cardboard taped into place

Plastic bottle base covered with rough layer of laminated papier mâché before applying papier mâché molding

Shape built up with pulped papier mâché (page 20)

Expanded polystyrene base

Trim off surplus plastic beyond the rim of the hat

Rolls of papier mâché

Strip of plastic bottle. If it is not stiff enough, tape a central wire reinforcement and staple ends to the body

Link all parts with laminated papier mâché

Cover the whole structure with laminated papier mâché (see page 20), ensuring that the joins are well covered, laminating across the junctions. Once thoroughly dry, paint glossy black

For coal, cut irregular shapes of polystyrene, paint with P.V.A. (white flexible glue) mixed with black paint or acrylic paint using a gloss medium

---

4 Assorted picture frames

Cut two identical shapes, one from cardboard and one from wadding, thin foam rubber, or cotton wool

Stretch over velvet, and secure

Cut a central star shape pulling and gluing the points to the back

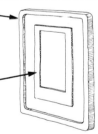

Curtain ring

Hide tape and string behind the braid

Gold braid glued to a cardboard oval

Polythene lids from ice cream containers have raised edges, ideal for frames

Rectangular colored mount, glued into position

Spray gold

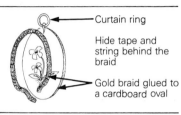

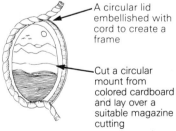

A circular lid embellished with cord to create a frame

Cut a circular mount from colored cardboard and lay over a suitable magazine cutting

---

Use felt shapes as decoration (see page 89)

Use an existing frame to create new molding from plaster (page 35)

Construct a frame from mitered packaging tubes (see page 69)

147

Victorian England

5 Standard lamp

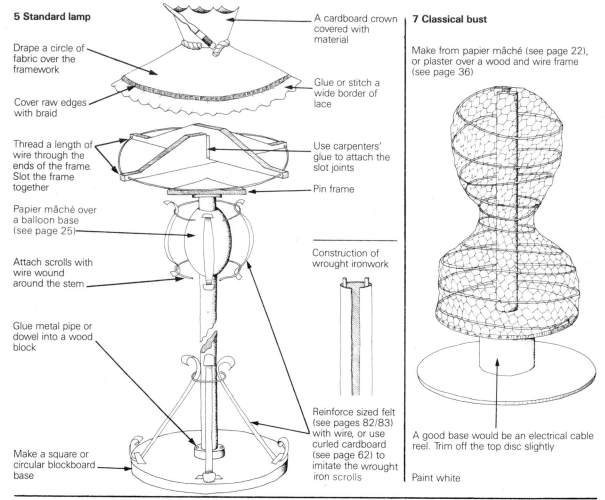

A cardboard crown covered with material

Drape a circle of fabric over the framework

Glue or stitch a wide border of lace

Cover raw edges with braid

Thread a length of wire through the ends of the frame. Slot the frame together

Use carpenters' glue to attach the slot joints

Pin frame

Papier mâché over a balloon base (see page 25)

Attach scrolls with wire wound around the stem

Construction of wrought ironwork

Glue metal pipe or dowel into a wood block

Reinforce sized felt (see pages 82/83) with wire, or use curled cardboard (see page 62) to imitate the wrought iron scrolls

Make a square or circular blockboard base

7 Classical bust

Make from papier mâché (see page 22), or plaster over a wood and wire frame (see page 36)

A good base would be an electrical cable reel. Trim off the top disc slightly

Paint white

6 Small oil lamp

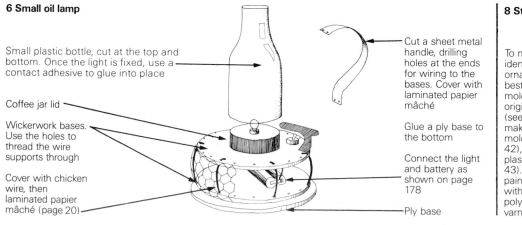

Small plastic bottle, cut at the top and bottom. Once the light is fixed, use a contact adhesive to glue into place

Coffee jar lid

Wickerwork bases. Use the holes to thread the wire supports through

Cover with chicken wire, then laminated papier mâché (page 20)

Cut a sheet metal handle, drilling holes at the ends for wiring to the bases. Cover with laminated papier mâché

Glue a ply base to the bottom

Connect the light and battery as shown on page 178

Ply base

8 Staffordshire dogs

To make two identical ornaments, it is best to use a mold. Make an original from clay (see page 40), make a plaster mold (see page 42), and cast in plaster (see page 43). Use gloss paint or watercolor with a polyurethane varnish

9 Iron

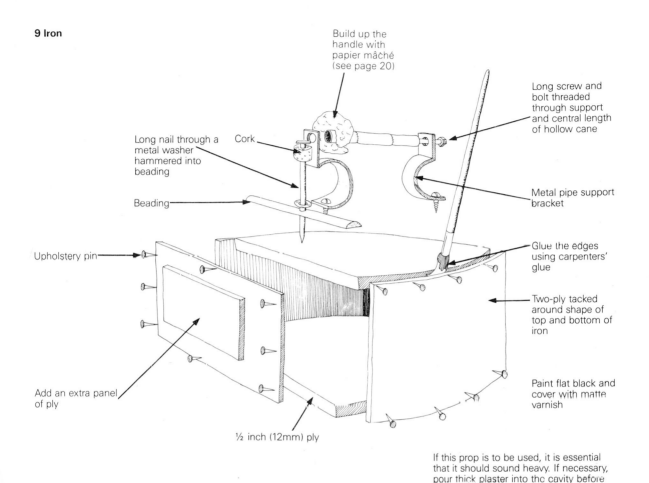

Build up the handle with papier mâché (see page 20)

Long screw and bolt threaded through support and central length of hollow cane

Long nail through a metal washer hammered into beading

Cork

Metal pipe support bracket

Beading

Upholstery pin

Glue the edges using carpenters' glue

Two-ply tacked around shape of top and bottom of iron

Add an extra panel of ply

Paint flat black and cover with matte varnish

½ inch (12mm) ply

If this prop is to be used, it is essential that it should sound heavy. If necessary, pour thick plaster into the cavity before tacking the rectangular panel into position

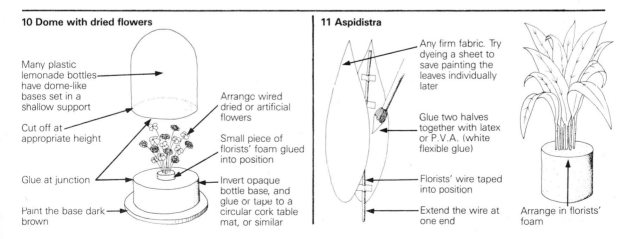

10 Dome with dried flowers

Many plastic lemonade bottles have dome-like bases set in a shallow support

Cut off at appropriate height

Glue at junction

Paint the base dark brown

Arrange wired dried or artificial flowers

Small piece of florists' foam glued into position

Invert opaque bottle base, and glue or tape to a circular cork table mat, or similar

11 Aspidistra

Any firm fabric. Try dyeing a sheet to save painting the leaves individually later

Glue two halves together with latex or P.V.A. (white flexible glue)

Florists' wire taped into position

Extend the wire at one end

Arrange in florists' foam

The Twentieth Century

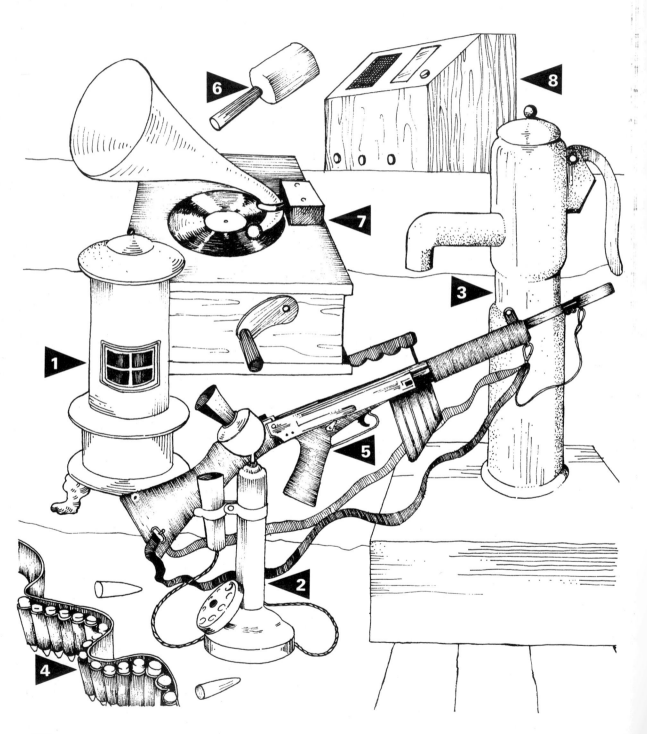

1 Paraffin heater

A ping pong ball or bead etc. placed on top. Use contact adhesive

Use an old saucepan lid, otherwise a section from a balloon-based papier mâché dome (see page 25)

Ply or cardboard

String glued to the surface to imitate panelling or ornamentation

Use strong cardboard for both drums, carefully rolling it over an existing curve to avoid folds or creases

Use red plastic filter material (see page 72). Glue to the inside of the prop

Cut a window while cardboard is flat. Paper fasteners or bolts can be glued around the edge

Tape a central black line

Extra molding can be created from pulped papier mâché (see page 20)

Utilize a battery source if a 'flare' is required (see page 178)

Make the lower drum wider than the top drum with rolled cardboard stapled and tabbed into place

Use an old cable reel (it may be made of heavy cardboard or ply)

Paint with black gloss

Build up the feet with pulped papier mâché (see page 20). Make the effect knobbly

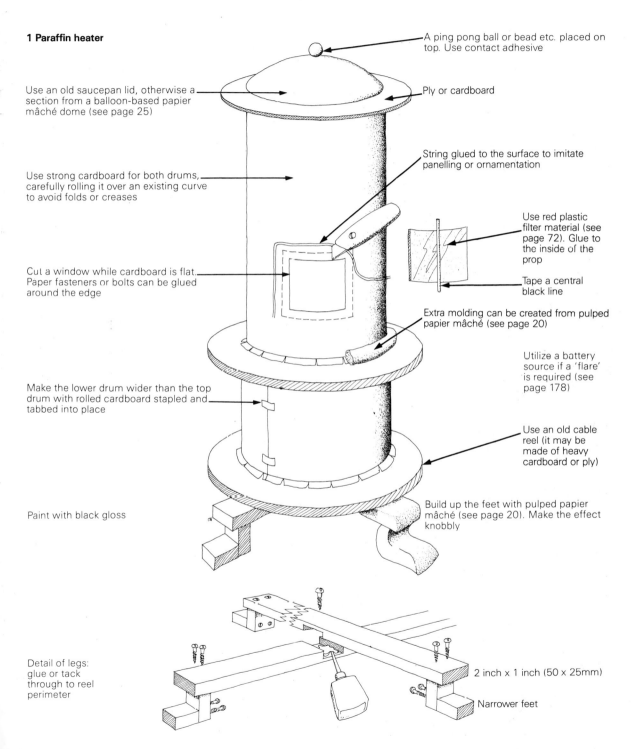

Detail of legs: glue or tack through to reel perimeter

2 inch x 1 inch (50 x 25mm)

Narrower feet

151

The Twentieth Century

2 Telephone

Plastic bottle top

Coffee jar top

Half a rubber ball

Narrow dowel threaded through cotton reels and inserted into a circular ply base

Odd pieces of toy car wheels

Cover reels with cardboard tube to disguise the edges

White sticky marker discs are a quick way to reproduce a dial

Glue a cardboard cone shape around a flared bottle top

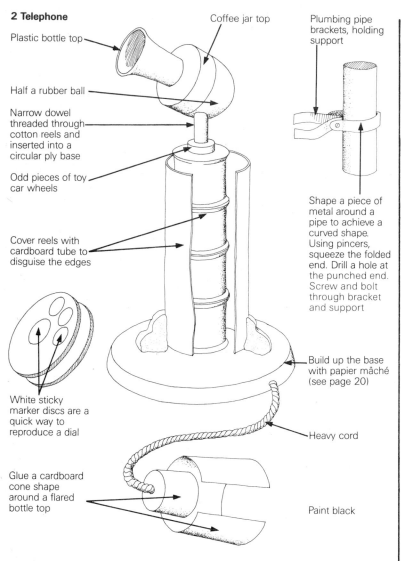

Heavy cord

Paint black

Plumbing pipe brackets, holding support

Shape a piece of metal around a pipe to achieve a curved shape. Using pincers, squeeze the folded end. Drill a hole at the punched end. Screw and bolt through bracket and support

Build up the base with papier mâché (see page 20)

3 Pump

Make the pump using papier mâché over a wood and wire frame (see page 36)

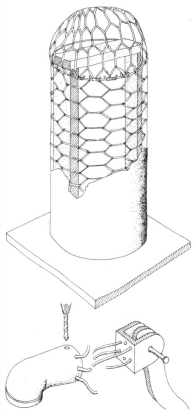

Section of plastic plumbing pipe with holes drilled at junction and threaded with wire to tie to main prop

Simple ply structure tacked together. Pivot arm on a long bolt. Screw through to the frame and wire into the chicken wire

---

4 Ammunition

Sharpen short lengths of doweling using a pencil sharpener (for jumbo-sized pencils); otherwise shave off roughly with a chisel

Sand off the point and curve the shape

Metallic paint

Glue between two canvas straps

5 Guns

See page 109. Extend the butt with wood mortised into place. Add sights using odd pieces of metal. For a handle, use doweling covered with a bicycle handlebar grip

6 Grenade

Fill an old can with plaster, place a small length of dowel centrally. When set, coat with a thick mix of P.V.A. (white flexible glue) and dark green powder paint

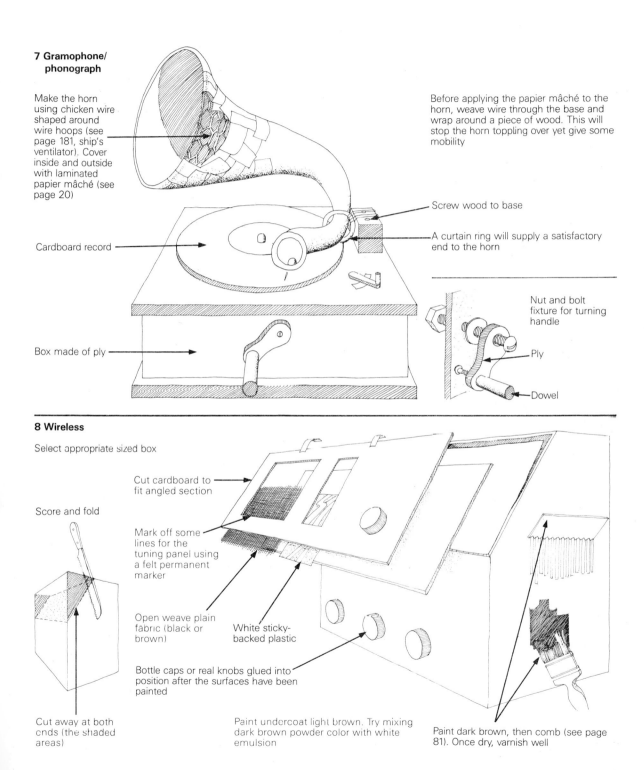

7 Gramophone/ phonograph

Make the horn using chicken wire shaped around wire hoops (see page 181, ship's ventilator). Cover inside and outside with laminated papier mâché (see page 20)

Before applying the papier mâché to the horn, weave wire through the base and wrap around a piece of wood. This will stop the horn toppling over yet give some mobility

Screw wood to base

Cardboard record

A curtain ring will supply a satisfactory end to the horn

Box made of ply

Nut and bolt fixture for turning handle

Ply

Dowel

8 Wireless

Select appropriate sized box

Score and fold

Cut cardboard to fit angled section

Mark off some lines for the tuning panel using a felt permanent marker

Open weave plain fabric (black or brown)

White sticky-backed plastic

Bottle caps or real knobs glued into position after the surfaces have been painted

Cut away at both ends (the shaded areas)

Paint undercoat light brown. Try mixing dark brown powder color with white emulsion

Paint dark brown, then comb (see page 81). Once dry, varnish well

Nativity

1 Angel

Make a strong wooden frame in the form of a cross, mortised and set in a wide board base (see page 36)

Cut wings from expanded polystyrene (see page 50). Decorate (see page 51). For companies with strict fire regulations, cover the polystyrene with papier or cloth mâché and treat with a fire retardant

Wire the wings into place, camouflage the join with plaster or papier mâché

Cast on a face mask using the dental moulage process (see page 44), or make a face mask from papier mâché (see page 31), or plaster (see page 38). While the plaster is still wet, press wire hooks into the back ready to secure to the frame

Wire the mask to the chicken wire base. Plaster around the edges, filling any gaps

Dip lengths of wool in plaster and arrange a hairstyle around the exposed netting on the head. Do not apply the strands singly, but in groups or skeins

Cast hands (see page 59); build up on a wire frame using plaster (see page 38); or papier mâché (see page 20); or try wiring some gloves and dipping these in plaster. Tie on to the frame with wire and tape with plastered scrim for added security

Bulk out the body, legs, arms, and head with chicken wire and roughly cover with laminated papier mâché (see page 22) or plastered scrim (see page 38). Leave the chicken wire exposed at the back to wire on to the wings later

Dip sheets and parts of old shirts etc. in plaster, and drape over the statue to simulate the natural fall of a garment

Paint with white emulsion

Nativity

2 Casket

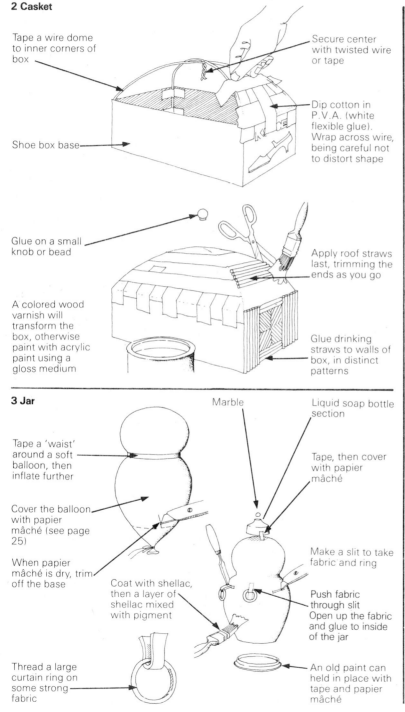

Tape a wire dome to inner corners of box

Shoe box base

Secure center with twisted wire or tape

Dip cotton in P.V.A. (white flexible glue). Wrap across wire, being careful not to distort shape

Glue on a small knob or bead

A colored wood varnish will transform the box, otherwise paint with acrylic paint using a gloss medium

Apply roof straws last, trimming the ends as you go

Glue drinking straws to walls of box, in distinct patterns

3 Jar

Marble

Liquid soap bottle section

Tape a 'waist' around a soft balloon, then inflate further

Cover the balloon with papier mâché (see page 25)

When papier mâché is dry, trim off the base

Coat with shellac, then a layer of shellac mixed with pigment

Thread a large curtain ring on some strong fabric

Tape, then cover with papier mâché

Make a slit to take fabric and ring

Push fabric through slit
Open up the fabric and glue to inside of the jar

An old paint can held in place with tape and papier mâché

4 Onyx jar

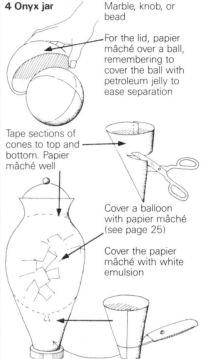

Marble, knob, or bead

For the lid, papier mâché over a ball, remembering to cover the ball with petroleum jelly to ease separation

Tape sections of cones to top and bottom. Papier mâché well

Cover a balloon with papier mâché (see page 25)

Cover the papier mâché with white emulsion

Tape, then papier mâché a 'foot' made from an old jar top

Prepare a shallow tray or dish ready for marbling (see page 79)

Roll the jar on the surface of the marbling solution, until the outside surface is covered. Repeat for lid

Varnish the marbled surface with polyurethane lacquer or shellac

5 Animal masks   See page 66

6 Crook   Follow method to make a flail (see page 116). Insert a shaped wire in the end of a cane, then build up with papier mâché (see page 20)

7 Stars

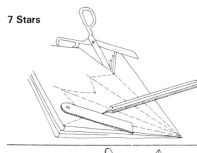

A many pointed star can be created by cutting and folding as illustrated.

(see page 64 for an alternative design)

Star shapes can be cut from ply or, even better, plexiglass

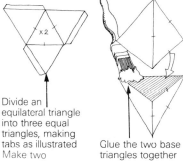

Divide an equilateral triangle into three equal triangles, making tabs as illustrated Make two

Glue the two base triangles together

Three-dimensional stars can be assembled from paper pyramids

Glue the rays of the star into position, matching the base facets with the bases of the isosceles pyramids

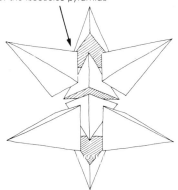

A stylized star can be made using plexiglass rods, which will glint in the light

Cover a ball of oasis (florists' foam) with silver foil and glue with P.V.A. (white flexible glue)

Arrange lengths of acrylic or plexiglass rods, spearing them into the ball

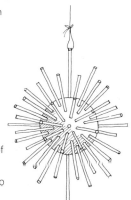

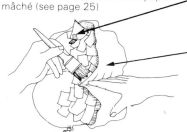

Make six triangular isosceles pyramids, the base triangle equalling the dimensions of the base facets

8 Crowns

A Tape two balloons together, the top one under-inflated. Cover with papier mâché (see page 25)

Tape on cardboard cone

Drape fine material, such as nylon, gauze, lurex, cheesecloth, and georgette around the base

Fold the fabric turban-style, gluing at intervals to secure around the base of the crown

Check diameter with actor's head measurement

Trim away spare papier mâché. Line inside with a strip of foam rubber or felt

B Make crowns from sized felt (see page 89)

C Make crowns from sized string over a balloon (see page 93)

9 Crib

Assemble as illustrated. Use only rough cut wood or scraps for economy. Paint with a dark wood stain

Two nails at crossing to stop rocking

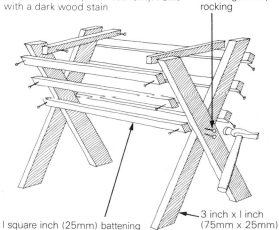

I square inch (25mm) battening

3 inch x I inch (75mm x 25mm)

Pantomime

Pantomime

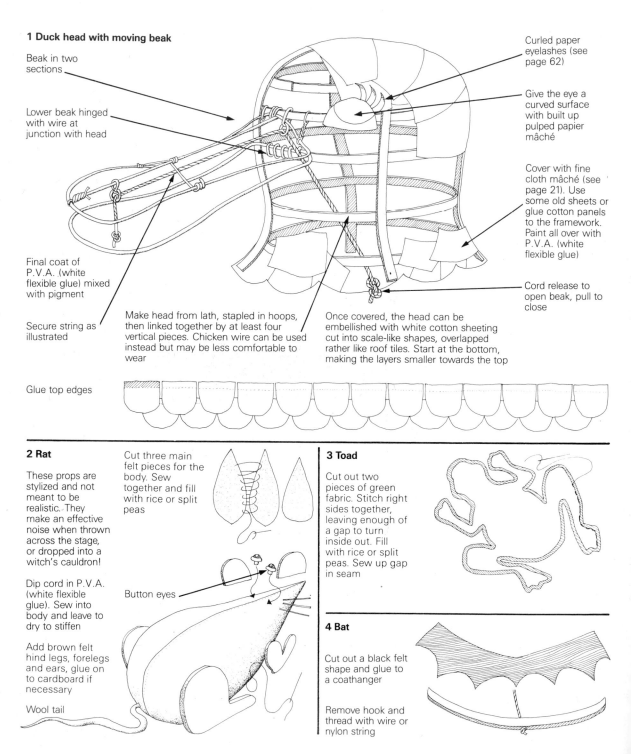

1 Duck head with moving beak

Beak in two sections

Lower beak hinged with wire at junction with head

Final coat of P.V.A. (white flexible glue) mixed with pigment

Secure string as illustrated

Make head from lath, stapled in hoops, then linked together by at least four vertical pieces. Chicken wire can be used instead but may be less comfortable to wear

Once covered, the head can be embellished with white cotton sheeting cut into scale-like shapes, overlapped rather like roof tiles. Start at the bottom, making the layers smaller towards the top

Curled paper eyelashes (see page 62)

Give the eye a curved surface with built up pulped papier mâché

Cover with fine cloth mâché (see page 21). Use some old sheets or glue cotton panels to the framework. Paint all over with P.V.A. (white flexible glue)

Cord release to open beak, pull to close

Glue top edges

2 Rat

These props are stylized and not meant to be realistic. They make an effective noise when thrown across the stage, or dropped into a witch's cauldron!

Dip cord in P.V.A. (white flexible glue). Sew into body and leave to dry to stiffen

Add brown felt hind legs, forelegs and ears, glue on to cardboard if necessary

Wool tail

Cut three main felt pieces for the body. Sew together and fill with rice or split peas

Button eyes

3 Toad

Cut out two pieces of green fabric. Stitch right sides together, leaving enough of a gap to turn inside out. Fill with rice or split peas. Sew up gap in seam

4 Bat

Cut out a black felt shape and glue to a coathanger

Remove hook and thread with wire or nylon string

5 Cheese

Wedge of softwood

Use countersink drill to make large holes

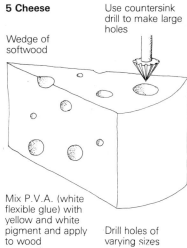

Mix P.V.A. (white flexible glue) with yellow and white pigment and apply to wood

Drill holes of varying sizes

6 Beanstalk

Tie with strong nylon or wire

Paint green, or bind green tape around and glue

Extend the wire spine

Wrap strong clothbacked sticky tape around

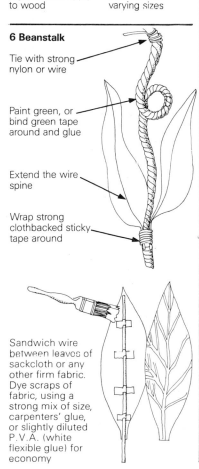

Sandwich wire between leaves of sackcloth or any other firm fabric. Dye scraps of fabric, using a strong mix of size, carpenters' glue, or slightly diluted P.V.A. (white flexible glue) for economy

7 Stylized foliage

This can be made from ½ inch (12mm) foamboard

Always try to cut against a hard edge

Saucers, saucepan lids etc. are good cutting guides for curved edges

Tape supports in position

Cut a wavy-edged baseboard

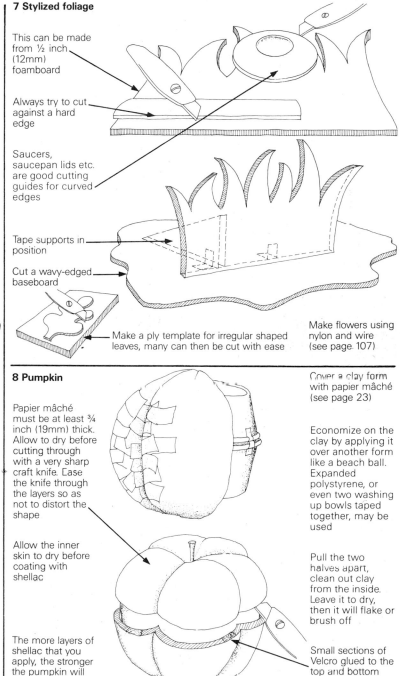

Make a ply template for irregular shaped leaves, many can then be cut with ease

Make flowers using nylon and wire (see page 107)

8 Pumpkin

Papier mâché must be at least ¾ inch (19mm) thick. Allow to dry before cutting through with a very sharp craft knife. Ease the knife through the layers so as not to distort the shape

Allow the inner skin to dry before coating with shellac

The more layers of shellac that you apply, the stronger the pumpkin will be. Allow to dry between layers

Split peas create a warty surface

Cover a clay form with papier mâché (see page 23)

Economize on the clay by applying it over another form like a beach ball. Expanded polystyrene, or even two washing up bowls taped together, may be used

Pull the two halves apart, clean out clay from the inside. Leave it to dry, then it will flake or brush off

Small sections of Velcro glued to the top and bottom will keep the two halves together

Pantomime

9 Wishing well

See page 65 for basic instructions

Tiles, corrugated side up

Softwood frame

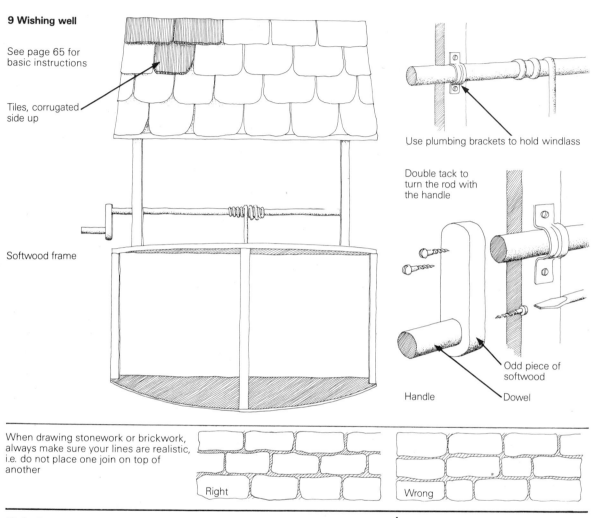

Use plumbing brackets to hold windlass

Double tack to turn the rod with the handle

Odd piece of softwood

Handle

Dowel

When drawing stonework or brickwork, always make sure your lines are realistic, i.e. do not place one join on top of another

Right

Wrong

---

10 Cauldron

Papier mâché over a chicken wire frame is the best method. See page 24

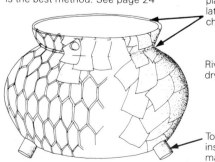

Use hoops of plastic, cane or lath taped to the chicken wire

Rivet through the dry papier mâché

Hook a wire handle through the rivet holes and wrap a few layers of laminated papier mâché around

Toilet roll tubes inserted in wire make good legs

11 Boulders See page 50

Cover with rough papier mâché or cloth mâché. Try to shape the expanded polystyrene in smooth facets

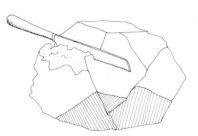

12 Milestone

Expanded polystyrene, cut with a hot knife (see page 50)

Bend a wire in a sharp 'V', heat and gouge out the lettering

Add stylized foliage if desired (see page 161)

Glue to a blockboard base using P.V.A. (white flexible glue)

Paint using a mixture of water, pigment, P.V.A., and plaster. Paint quickly, covering the whole surface.

Do not flood the wording. Fill in the lettering with a slightly darker color.

13 Tree stump

Pivot a comb to create rings (see page 81)

Papier mâché over a wood and wire frame (see pages 21 and 24)

Add sized string or pulped papier mâché to create a bark effect on the tree

Torn sections of corrugated paper add to the surface texture

14 Celestial bodies

Scraps of polystyrene snow

Cover with a thin layer of papier mâché (see page 20)

Using P.V.A. (white flexible glue), glue plastic knitting needles into position

Folded paper attached to the disc with tabs (see page 63)

Cover with a thin layer of papier mâché

Cut these shapes out of expanded polystyrene (see page 50)

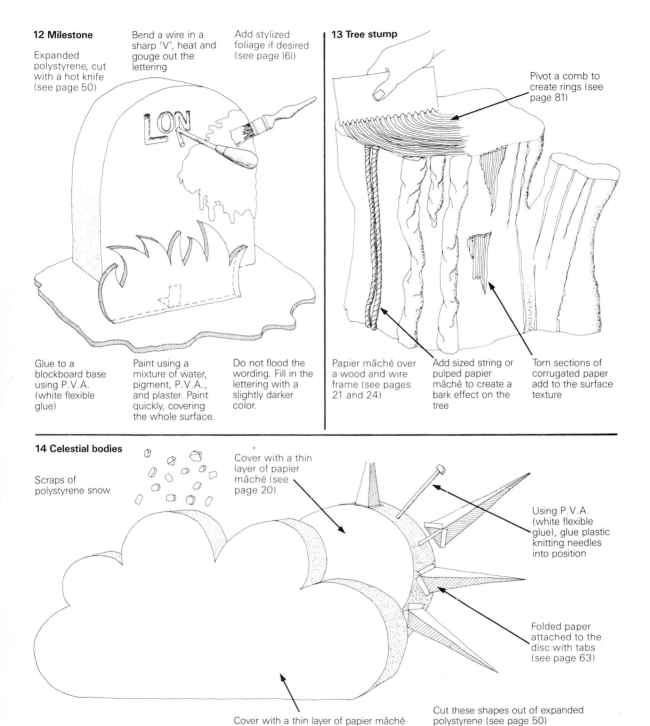

The Orient

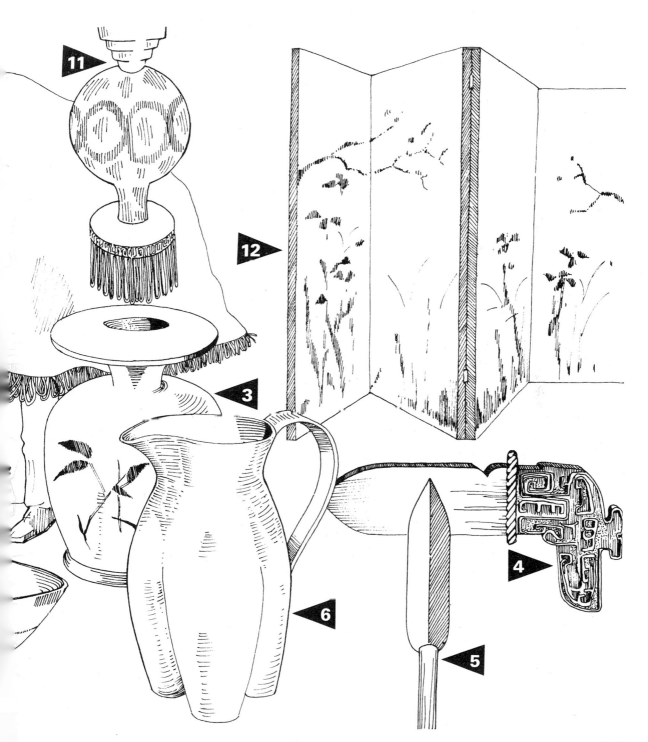

The Orient

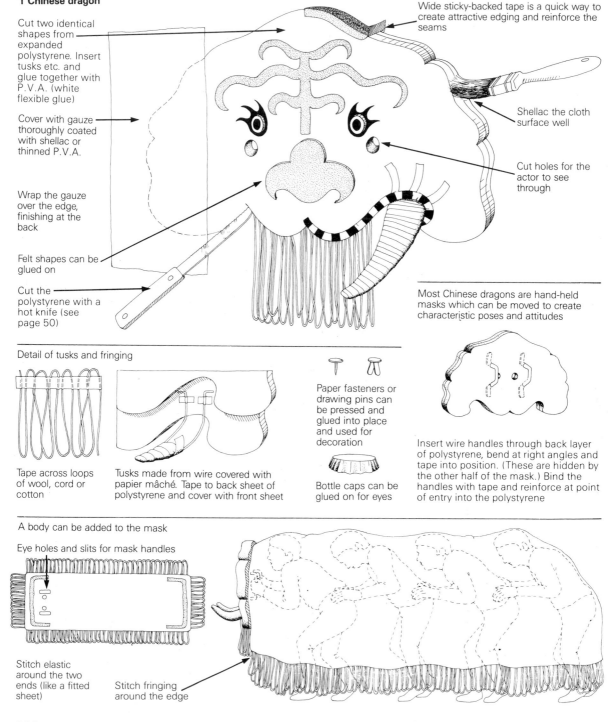

1 Chinese dragon

Cut two identical shapes from expanded polystyrene. Insert tusks etc. and glue together with P.V.A. (white flexible glue)

Cover with gauze thoroughly coated with shellac or thinned P.V.A.

Wrap the gauze over the edge, finishing at the back

Felt shapes can be glued on

Cut the polystyrene with a hot knife (see page 50)

Wide sticky-backed tape is a quick way to create attractive edging and reinforce the seams

Shellac the cloth surface well

Cut holes for the actor to see through

Most Chinese dragons are hand-held masks which can be moved to create characteristic poses and attitudes

Detail of tusks and fringing

Tape across loops of wool, cord or cotton

Tusks made from wire covered with papier mâché. Tape to back sheet of polystyrene and cover with front sheet

Paper fasteners or drawing pins can be pressed and glued into place and used for decoration

Bottle caps can be glued on for eyes

Insert wire handles through back layer of polystyrene, bend at right angles and tape into position. (These are hidden by the other half of the mask.) Bind the handles with tape and reinforce at point of entry into the polystyrene

A body can be added to the mask

Eye holes and slits for mask handles

Stitch elastic around the two ends (like a fitted sheet)

Stitch fringing around the edge

2 Hints on imitating Chinese brushwork

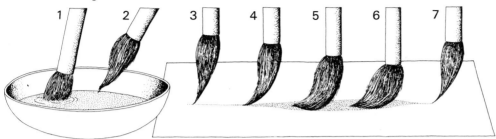

To obtain the right effect, it is necessary to draw with a genuine Chinese brush. Use a generous amount of paint, and always keep the brush vertical. Variations in line thickness are achieved by pushing the brush down or drawing it away from the paper. Avoid jerky movements and practice using the brush so that each line is drawn in one smooth action

1 Dip and fill with paint

2 Twirl brush to make a point while squeezing out surplus paint

3 Drag the brush gently, making a thin line

4 and **5** Rapidly lower the brush, allowing the line to thicken

6 and **7** Quickly lift up the brush using a twirling action before the brush leaves the surface

Once you have mastered straight lines and are able to control the width of line, try painting curves

Sometimes you may like to reverse the process described above. Press the brush down firmly on to the paper and gradually lift up using a sweeping movement

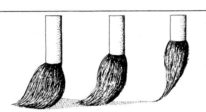

---

3 Wide-necked jar

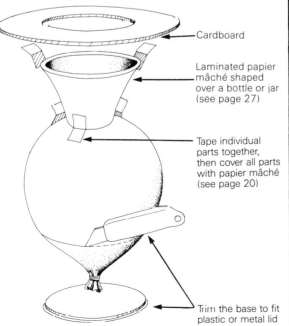

Cardboard

Laminated papier mâché shaped over a bottle or jar (see page 27)

Tape individual parts together, then cover all parts with papier mâché (see page 20)

Trim the base to fit plastic or metal lid

4 Dagger

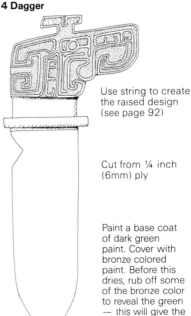

Use string to create the raised design (see page 92)

Cut from ¼ inch (6mm) ply

Paint a base coat of dark green paint. Cover with bronze colored paint. Before this dries, rub off some of the bronze color to reveal the green — this will give the effect of old, tarnished bronze

5 Spear

Ply. Paint in two sections, one half slightly darker than the other

Dowel with slot cut in the end to take the spear head

The Orient

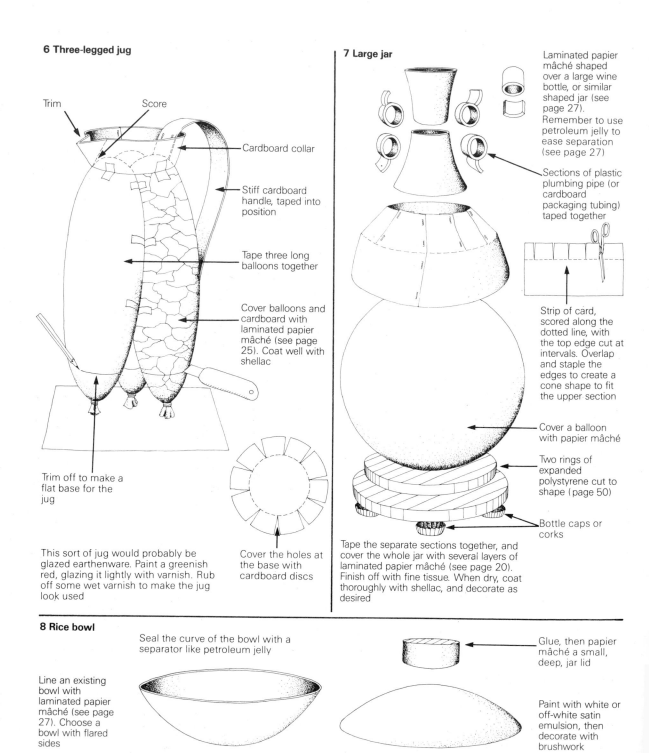

6 Three-legged jug

Trim

Score

Cardboard collar

Stiff cardboard handle, taped into position

Tape three long balloons together

Cover balloons and cardboard with laminated papier mâché (see page 25). Coat well with shellac

Trim off to make a flat base for the jug

This sort of jug would probably be glazed earthenware. Paint a greenish red, glazing it lightly with varnish. Rub off some wet varnish to make the jug look used

Cover the holes at the base with cardboard discs

7 Large jar

Laminated papier mâché shaped over a large wine bottle, or similar shaped jar (see page 27). Remember to use petroleum jelly to ease separation (see page 27)

Sections of plastic plumbing pipe (or cardboard packaging tubing) taped together

Strip of card, scored along the dotted line, with the top edge cut at intervals. Overlap and staple the edges to create a cone shape to fit the upper section

Cover a balloon with papier mâché

Two rings of expanded polystyrene cut to shape (page 50)

Bottle caps or corks

Tape the separate sections together, and cover the whole jar with several layers of laminated papier mâché (see page 20). Finish off with fine tissue. When dry, coat thoroughly with shellac, and decorate as desired

8 Rice bowl

Seal the curve of the bowl with a separator like petroleum jelly

Line an existing bowl with laminated papier mâché (see page 27). Choose a bowl with flared sides

Glue, then papier mâché a small, deep, jar lid

Paint with white or off-white satin emulsion, then decorate with brushwork

9 Wallhanging

A length of material stapled to the back of dowel rods

Copy some existing lettering for authenticity

Glue a tailor's 'frog' on to a clothes peg, and attach to the fabric. Alternatively, create a pattern by gluing string to a piece of cardboard and gluing this to a peg

Buff or gold colored paper glued on

10 Buddha

Construct a wood and wire frame (see page 36). Cover with plaster (see page 38), or papier mâché (see page 21)

11 Hanging lantern

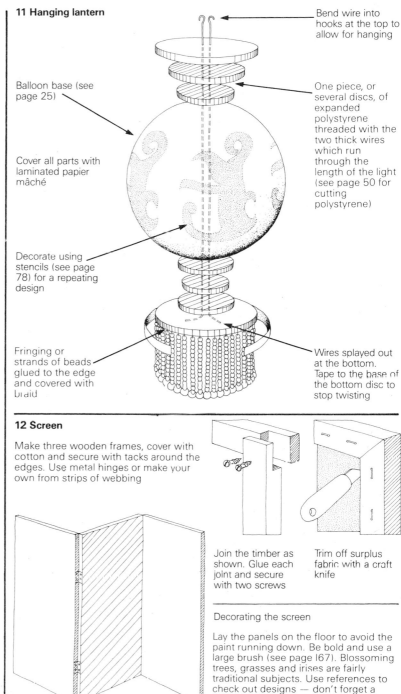

Bend wire into hooks at the top to allow for hanging

Balloon base (see page 25)

One piece, or several discs, of expanded polystyrene threaded with the two thick wires which run through the length of the light (see page 50 for cutting polystyrene)

Cover all parts with laminated papier mâché

Decorate using stencils (see page 78) for a repeating design

Fringing or strands of beads glued to the edge and covered with braid

Wires splayed out at the bottom. Tape to the base of the bottom disc to stop twisting

12 Screen

Make three wooden frames, cover with cotton and secure with tacks around the edges. Use metal hinges or make your own from strips of webbing

Join the timber as shown. Glue each joint and secure with two screws

Trim off surplus fabric with a craft knife

Decorating the screen

Lay the panels on the floor to avoid the paint running down. Be bold and use a large brush (see page 167). Blossoming trees, grasses and irises are fairly traditional subjects. Use references to check out designs — don't forget a Chinese signature!

The Wild West

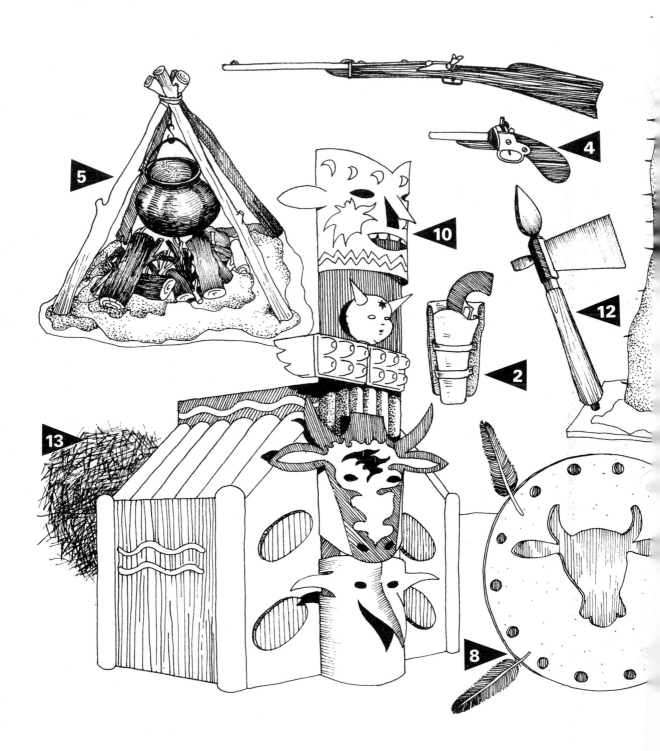

WANTED

00 REWARD

DEAD OR ALIVE

The Wild West

1 Chaps

Using felt, cut and sew the garment using the following dimensions

A-B = crotch to ankle
A-C = circumference of leg top
D-E = waist measurement

CUT 2

CUT 1

A   C

B

Position hooks, adjusting to fit the actor

Once the garment has been assembled, convert the felt into mock leather (see page 84). Use a length of heavy cord or shoe lace to tie the front waistband together

Rivet holes   D

E

Stitch chaps to inside of the waistband

Glue buckram or sackcloth to waistband back, using latex

Add buttons for decoration

Decorate with large stitching using a light colored cord after the felt has been 'converted' to leather

3 Powder horn

Shape chicken wire, then cover with laminated papier mâché (see page 20)

Make the chicken wire shape to fit available lids and bottle caps, not the other way around

Plastic, brass or metal ring must be an exact fit for stopper made from a bottle cap, built up with pulped papier mâché

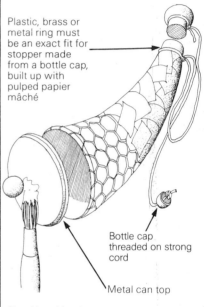

Bottle cap threaded on strong cord

Metal can top

Glued bead knob

Paint the horn yellow or greeny white. Smear pure white in a streak along the middle to give a translucent quality

2 Holster

Cut felt for main part and two pieces for the straps

Punch holes in the leather

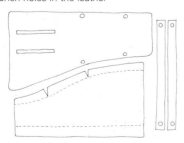

Convert the felt into mock leather (see page 84)

Stitch and glue into place

Paper fasteners will hold the straps in place

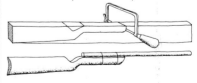

4 Guns

See page 109 or the guns detailed in the 17th and 18th Century section on page 140

For the stocks, cut the basic shape from wood and shape with a rasp

Wire scrap metal tubing to the stock

There are many suitable toy guns

5 Campfire with pot

Assemble a four-sided pyramid from softwood and mount on a blockboard base

Cover three sides of the pyramid with red or orange fireproof plastic filter material (see page 72). Glue or staple into place

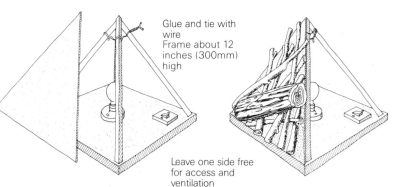

Glue and tie with wire
Frame about 12 inches (300mm) high

Leave one side free for access and ventilation

Arrange sticks, twigs and logs, gluing or tying into place. Brown or black clothbacked adhesive tape is useful for this and less difficult to camouflage

Leave enough gaps to allow glow to show through

Screw in a lightbulb and socket with a switch connection. Make provision for a battery connection (see page 178), or connect to mains. (Wire on stage is a hazard: be careful)

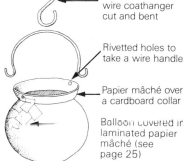

Hook made from a wire coathanger cut and bent

Rivetted holes to take a wire handle

Papier mâché over a cardboard collar

Balloon covered in laminated papier mâché (see page 25)

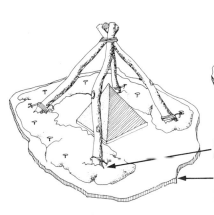

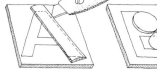

When making the base to take the fire, leave enough flat space for the pyramid

Embed sticks in the plaster or papier mâché, tying with wire to nail

Blockboard base keyed with tacks and partially covered with lumpy plaster or pulped papier mâché

---

6 Posters

Use sheet expanded polystyrene to reproduce detail on large posters. Many can be reproduced in this way

A sheet of heavy cardboard or particle board makes a good base on which to glue the polystyrene. Use P.V.A. (white flexible glue)

Roll ink carefully over the raised areas only (see page 77)

Lightweight corrugated cardboard

String

This type of poster lends itself to stenciling (see page 78), although it would be rather expensive to use a lino cut

Cut against a metal rule where possible

For curves, find metal egg cups, can tops, jam pot covers etc. to draw around

Cut out the letters, right way around, then reverse and glue to printing block

Print, following instructions on page 77. You can print two colors at once with careful application of the printing ink

The Wild West

7 Quiver

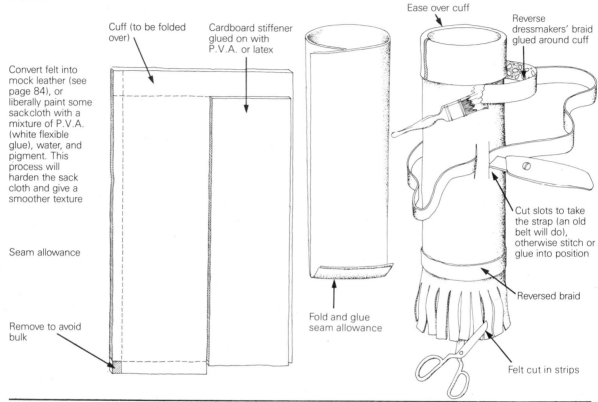

Convert felt into mock leather (see page 84), or liberally paint some sackcloth with a mixture of P.V.A. (white flexible glue), water, and pigment. This process will harden the sack cloth and give a smoother texture

Cuff (to be folded over)

Cardboard stiffener glued on with P.V.A. or latex

Ease over cuff

Reverse dressmakers' braid glued around cuff

Seam allowance

Remove to avoid bulk

Fold and glue seam allowance

Cut slots to take the strap (an old belt will do), otherwise stitch or glue into position

Reversed braid

Felt cut in strips

8 Sioux shield

Sackcloth glued to hardboard. Soak first with woodworkers' glue for adhesion and change of surface

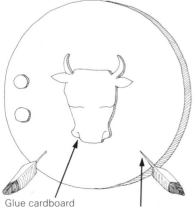

Leather or P.V.C. strap stapled to back

Glue cardboard cutouts using P.V.A.

Dip feather ends in dye. Staple or glue

Paint using earthy, natural colors — red, brown, cream, mustard etc.

9 Peace pipe

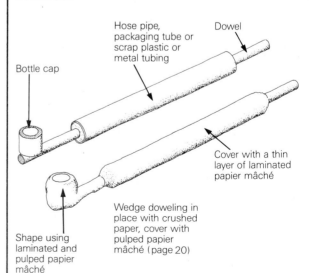

Hose pipe, packaging tube or scrap plastic or metal tubing

Dowel

Bottle cap

Cover with a thin layer of laminated papier mâché

Shape using laminated and pulped papier mâché

Wedge doweling in place with crushed paper, cover with pulped papier mâché (page 20)

10 Totem pole

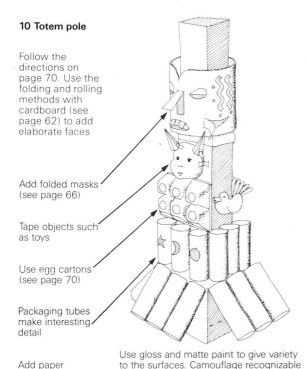

Follow the directions on page 70. Use the folding and rolling methods with cardboard (see page 62) to add elaborate faces

Add folded masks (see page 66)

Tape objects such as toys

Use egg cartons (see page 70)

Packaging tubes make interesting detail

Add paper sculpture (see page 64)

Use gloss and matte paint to give variety to the surfaces. Camouflage recognizable objects with unusual color combinations, or break up the shape with different colors

11 Container

Make this on the same principle as the barrel on page 142; otherwise an old paint can (2.5 or 5 litre size) will actually hold fluid

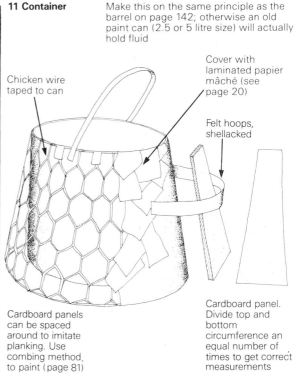

Chicken wire taped to can

Cover with laminated papier mâché (see page 20)

Felt hoops, shellacked

Cardboard panels can be spaced around to imitate planking. Use combing method to paint (page 81)

Cardboard panel. Divide top and bottom circumference an equal number of times to get correct measurements

12 Axe

Follow basic principles of making a ceremonial pole axe (see page 141). Build up handle with papier mâché (see page 20). Fold and score cardboard to imitate faceted central section (see page 62)

13 Tumbleweed

Roll a small ball of dried grass in some watered-down P.V.A. (white flexible glue). Keep repeating this process, occasionally tying with thin twine

14 Cactus

Assemble and shape expanded polystyrene with a hot knife (see page 50)

Cover using cloth mâché (see page 21). Use a fine cloth, such as cheesecloth, cut on the cross. This will stretch well around the curved shapes. Paint green

Glue polystyrene to a particle board base. It could be impaled on a vertical wooden strut, mortised to the base

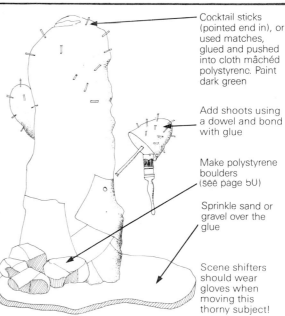

Cocktail sticks (pointed end in), or used matches, glued and pushed into cloth mâchéd polystyrene. Paint dark green

Add shoots using a dowel and bond with glue

Make polystyrene boulders (see page 50)

Sprinkle sand or gravel over the glue

Scene shifters should wear gloves when moving this thorny subject!

175

Ships and the Sea

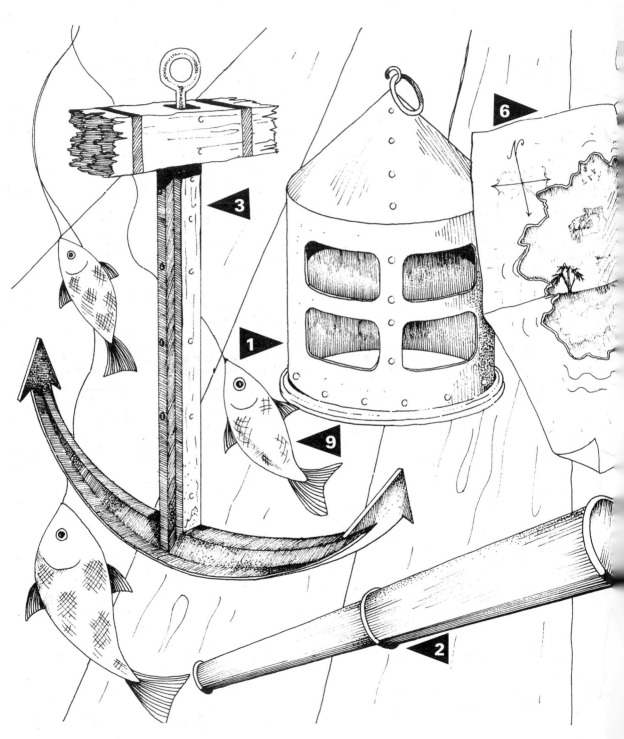

Ships and the Sea

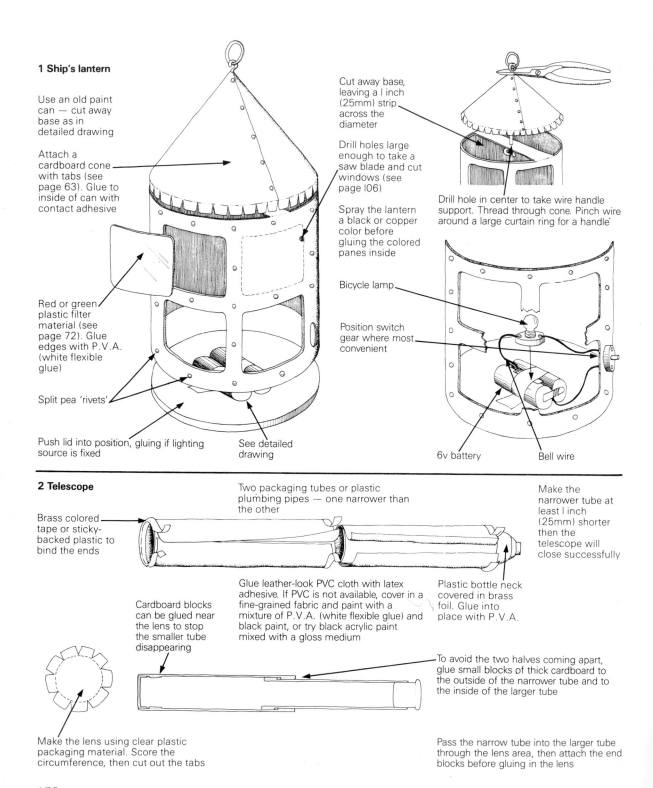

1 Ship's lantern

Use an old paint can — cut away base as in detailed drawing

Attach a cardboard cone with tabs (see page 63). Glue to inside of can with contact adhesive

Red or green plastic filter material (see page 72). Glue edges with P.V.A. (white flexible glue)

Split pea 'rivets'

Push lid into position, gluing if lighting source is fixed

See detailed drawing

Cut away base, leaving a I inch (25mm) strip across the diameter

Drill holes large enough to take a saw blade and cut windows (see page l06)

Spray the lantern a black or copper color before gluing the colored panes inside

Bicycle lamp

Position switch gear where most convenient

Drill hole in center to take wire handle support. Thread through cone. Pinch wire around a large curtain ring for a handle

6v battery

Bell wire

2 Telescope

Brass colored tape or sticky-backed plastic to bind the ends

Two packaging tubes or plastic plumbing pipes — one narrower than the other

Make the narrower tube at least I inch (25mm) shorter then the telescope will close successfully

Cardboard blocks can be glued near the lens to stop the smaller tube disappearing

Glue leather-look PVC cloth with latex adhesive. If PVC is not available, cover in a fine-grained fabric and paint with a mixture of P.V.A. (white flexible glue) and black paint, or try black acrylic paint mixed with a gloss medium

Plastic bottle neck covered in brass foil. Glue into place with P.V.A.

To avoid the two halves coming apart, glue small blocks of thick cardboard to the outside of the narrower tube and to the inside of the larger tube

Make the lens using clear plastic packaging material. Score the circumference, then cut out the tabs

Pass the narrow tube into the larger tube through the lens area, then attach the end blocks before gluing in the lens

3 Anchor

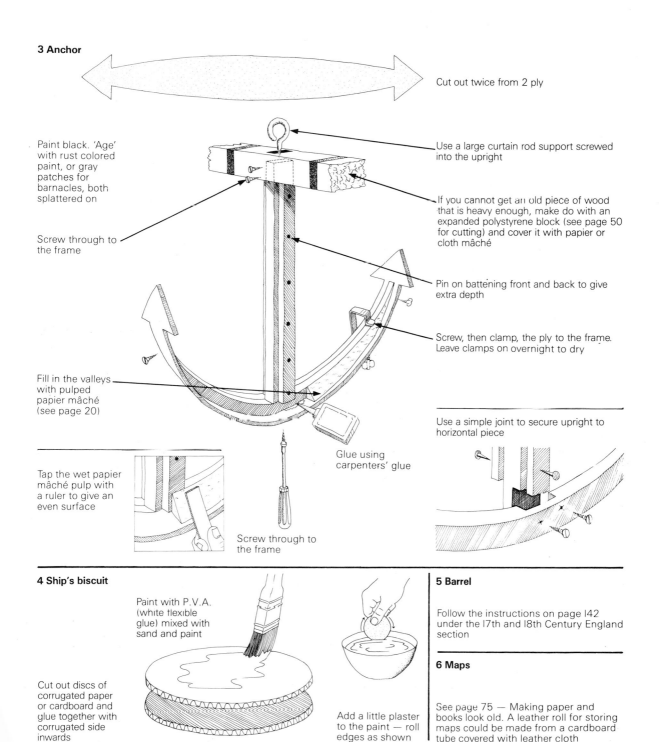

Cut out twice from 2 ply

Paint black. 'Age' with rust colored paint, or gray patches for barnacles, both splattered on

Use a large curtain rod support screwed into the upright

Screw through to the frame

If you cannot get an old piece of wood that is heavy enough, make do with an expanded polystyrene block (see page 50 for cutting) and cover it with papier or cloth mâché

Pin on battening front and back to give extra depth

Screw, then clamp, the ply to the frame. Leave clamps on overnight to dry

Fill in the valleys with pulped papier mâché (see page 20)

Use a simple joint to secure upright to horizontal piece

Tap the wet papier mâché pulp with a ruler to give an even surface

Glue using carpenters' glue

Screw through to the frame

4 Ship's biscuit

Paint with P.V.A. (white flexible glue) mixed with sand and paint

Cut out discs of corrugated paper or cardboard and glue together with corrugated side inwards

Add a little plaster to the paint — roll edges as shown

5 Barrel

Follow the instructions on page 142 under the 17th and 18th Century England section

6 Maps

See page 75 — Making paper and books look old. A leather roll for storing maps could be made from a cardboard tube covered with leather cloth

Ships and the Sea

7 Capstan

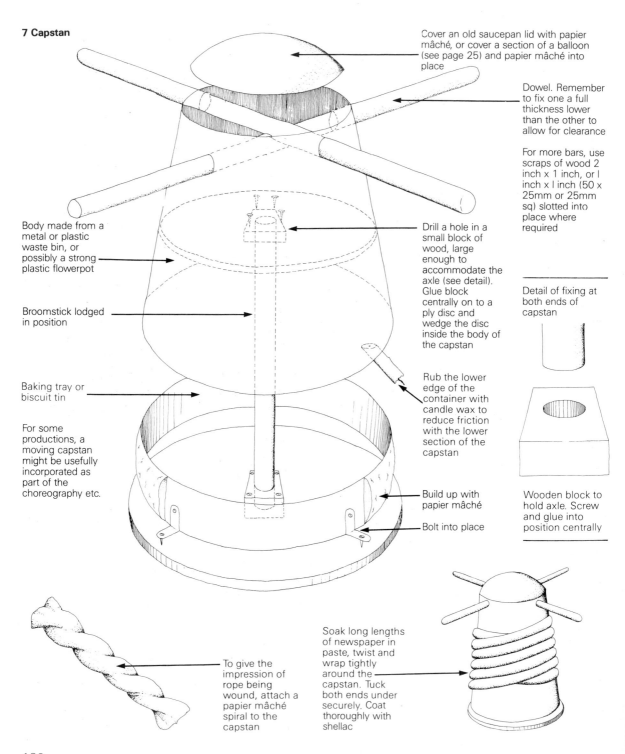

Cover an old saucepan lid with papier mâché, or cover a section of a balloon (see page 25) and papier mâché into place

Dowel. Remember to fix one a full thickness lower than the other to allow for clearance

For more bars, use scraps of wood 2 inch x 1 inch, or I inch x I inch (50 x 25mm or 25mm sq) slotted into place where required

Body made from a metal or plastic waste bin, or possibly a strong plastic flowerpot

Drill a hole in a small block of wood, large enough to accommodate the axle (see detail). Glue block centrally on to a ply disc and wedge the disc inside the body of the capstan

Detail of fixing at both ends of capstan

Broomstick lodged in position

Baking tray or biscuit tin

Rub the lower edge of the container with candle wax to reduce friction with the lower section of the capstan

For some productions, a moving capstan might be usefully incorporated as part of the choreography etc.

Build up with papier mâché

Bolt into place

Wooden block to hold axle. Screw and glue into position centrally

To give the impression of rope being wound, attach a papier mâché spiral to the capstan

Soak long lengths of newspaper in paste, twist and wrap tightly around the capstan. Tuck both ends under securely. Coat thoroughly with shellac

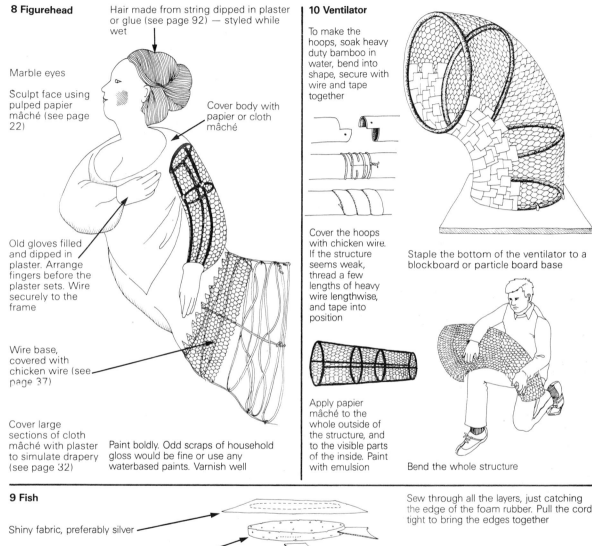

8 Figurehead

Hair made from string dipped in plaster or glue (see page 92) — styled while wet

Marble eyes

Sculpt face using pulped papier mâché (see page 22)

Cover body with papier or cloth mâché

Old gloves filled and dipped in plaster. Arrange fingers before the plaster sets. Wire securely to the frame

Wire base, covered with chicken wire (see page 37)

Cover large sections of cloth mâché with plaster to simulate drapery (see page 32)

Paint boldly. Odd scraps of household gloss would be fine or use any waterbased paints. Varnish well

10 Ventilator

To make the hoops, soak heavy duty bamboo in water, bend into shape, secure with wire and tape together

Cover the hoops with chicken wire. If the structure seems weak, thread a few lengths of heavy wire lengthwise, and tape into position

Apply papier mâché to the whole outside of the structure, and to the visible parts of the inside. Paint with emulsion

Staple the bottom of the ventilator to a blockboard or particle board base

Bend the whole structure

9 Fish

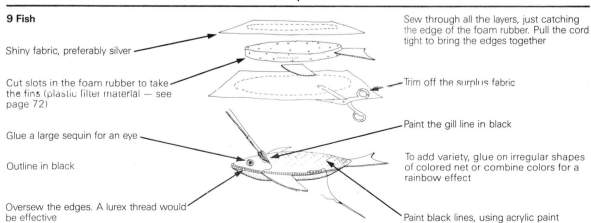

Shiny fabric, preferably silver

Cut slots in the foam rubber to take the fins (plastic filter material — see page 72)

Glue a large sequin for an eye

Outline in black

Oversew the edges. A lurex thread would be effective

Sew through all the layers, just catching the edge of the foam rubber. Pull the cord tight to bring the edges together

Trim off the surplus fabric

Paint the gill line in black

To add variety, glue on irregular shapes of colored net or combine colors for a rainbow effect

Paint black lines, using acrylic paint

181

Science Fiction

1 Console

Assemble framework, with simple carpentry joints, screws or corrugated fasteners. Add corner supports where necessary

Odd electric switches

Sliding gear: make 'H' shaped slides to fit into slots within egg box lid cover. Strengthen the cross piece with wire and cover with metalized sticky-backed tape

Colored metallic plastic, glued down on panels

Unusual telephones made from the hollow handles of large plastic containers (seal up the exposed ends with layers of cardboard). Shellac with pigment thoroughly

Build up with papier mâché (see page 20)

Tack or staple on hardboard, corrugated cardboard or any odd packaging pieces

Clock faces cut from magazines and mounted on metal lids

Paint roller handles taped to back of board

Add telephone wire or make your own spiral cord:

1 Smother a length of dowel with petroleum jelly

2 Dip cord in slightly diluted P.V.A. (white flexible glue) and wrap around dowel. Do not let string coils touch each other

3 Allow to dry, then slide off pole The cord should keep its spiral for a short time but is not suitable for prolonged practical use

Glue down ceramic or plastic tesserae for telephone buttons

Plastic lemonade bottle bottoms make good domes for very small battery-powered lights

Reels (two-color to show movement) can be linked up to slow-running barbecue motors, powered by mains or battery

Sections of packaging tubing help to give variety to the surfaces

Pin down a variety of surfaces. Use corrugated paper, pinboard, fruit packaging etc.

Use small boxes to create recesses, taping them to the frame and tacking or stapling where possible

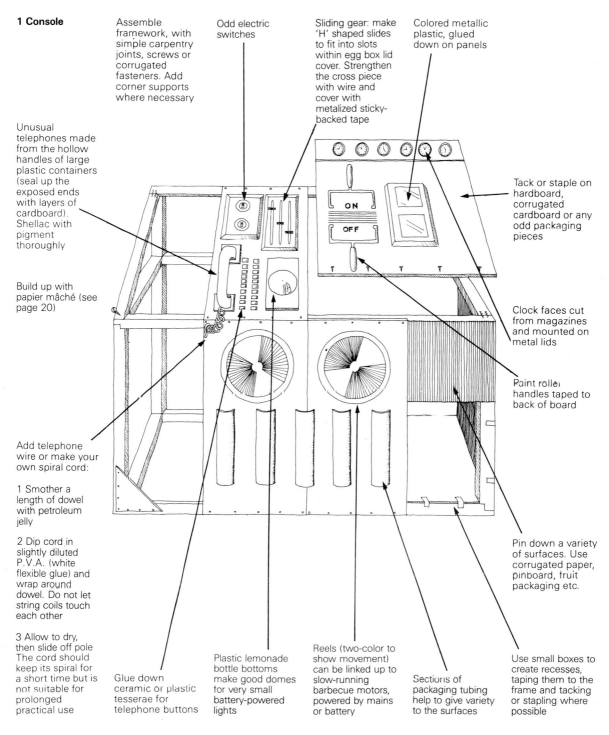

Science Fiction

2 Two face masks

This face mask is a lightweight, papier mâché shell formed over a clay shape (see page 23)

Holes to correspond with actor's eyes and covered with see-through gauze

Red marble eyes anchored in position while papier mâché is still wet

An alternative mask based on papier mâché over a chicken wire frame (see page 24), or over a balloon, extending it with a cardboard collar (see page 25)

Check dimensions with actor's measurements

Liquid soap bottle tops

Sized felt detail

Doweling

Bolts

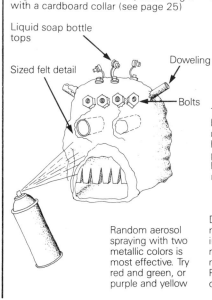

Fun fur balaclava or hood shape attached with Velcro

Split peas glued on will give a warty surface

Final layer of cheesecloth soaked in size, shellac or P.V.A. (white flexible glue). Arrange the fabric, pressing into the hollows and gathering it to simulate folds of flesh where appropriate

Toilet roll tubes built up with papier mâché. Make eye holes through the papier mâché base, once the mask is dry

Random aerosol spraying with two metallic colors is most effective. Try red and green, or purple and yellow

Decoration need not be embedded in the wet papier mâché. Once the mask is dry, use P.V.A. or contact cement

3 Space helmet

Papier mâché over a chicken wire base (see page 24), or cover a balloon which has a cardboard collar extension (see page 25), or an old motorcycle helmet can be extended in much the same way

Make a cross of wire and cover with metallic tape to give a window pane appearance

Foam rubber insulating tubing

Glue odd pieces of metal gauze over a small packaging box

Bind edges using metallic sticky-backed tape

Hose from a backpack can be linked into helmet. Hook it on for easy detachment. Camouflage hook with a 'washer' made from a disc of silver PVC cloth

Countersink plastic bottle caps Mâché over join

Clothbacked adhesive tape linking foam rubber to papier mâché. Stab stitch as an extra precaution. Cover with cloth mâché, using a fine material (see page 21)

Using stab stitches of heavy cord, link the two circles of foam rubber.
(An upholsterer's curved needle might be useful when stitching at awkward angles)

4 Ray gun

Wire knitting needles together

Use sized string for decorative 'turning'

Hollow handle from plastic container

Paint with shellac mixed with metallic pigment or spray

There are many metallic adhesive tapes available. These would certainly brighten up the prop

Assemble the individual components together, using strong tape, clothbacked adhesive tape or masking tape

Build up shape with pulped papier mâché (page 20)

Pack pulped papier mâché in tube to hold doweling and needles in position

Doweling

Small box

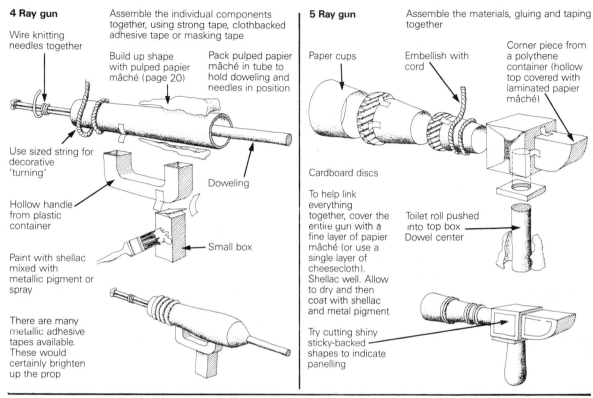

5 Ray gun

Assemble the materials, gluing and taping together

Paper cups

Embellish with cord

Corner piece from a polythene container (hollow top covered with laminated papier mâché)

Cardboard discs

To help link everything together, cover the entire gun with a fine layer of papier mâché (or use a single layer of cheesecloth). Shellac well. Allow to dry and then coat with shellac and metal pigment

Try cutting shiny sticky-backed shapes to indicate panelling

Toilet roll pushed into top box Dowel center

6 Backpack

Glue two large plastic containers together

Box with dials glued on

Hose (from a cleaner, or use garden hose)

Box

Wire twisted around handle

Knitting needle

Papier mâché over a saucer (see page 27)

Plastic lemonade bottle with base removed

Old ventilator

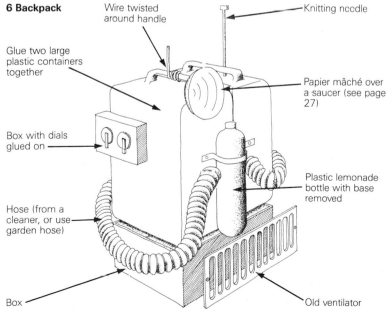

7 Handset with moving antenna (aerial)

Motor-driven children's toys can be adapted for gadgets such as this rotating antenna

Bed spring, taped to a wheel

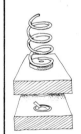

Pack in a box covered with sticky-backed plastic. Add buttons, knobs etc.

8 Shapes

Make astrological shapes using paper sculpture (see page 64) with the varied textured papers available. Some are metalized or plasticized. Ask in your local shops: often parts of their window displays will be an invaluable source of paper props

Science Fiction

9 Robot

Make this large enough to accommodate an actor, if necessary

Papier mâché over a beach ball. Follow the same principles for covering a balloon (see page 25). Make eye holes where appropriate

Using upholsterers' webbing, make two straps across the top hoop to rest on actor's shoulders. Tape into place

Make hoops large enough to give the actor room to move

Cover with chicken wire

Cover with cloth or papier mâché

Purchased hoops (plastic or cane), or wire plastic flexible curtain rod

Plastic bottle bottom

Battery-driven flashing light

Turret

Split pea rivets

Metallic spray

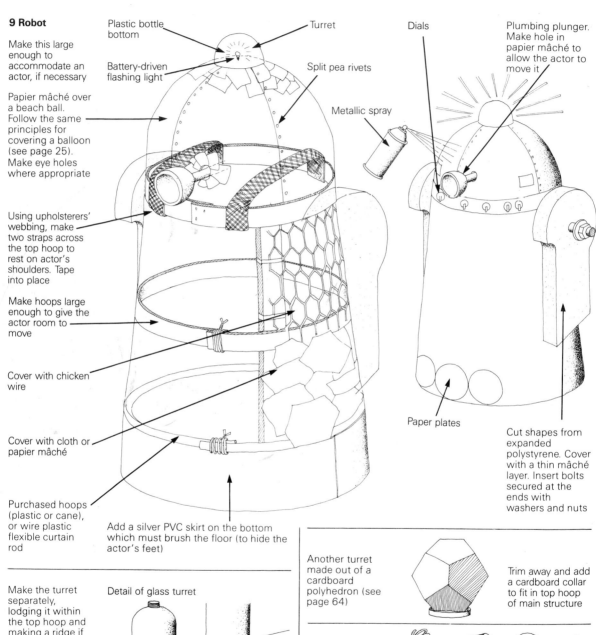

Dials

Plumbing plunger. Make hole in papier mâché to allow the actor to move it

Paper plates

Cut shapes from expanded polystyrene. Cover with a thin mâché layer. Insert bolts secured at the ends with washers and nuts

Add a silver PVC skirt on the bottom which must brush the floor (to hide the actor's feet)

Make the turret separately, lodging it within the top hoop and making a ridge if necessary to ensure a good fit

Remove plastic base

Detail of glass turret

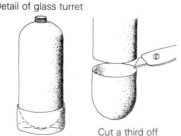

Cut a third off

Another turret made out of a cardboard polyhedron (see page 64)

Trim away and add a cardboard collar to fit in top hoop of main structure

Many familiar things can be used as sci-fi gadgetry

Spotlight sockets

Bedsprings

Child's windmill

10 Module

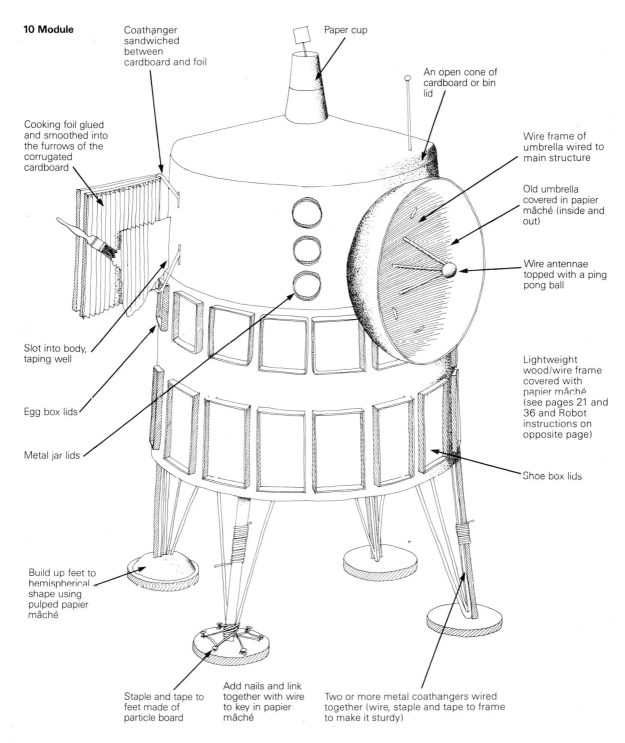

Coathanger sandwiched between cardboard and foil

Paper cup

An open cone of cardboard or bin lid

Cooking foil glued and smoothed into the furrows of the corrugated cardboard

Wire frame of umbrella wired to main structure

Old umbrella covered in papier mâché (inside and out)

Wire antennae topped with a ping pong ball

Slot into body, taping well

Egg box lids

Metal jar lids

Lightweight wood/wire frame covered with papier mâché (see pages 21 and 36 and Robot instructions on opposite page)

Shoe box lids

Build up feet to hemispherical shape using pulped papier mâché

Staple and tape to feet made of particle board

Add nails and link together with wire to key in papier mâché

Two or more metal coathangers wired together (wire, staple and tape to frame to make it sturdy)

Compiling Information

One of the fascinating aspects of making props is the discovery of a new awareness of people and their way of life. Carefully chosen props in an historical setting give us an insight into the domestic and social conditions of the time.

Research extensively using newspapers, magazines, pictures, books, postcards, photographs, sketches and so on. Having found your references, organise and as-semble them into a scrapbook. This is not only a useful exercise to gather your thoughts and ideas together, but may be invaluable as a reference for the future. Children's history books are particularly useful for research. They convey the essence of a period simply and directly.

Sort out your ideas and discuss your thoughts with the rest of the production team. Consider speci-fically which techniques are neces-sary for the props in the produc-tion. If you are using a technique that is new to you, it is a good idea to note down the details of the pro-cess, how long it took and any problems that were encountered. These notes could save you time at a later date when you may have to work on a similar project.

Make a box file, indexed under items rather than processes.

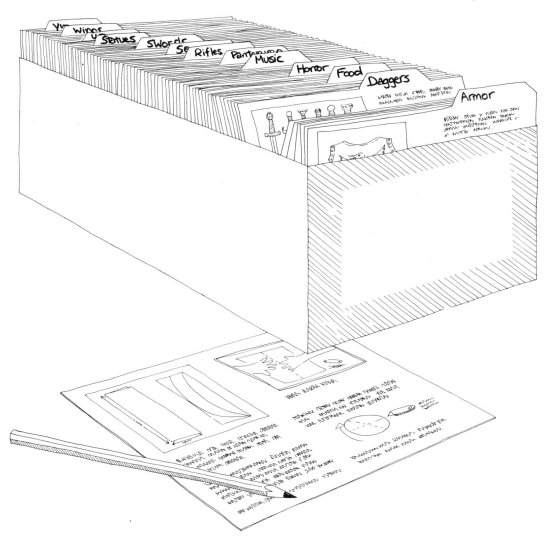

Bibliography

Carson, Richard **Stage Make-Up** USA — Prentice-Hall, Inc, 1981

Johnson, Pauline **Creating with Paper** UK — Nicholas Kaye Limited, 1960

Alkema, Chester J **Mask Making** USA — Sterling Publishing Co, Inc, 1981, UK — distributed by Ward Lock Limited, 1981

Bruun-Rasmussen, Ole and Peterson, Grete **Make-Up, Costumes & Masks for the Stage** USA — Sterling Publishing Co, Inc, 1976, UK — distributed by Ward Lock Limited, 1976

Griffiths, Trevor R **Stagecraft** USA — Chartwell Books Inc, 1982, UK — Phaidon Press Limited, 1982

Boyes, Janet **Making Paper Costumes** USA — Plays Inc, 1972, UK — B T Batsford Limited, 1974

Burleson, Bonny Schmid **The Technique of Macrâmé** USA — Brandford, 1972, UK — B T Batsford Limited, 1974

Powell, Anton and Varnags, Patricia **A Closer Look at Ancient Greeks** USA — Franklin Watts, Inc, UK — Hamish Hamilton Limited, 1978

Harris, Nathaniel **History Around Us** UK — Hamlyn Books, 1979

Middleton, Haydn **Everyday Life in the Sixteenth Century** USA — Silver Burdett, 1984, UK — Macdonald & Co (Publishers) Limited, 1982

McLaughlin, Terence **Papier Mâché Work** UK — Pelham Books Limited, 1974

Kenton, Warren **Stage Properties and How to Make Them** USA — Drama Book Publishers, 1964, UK — A & C Black (Publishers) Limited, 1974

Unstead, R J **Looking at History** UK — A & C Black (Publishers) Limited

Han, David de **Antique Household Gadgets** UK — Blandford Press, 1977

Covey, Elizabeth **Costumers Handbook** USA — Prentice-Hall, Inc, 1980

Taylor, Boswell and Bareham, John D **Ancient Egyptians** UK — © Brockhampton Press Limited (Hodder & Stoughton Childrens Books), 1970

Jackson, Brenda B **Models Made from Junk** UK — Evans Brothers, 1971

McCullum, Andrew **Fun with Stagecraft** UK — Kaye & Ward, London, 1977

Hoare, Robert J **When the West was Wild** UK — A & C Black (Publishers) Limited, 1973

Conolly, Peter **Pompeii** UK — Macdonald Educational, 1979

Schafer, Edward H **Ancient China** UK — Time-Life International (Nederland) B.V., 1970

Index